THE ENVIRONMENTAL MAFIA

THE ENVIRONMENTAL MAFIA

The Enemy is Us

Richard O'Leary

Algora Publishing
New York

ISBN: 0-87586-220-9 (softcover)
ISBN: 0-87586-159-8 (hardcover)

Library of Congress Cataloging-in-Publication Data

O'Leary, Richard, 1949-
Environmental mafia : when greens go too far / Richard O'Leary
    p. cm
Includes bibliographical references and index.
0-87586-159-8 (alk. paper) 0-87586-220-9 (pbk. : alk. paper)
1. Green movement — political aspects. 2. Environmentalism — Political aspects.
3. Ecoterrorism. I. Title.

GE195 .O54 2003
333.7'2'0973—dc21

                                2003011308

Printed in the United States

TABLE OF CONTENTS

INTRODUCTION

In its early days, the environmental movement tapped a current of concern in the public who saw their woods and water being dirtied or destroyed, and spurred a healthy interest in developing cleaner, more efficient practices. But the ideology of the early movement has been kidnapped by extremists. Now, working under the cover of some of America's most respected institutions, these extremists have implemented national legislation and local laws that needlessly and pointlessly restrict Americans' rights and in many cases deprive them of a livelihood.

Environmental policy makers, and those who carry out the dictums of these elitist groups and individuals, have developed a strategy that incorporates a range of "hot button" issues that are designed to win public support. These issues are used to carry out their meticulously engineered campaign to achieve a hidden agenda, objectives which are inimical to the American way of life and the sovereignty of the United States of America. This book has been written to expose that agenda, a task that should have already been accomplished by our mainstream media — but, unfortunately, has not been.

The copious information that the movement disseminates appears, on the surface, to describe the noblest of moral causes, but this facade is carefully fabricated, a disguise to conceal the true agenda of the deep ecologists who spearhead this massive and extremely powerful juggernaut. If they were what they represent themselves to be, I would be one of their most ardent supporters; but they are not.

It is impossible to present this material in a comprehensive text without some repetition, for which I apologize. I have attempted to categorize the distinct aspects of the subject so as to provide the reader with a panoramic view of the entire spectrum of this enormous conspiracy. This has not been a simple task, for the pervasive influence of the environmental cartel is worldwide in its scope, and also highly personal, reaching into the homes of every American.

Many of the issues I address are well known, household words in many cases. Some who read this book will be challenged to remain objective and withhold judgment until they have digested what is written here. Many sincere and well-meaning Americans have invested their trust in environmental non-profit organizations because they believe these entities represent our interests in environmental matters.

This book is divided into two sections: Commentary, which embodies, for the most part, my personal experiences and observations in regard to the environmental movement over a 40-year period, and Documentation, which is selected material regarding the subject from a roster of professional men and women in the fields of law, education, journalism, government, law enforcement and earth sciences.

The following summary is a thumbnail sketch of the entire spectrum of evidence found in this book. The agenda is far reaching and extremely ambitious.

SOME BASIC FACTS

1. The true agenda of the environmentalist is "re-wilding" America, not, as we have been led to believe, merely monitoring our use of natural resources. This enormous project (called The Wildlands Project) calls for the forced relocation of our rural population by governmental fiat using regulatory tyranny as their stimulus. The Wildlands Project doctrine demands that every farmer and rancher in targeted areas be removed from their farms and ranches and the land returned to the indigenous "biosphere."

Farmers and ranchers, miners and loggers in the entire western United States are suffering from the needless incursion of the eco-establishment and their federal allies. The states of Washington, Oregon, Idaho, Montana, North and South Dakota, Colorado, Utah, Wyoming, Arizona, Nevada, New Mexico, Oklahoma and Kansas are struggling with stagnant economies, thanks in part to environmentalist meddling, and things will get much worse, because:

2. Environmentalists are leading an all-out campaign to dismantle our free market economy, which they regard as an evil that will eventually destroy the environment. They not only oppose ANY use of natural resources whatsoever, but they subscribe to a socialistic model for our future in which we "travel light," use far less natural resources and suffer a dramatically diminished lifestyle. They also view the economy as a strategic means of forcing millions of Americans out of small rural towns by closing down farming, logging, ranching, mining, fishing, and oil production, the industries that constitute the tax base and economic mainstay of those communities.

3. The dogma that drives "deep ecology" is their obsession with an ancient pagan religion, the worship of "Gaia," *aka* Mother Earth, a cult that predates Greek mythology. The name they have coined for this faith is "New Age Spiritualism," but there is nothing "new" about it. Gaia worship is believed to have its origins in Eastern mysticism, but regardless of where it came from, taken to extremes it is inimical to human life on earth.

Keep an eye open, and you will see the terms "Gaia" and "Mother Earth" crop up many times in environmentalist literature. Many of the contributors to this book also allude to them.

Adherents to New Age Voodoo have exalted the natural order to the status of a deity and assigned it the right to exist for its own sake, the whole of nature making up a living entity in all its divergent species. Every animal and plant has rights, and man is considered a parasite with subordinate rights. Man is a freak that contributes nothing to nature, but only uses it for his own selfish needs. This hostile contention is evident, once you are aware of it, in all they do and support.

4. Environmentalists openly acknowledge in their literature and public speeches to the Faithful that there is no factual basis for the theory of "global warming" or the catastrophic depletion of the ozone layer. In fact, as I have documented in an entire chapter, they use these doomsday scenarios to instill fear in society as a means of reaching their objectives, already made quite clear above. They encourage those in their movement to ignore the truth and say whatever has the most effective impact.

But this intention to deliberately deceive our society goes far beyond the greenhouse Chicken Little scenario. Page after page of investigative reports and Congressional testimony herein reveal the blatant distortion of facts (lying), use of junk science, planting bogus evidence, and even strong-arming civil servants working within our government agencies to illegally lobby members of Congress for resolutions favorable to the eco-movement.

5. Contrary to what even I believed, for many years, the environmental movement as it exists today was not a grassroots phenomenon, but an organized, well-funded alliance of some of the wealthiest individuals on this planet. The ranks of those Bambi loving granolas who *were* grassroots were absorbed by the upscale eco-movement. It is easy, therefore, to misunderstand the makeup of the movement as it exists today. Most Americans are not aware that the grassroots environmental crusade was hijacked by The Rockefeller Foundation and other outlets for elitist funding.

There is copious evidence of this fact, but as any astute political aficionado will agree, the ease with which the environmental cartel infiltrated the highest offices of government and gained control of the most powerful agencies in Foggy Bottom was not the work of ecological flower children. We have financial records tracking the billions of dollars that fund the mega-powerful eco-organizations as they are channeled through private foundations and other sources.

6. An even more sinister long range objective of the eco-elite is now coming into clear focus: the subjugation of the American people to an international ruling body whose environmental charter will supercede our Constitution and Bill of Rights. The Kyoto Protocol was the first shot fired across our bow, and examining the tenets of that treaty, signed by Bill Clinton, reveals that it is simply the extension of environmentalist socialism designed to embrace the entire globe.

Under the articles and mandates of Kyoto, America, as the wealthiest nation on earth, and the most prolific "polluter," would be obligated to fund the lion's share of the multi-billion dollar regime, but more alarming, the forced restrictions on the production of "greenhouse gases" would cost our society an estimated $400,000,000,000.00 (that's 400 billion), and the loss of 5 million jobs.

The United Nations in its socialistic desire to redistribute resources is driving to capture American public opinion and force our leaders to surrender our national sovereignty to this mass paranoia.

When I say "paranoia," my assertion is supported by the Petition Project, signed by 19,200 distinguished scientists in the fields of earth science. Over 75 of those gentlemen are Nobel Prize winners. Their petition, and a link to an Internet listing of all their names, is published herein.

Their conclusion, in a few words, was that "global warming" is totally overblown and should be a non-issue.

7. Perhaps the most despicable aspect of the environmental movement is their brainwashing of our children. Any parent who has seen Captain Planet, or any number of other eco-sponsored cartoon programs, has seen the red-eyed dozer operators destroying precious rain forest until the muscle-bound hero comes swooping down to banish them. Even Mr. Green Jeans and his benign chum, Mr. Rogers, are purveyors of activist propaganda for our children's consumption.

Almost every textbook in our educational system is rife with environmental innuendos. Even math books pose problems with an environmental slant. For those who are conversant with the Internet, one can find dozens of websites targeting children with their subtle (and many times not so subtle) anti-capitalistic cant. They encourage our kids to develop skills as young activists, even teach them how to write hardball rhetoric in letters and mail them to their representatives in government.

8. Population reduction is another major goal of environmentalism, including government controlled birth quotas, and punishment for those who have a child "illegally," and support for regimes that are starving their citizens or committing genocide. As incredible as it sounds, the evidence is all here.

It all comes down to one simple conclusion: *We have entrusted the responsibility of nurturing our environment to the wrong people.*

A Note from the Author

When I was ten years old, my family was living in a comfortable middle class home in Aurora, Colorado, a suburb of Denver. The year was 1956. That summer Mom and Dad took an extended vacation to British Colombia. On the way they drove through Libby, Montana, a beautiful mountain town with a population of 3,000.

Somehow they ended up talking with Florence Tisher, a local real estate saleslady. Some of her listed properties were located 50 miles from Libby, over rough gravel roads, in the remote Yaak River Valley. It was a three hour trip then, up Pipe Creek Road, winding through the scenic Cabinet Range, until it intersected with the Yaak Road at a quaint establishment called The Dirty Shame Saloon.

Twelve miles further on was a 150-acre ranch situated right on the east fork of the Yaak River. My folks arranged to purchase the land and they broke the news to us on their return to Denver.

For me, it was the beginning of the greatest adventure of my life. We moved north the following summer.

There were several buildings on the Yaak place, a two-story main house that was built with huge logs, a garage, barn, chicken house and harness shed, with a one-room cabin just a stone's throw from the front door of the house. There was also a woodshed behind the house that was big enough to store enough wood to last an entire winter.

About a mile from the main homesite was a 25-acre hay meadow, lying in the shadow of Lick Knob, with a comfortable log cabin in one corner that had been built years before by one of the original homesteaders of the Yaak basin. It was a postcard setting, with the Yaak flowing along one side of the meadow, and stately aspen and yellow pine shading the cabin site, and towering larch and lodge pole that grew right up to the edges of the open field. I spent many summers there, alone, in the unspoiled splendor of the wilderness.

Life in the Yaak was primitive. We had no running water, electricity, telephone or indoor facilities. We used kerosene lamps for light and I carried water by the bucketful from the river, just yards away from the back porch.

The most dreaded day of the week, for me, was wash day. There was a huge claw foot tub in the cabin near the house, and a pot bellied stove. We designated it the "wash house" and Dad bought a gasoline-powered Maytag and put it in there. Being the oldest son, it was my job to carry water for wash day, and while Mom was tending to those chores, we heated water for a community bath. My five siblings would splash around in the tub while Mom toiled at the washer and big brother raised blisters carrying water.

Me? I took a dip in the icy Yaak to clean my hide.

Dad took a job for the Stevens Brothers at their tie mill on the Community Hall sale, and later for the U.S. Forest Service. I divided my time between two responsibilities, harvesting wood for the winter and providing meat for the table.

At least three days a week I would crank up the ancient McCormick Deering tractor and head for the timber with the chainsaw on board. There was abundant dead fall, lodge pole mostly, about telephone-pole size and larger. I would skid several logs to the house and buck them into 18" rounds, then stack them in the woodshed. The remainder of the week you would find me ranging a five-mile stretch of river, fishing my favorite holes. I would return in the afternoon with a mess of trout for supper.

There were hundreds of roughed grouse in the timber, where they dined on kinikinick berries. I came to know every foot of that country like my own bedroom, and I knew right where to go when Mom wanted "chickens" for dinner. Dad taught me to pick roosters; and we never hunted birds in the spring when they were mating, not until their chicks big enough to survive on their own.

Venison was plentiful, and I would bring home a fat white tail once a month. We shared a portion of every deer with our nearest neighbor, old Gus Schultz, five miles away. In the summer, the meat would spoil if we kept it all; and Gus's eyes were bad, so he was unable to hunt anymore. We looked out for him.

To keep perishables, we had an antique ice box. During the winter, when the ice on the river was a foot thick, we used the chainsaw to cut big blocks and skid them to the harness shed, where we buried them in sawdust. We still had ice left at the end of the summer.

As enjoyable as the lazy summer months were, with winter and spring came an ordeal that required almost superhuman energy and hard work just to survive. Snowfalls would bury the fence posts, four feet high, until the ends were just nubs on the surface. Temperatures dropped to 40° below zero. There were no county services that far up. It was up to us to make it on our own. Of course, we had to be in school every day, an eleven-mile trip down the road, and Dad had to get to work. We couldn't afford the luxury of holing up after a heavy snow.

Dad had a system. In weather that severe, the vehicles wouldn't even turn over, much less start, so Dad nosed the rigs up to the house, near the windows, and we disconnected the batteries and took them inside to sit near the fireplace. I was the lucky slob who got up early to make the fires in the morning. When it was really cold, I slept with my clothes on, in a sleeping bag, because I hated poking my feet into two blocks of ice.

The house was cold enough to freeze an inch of ice on top of the water bucket, and I hunkered near the kindling blaze, shivering until the fires caught and came to life. After breakfast I would go outside to ready the rigs for starting. I took a regular coffee can with about an inch of gas in the bottom and pushed it under the oil pan, then dropped a lighted match into it. A nifty flame sprang up, about two inches above the top, and tickled the bottom of the pans. By the time we hooked up the batteries, the oil would be boiling and those engines roared to life on the first turn. (Kids, don't try this at home! If you light the gas first and try to push it under the pan, you can tip it over and probably incinerate your vehicle.)

I used to love those trips down the valley when there was a new snow. It was pristine, untouched, like a sea of gentle swells, rolling across the road and timber and meadows in the morning sun, glittering like a vast ocean of diamonds. The world under a blanket of new snow is clean, virginal, pure.

The marvelous thing about heavy snow is the way it tames a rough dirt road. It's like flying on a cloud in stealth mode, silent, smooth as a Rolls Royce on the interstate. The bumper sent a constant sheet of snow over the hood. It was like gliding through a fairytale world.

When the snow was packed, there was black ice to contend with. We had to chain up all four tires and creep along at 20 mph to stay on the road. I've seen it so slick that men were on their hands and knees crawling up the slight incline from the parking area to the porch of the Dirty Shame, and they weren't making much headway, either. Buster, the proprietor, would stand on the porch and toss them a rope.

Spring was the worst for driving. We called it "breakup." The melting snow and thawing earth created an obstacle course that only the hardiest souls would attempt to travel (and that meant us). The mail lady wouldn't come farther than the Dirty Shame during breakup.

Where there were plugged culverts, water would lie in low spots as deep as three feet. Dad would skirt the biggest puddles on one side, with just two wheels submerged. In other spots, where there was little rock in the ground, the ruts in the mud would be knee deep. You had to pick the best path you could see, put the gas to the floor, and ride it out.

This was a daily routine for us.

After Dad took a job with the Forest Service, I began learning conservation. He was promoted to fire dispatcher, but much of his time was spent cruising timber sales and coordinating with logging contractors.

The environment was more than a lovely scenic panorama to us, it was our life. We learned to savor the beauty of it, and survive its formidable power. In those primitive surroundings I found a harmony with the earth, and my fondest memories are of jogging along the timber trails, fly fishing in the red cast of evening, or trailing a deer through a light snow. There is no music on earth so beautiful as waking to the sound of the river and the birds heralding the new day. The sun breaking over the crest of Wood Mountain reflected from dew on the knee-high timothy hay and painted the horse pasture with a brilliant display of glistening gems. It was my paradise.

This book is not written by someone who has learned about nature from a book, or camping on long weekends. My knowledge of the wilderness comes from living in the wild without the amenities that make life easier. With the exception of automobiles and chainsaws, we lived a life exactly like the early pioneers, living off the land, isolated, dependent upon our own wits and endurance. While my contemporaries were sledding down the hill at the city park, I was on snowshoes with my rifle, hunting for meat.

This book is not an attack on the millions of Americans who, like myself, share a love for the environment. To the contrary. It is an expose of the most virulent attack on the freedom of the American people ever to take place. The people who represent themselves as champions of the natural order are wolves in sheep's clothing. As the pages of this book will reveal, their objectives are not protecting the environment, as they claim.

I know what is good for the environment, from experience, and these elitist fanatics are not protecting a damn thing, except their insane vision of a new social order.

The finest tradition in American culture is the right of the people to speak freely about issues that concern them. So long as we enjoy the privilege to organize and present our views in a public forum, and make ourselves heard, we, the people, hold power and responsibility to correct the wrongs in our society.

In the case of environmental extremism, we are pitted against an enemy that is elusive, masters of disinformation, with the political and legal savvy to force their onerous mandates on all citizens. To combat their expertise, their far-reaching influence, and legal gambits, we must unite and speak with one voice in defense of our inalienable rights.

We must also be well informed, vigilant in our daily lives, and resolved to stand up and be counted when and if the occasion demands. Our vote is our power, and we must use it to remove any official from office that does not acknowledge these issues, and choose a candidate who is strongly pro-rights.

CHAPTER 1: THE ENEMY IS US

Let's start with an introduction to a few of the individual luminaries in the environmental establishment whose philosophies have contributed to the crisis we are facing today. These excerpts were extracted from environmentalist literature and speeches:

"You live in a world of wounds, a world infected by us human beings. . . " [David Foreman, founder, The Wildlands Project]

"Childbearing [should be] a punishable crime against society, unless the parents hold a government license. . . . All potential parents [should be] required to use contraceptive chemicals, the government issuing antidotes to citizens chosen for childbearing." [David Brower, Friends of the Earth]

"The right to have children should be a marketable commodity, bought and traded by individuals but absolutely limited by the state." [Keith Boulding, originator of the "Spaceship Earth"]

"We in the Green movement aspire to a cultural model in which the killing of a forest will be considered more contemptible and more criminal than the sale of 6-year-old children to Asian brothels." [Carl Amery, Green Party of West Germany]

"I got the impression that instead of going out to shoot birds, I should go out and shoot the kids who shoot birds." [Paul Watson, founder of Greenpeace and Sea Shepherd]

"Phasing out the human race will solve every problem on earth, social and environmental." [Dave Foreman, founder of Earth First!, and presently a member of the Board of Directors of the Sierra Club]

At the heart of environmentalist doctrine is a pathological hatred for mankind, as demonstrated by the sampling of quotes above. There is more to this enmity than the reasons most of us would normally have for despising another person, and I will explain this anomaly in full; but for the present I want to make a clear and rational statement regarding the relationship between man and nature, and I believe the vast majority of Americans will agree with me.

MAN AND THE ENVIRONMENT

In spite of his misadventures and poor judgment over the centuries, his lapses into needless violence and despotic rule, one of the admirable facets of man's nature is that which drives him to innovate, to invent.

It is this marvelous attribute that has prevailed in spite of sloth and corruption to lift humanity from a primitive existence to a highly civilized and cultured race. And it is this unique quality that sets him apart from the many other species which inhabit this planet.

Today the wonders of our ingenuity, and our ability to transform our dreams into reality, have overcome the dark frontiers of ignorance and thrust mankind into an age of illuminated thought, and all the benefits that come of it. Naturally, there are dangers as well.

It wasn't that long ago that doctors bled their patients to relieve suffering, and a barber doubled as a dentist. It took months for news of legislation in our Congress to reach the West Coast, and a journey across our nation was fraught with so many hazards that many died en route. Clumsy wagons drawn by oxen or mules lurched over the unforgiving terrain to carry those hardy souls, the American pioneers, to a new life in the golden west.

That was not so long ago. We've come far in a short 200 years.

But the marvels of our world today were not manufactured from thin air. They required the refinement of raw materials into the elements of a better and more sophisticated life. In these achievements we have come far, much farther then even the most brilliant minds of the past could have dreamed.

We have harnessed the power of the tiniest unit of matter, the atom, devised processes to transform raw minerals into steel for our automobiles, aircraft and ships. We have formulated new materials, such as plastics, to create cheaper and more durable products. We have discovered uses for chemical elements that prolong life, control mental illness, and relieve pain.

Innovations in herbicides and fertilizers have drastically increased our production of food. Pesticides control potentially deadly insects and rid us of insects that infest our homes.

I could go on for pages detailing the spectacular advances in technology, the enhancements that have provided us with a lifestyle beyond the wildest imagination of ancient cultures.

Of course, with the advances have come a measure of waste and destruction. But the answer to these liabilities also lies in the inherent genius of the human mind, under a system of freedom, in our quest to create a better and more secure world.

None of these advances would have been possible without using natural resources and harnessing the awesome power of nature, and we aren't finished yet, not by a long shot! We are now on the verge of a new frontier in power generation and cleaner technologies for industrial applications.

Every year researchers discover new and more effective medications, solve the riddles of crippling diseases, and even restore sight to the blind and hearing to the deaf. Discoveries in genetics and the mysteries of DNA may one day rid us of disease altogether, and perhaps even retard the aging process, make it possible to lose weight by taking a pill that alters metabolism, and even "grow" human organs from DNA cultures.

Eventually, and not that many years from today, we will look back on many of our current practices as crude and wasteful. But these conditions are not a matter of choice, but rather the necessary stages of progress that must transpire in our quest to improve our lifestyles and the world around us. We are not lodged in a stationary status quo, but constantly in the process of change, for the better. Certainly, we have made mistakes, caused harm to our environment, and wasted natural resources, but these errors serve the purpose of motivating us to discover better ways to produce and prosper.

It is common knowledge that our primitive ways cannot continue indefinitely. This awareness is a catalyst that energizes the dynamics of human intelligence to move on, and upward. To characterize businesses as evil is ludicrous. Businesses are managed and staffed by people who are inhabitants of this planet, and they are as anxious as anyone, even if only for the reason of self interest, to solve the problems of environmental degradation. In fact, most of those people are us! We are "business" — working Americans.

Besides, as several segments of this book will reveal, the biggest polluters aren't steel mills or mining operations, but the cities and communities, local governments that pump sewage into our rivers and lakes.

But we have an element in our society who resist advances in technology. They aggressively attack our use of natural resources as a means of innovation. They view our free enterprise system as an evil that must be dismantled, and insist that the use of our land for cultivating crops and raising livestock must be limited. They demand that Americans who live on the land must be run off, bankrupted, or otherwise forced to abandon their homes and livelihoods.

In the words of John Davis, editor of the official journal of the Wildlands Project, *Wild Earth*:

> Wilderness recovery must start now but continue indefinitely — expanding wilderness until the matrix, not just the nexus, is wild . . . Does [this] mean that Wild Earth and the Wildlands Project advocate the end of industrial civilization? Most assuredly. Everything civilized must go.

Normally, comments such as this one would be of no consequence. Many cults practice their eccentric beliefs in this country. However, this cult is not an isolated group of fanatics but a cadre of extremely powerful individuals that are literally the dictators of this country's environmental policy. Their influence reaches into the highest offices of our government and controls the most powerful agencies of the bureaucracy in Washington, D.C.

In the private sector the deep ecology movement is sponsored by the most wealthy non-profit organizations in America. Their combined revenues total an incredible $9 billion a year.

In their infancy these crusaders were embraced by the American people, supported by our dollars, and given the clout in terms of votes to sway the men and women in Congress who are responsible for the body of environmental law as it exists today. But the ideology of the early movement has undergone a drastic change that has gone largely unnoticed.

The grassroots crusade that focused upon concerns we all share has mutated and grown into a monster that is devouring our freedom, one bite at a time.

We have been deceived on a massive scale, for the agenda of these powerful organizations, both private and governmental, is inimical to our way of life, our future, and our freedom. They have won popular support with the claims that they represent our interests, but an examination of the facts exposes their deception. Our interests involve the harmonious existence of the human race with our natural surroundings — but this is not the objective of the eco-elite.

Mr. Davis summed up their objectives very well: the systematic dismantling of our economy and banishment of our rural populations in order to "rewild" America; to return the land to its pristine state. They make no bones about it! They have seized upon the issues that we, the mainstream population, are concerned about, in order to garner widespread support; but they have misused the prestige that we have bestowed upon them. In effect, they have betrayed us in a systematic campaign to create an environmental utopia devoid of human activity.

The laws they have successfully lobbied for are their weapons in the war against the ordinary citizen, and they use our dysfunctional court system against us very effectively. So outrageous are the persecutions of free Americans at the hands of this mafia that you, dear reader, will find it a challenge to believe them. But I assure you, the arrogant abuses of property rights and privacy that are compiled in this book are documented fact, not delusionary rhetoric.

Yet, millions of Americans pursue their daily lives, grappling with the concerns of the day, blissfully unaware that their jobs, their lifestyles, and their freedoms are the target of these fanatics. In fact, millions of us actually contribute to this insanity!

The material in this book reveals the scope of the environmentalist campaign and the very real dangers their efforts pose to our well-being, even our national sovereignty. The destruction of our economy alone will not satisfy them, for their dream is to bring every nation under the umbrella of one all-powerful body, an environmentally oriented body that, directly or indirectly, holds sway over the entire world. If that happens Americans will be denied the rights defined in our Constitution and Bill of Rights. We will be denied due process. An international police force will have the overriding authority to arrest us, fine us, and impose sanctions on our business sector and society at their whim.

As every chapter in this book will demonstrate, environmentalism is counter productive — not only to society, but to nature itself. Deep ecologists' misleading claim that they are concerned about every snail and bird obscures the fact that they could not care less if those creatures become extinct, so long as nature, itself, is the reason for their demise.

Obviously, thousands of animals and fish are destroyed in every forest fire, and although accurate records of wildlife mortality are impossible to compile, the United Nations report on Forest Fire Statistics puts the number of acres lost to forest fires in the U.S. at 152 million acres over a 17-year period (1982-1998), yet environmentalists advocate a "let it burn" policy. What they protest is man's involvement, pure and simple!

Many reasonable practices of years past were instrumental in reducing the likelihood of wildfire and significantly contributed to the well-being of our wildlife. But the deep ecologist is adamantly opposed to our tampering with nature in any way, even if our intervention is desirable and necessary for the maintenance of our environment.

The catastrophic fires that have destroyed hundreds of thousands of acres of prime forest lands and destroyed homes and human lives in the last couple of years are the direct result of twenty years of mismanagement under the auspices of environmentalist fanatics. These people have become entrenched in key positions in the Environmental Protection Agency, The Department of Interior, The United States Forest Service, The United States Fish and Wildlife Service, The National Park Service, The Bureau of Land Management, OSHA, and thousands of local branches of these agencies.

Contrary to environmentalist dogma, the means of protecting our environment is not the obliteration of our free enterprise system. It is this blessed presence in our society that will lead to a solution to our dilemma. As President Bush pointed out in his Clean Skies proposal: new technologies that ensure cleaner air and water are expensive, and only a prosperous economy can pay the cost of research and development that will eventually liberate us from our plight. Our free economy is the assurance of our deliverance, not the agent of our ruination.

Mr. Tom DeWeese is the President of the American Policy Center. He has been active in the battle to liberate America from the insidious influence of environmental extremism for many years. The following article offers Mr. DeWeese's astute observations regarding the subject at hand.

"Sustainable Development" — The Environmentalist Elite's "Vision" For America's Future. UN Attacks Freedom's Foundations
(By Tom DeWeese, August 26, 2002, NewsWithViews.com)

"Name any aspect of your life that you believe is your right as an American citizen to determine and it will be taken away from you in the name of 'Sustainable Development.'

'Sustainable Development'" is the phrase that those who seek to control the world use to hide their totalitarian ambitions. Sustainable Development is a horror that hardly anyone in this nation understands or even cares to oppose. It can be ignored only at the peril of everything you hold dear, including individual liberty, private property, free enterprise, freedom to travel, freedom of association, and life itself.

"The World Summit on Sustainable Development, beginning August 26th in Johannesburg, South Africa, is the United Nations' plan to impose this Orwellian agenda on this nation and the world.

"Here is the definition of a sustainable community from the Report of the President's Council: 'Sustainable Communities encourage people to work together to create healthy communities where natural resources and historic resources are preserved, jobs are available, sprawl is contained, neighborhoods are secure, education is lifelong, transportation and health care are accessible, and all citizens have opportunities to improve the quality of their lives.'

"These noble sounding goals hide an agenda that would transfer power from elected representatives to a local committee or council that will set 'a vision' for the city. They will put a plan together for the future development of the community. The plan, however, will not be written by the committee. The blue print will come out of Washington, DC.

"Individual landowners and businessmen will have little or no real input. Instead, they will be stripped of their property rights in order to 'protect' open space and historic buildings. The committee will control the use of all private property. This right is so precious, it is protected by the Fifth Amendment of the U.S. Constitution.

"To insure the success of Sustainable Development, the committee will insure that everyone have the right attitudes, values and beliefs. These attitudes are already being taught in our nation's schools. This is why our educational system, so far as teaching the fundamentals of reading, writing and arithmetic, are in a total meltdown. It is no longer education: it is indoctrination.

"Utilizing a United Nations program as its guide, neighborhood by neighborhood, people will be taught how important it is to protect the environment, how evil sprawl can be to the Sustainable Development plans. Sustainable Development will also set up government-sponsored clinics with tax-paid healthcare.

"Sustainable Development believes that people must be weaned from the use of their own automobiles, so public transportation will be emphasized.

"It will emphasize building light rail trains and bus lines to get us around to our jobs. It will emphasize designing housing developments around the rail and bus lines so they are within walking distance for everyone. In time, cars will be banned from streets during certain hours of the day, then banned entirely. In his book, *Earth in the Balance*, former Vice President Al Gore advocates 'eliminating the internal combustion engine.'

"There are other things that the committee will find necessary to ban. Single family homes that 'waste' precious land will be deemed unnecessary. Any further suburban housing will be banned.

"The committee will also look after public health. People will be required to eat properly. That's why they will determine that precious farmland cannot be 'wasted' on raising cattle for beef consumption. Beef is harmful to your health, so it will be banned. Wheat and soy will be grown on that land instead. With our new healthy diet, as outlined by the committee, we will no longer need things like 7-11's and McDonald's and their unhealthy fast foods and snacks. They will be banned.

"Sustainable Development fears overpopulation. The committee will decide the proper number of people who can live in community limits. Some strict guidelines will be imposed for the sake of the community's well being and for the protection of the environment. Limits on the number of children a family can have will be imposed.

"This is not about 'preserving the environment for future generations.' This is about totalitarianism. It's about controlling every aspect of our lives with decisions made by committees that will grow more powerful and more oppressive with every passing day and with each new regulation proposed by empowered special interest groups. There will be no satisfying their lust for power. There will be no part of our lives that is overlooked or uncontrolled."

[Tom DeWeese is the publisher/editor of *The DeWeese Report* and President of the American Policy Center]

I bought my girls *Lion King* when it came out on video cassette and I couldn't help but think, as I sat and watched it with them, how far removed from reality the story was. In a sense, the environmentalist dream of a pristine wilderness is just as ludicrous; but these ecologists' vision is not entertainment for children, but a fantasy which they have parlayed into a nightmare for the people.

Nature is harsh, cruel in human terms, devoid of compassion or sympathy. From the beginning man has been forced to contend with the extremes of our environment to survive. You could say that we have emerged the victor, in most cases, in the struggle for domination; for either man or nature will rule. There is no such thing as a relationship between the two that is entirely compatible without considerable adjustments.

Given a choice, sane people would opt for man's preeminent status over nature, for the environment is without conscience or moral direction. Nature is also non-productive, except in a limited sense. Simply put, if we adopted a policy wherein we exist without intruding on the natural order, we willingly subject ourselves to a primitive lifestyle. Far better that we impose human values on our natural surroundings.

Nature provides the natural materials for progress and commerce, and these raw elements are only acquired by harvesting, digging, trimming, cutting, hunting and collecting. In most cases the things we need to build a better life and feed ourselves are renewable resources: timber, crops, water, fishing. Those materials that are in limited supply, like ore and petroleum, can be replaced with technological innovation in time. Before they are depleted,, we can have alternative sources, synthetics and advanced sources of power. We are very close to these realities even now.

But the environmentalist demands that we halt the very progress that will eventually make many of the practices we utilize today obsolete. Clean nuclear power will replace fossil fuels. Other technologies are already in the market place; the use of solar power, electro-magnetics, and other inventions will come out of humanity's relentless pursuit of a better life.

Yet, there is no compromising with the eco-mafia. Their inflexible demand that we cease using natural materials in any context is unchanged.

There is a logic in developing advanced technologies to replace traditional methods. If we continue to make progress in energy production and various forms of manufacture, for instance, we won't need coal any longer, nor gasoline, oil, steel. . . .You'd think that they would advocate an accelerated agenda for such innovations, yet one of the cornerstones of the environmental movement is the dismantling of our economy, hindering businesses that use raw materials, and closing public lands to grazing and farming.

In closing this chapter, I want to make the final point that Americans must wake up to the reality of this dilemma. Unless we take action with our votes and wherever we confront the issues discussed herein, the environmental juggernaut will only gain momentum; and friends, they have gained far too much ground already.

The ugly truth is: the enemy is us.

CHAPTER 2.
THE RELIGIOUS ROOTS OF ENVIRONMENTALISM

The outrageous demands of eco-activism have always confused and angered me. Putting animals and plant life ahead of the welfare of humanity is unnatural, degrading.

Even the motives of such men as Adolf Hitler had a twisted logic, barbaric as it was, that we could understand as psychopathic dementia. But the motives of environmentalists have defied understanding. Regardless of how I might stretch my imagination I have never been able to grasp what possible good could come of denying human beings the comforts and conveniences that technology can provide. The contention that shutting down a hydroelectric dam, or taking some other measure which imposes suffering on human beings, for the sake of a helpless animal is simply not a creditable argument when we study all the facts. In most cases the impact on the animals and plants they designate as "endangered" is not so threatening as they claim.

But even if there were a real possibility that we may snuff a species of toad, or eradicate a species of wild flower, the moral imperatives of providing security and prosperity for the human race take precedence. Certainly, if it is possible to make a reasonable sacrifice to save something, plant or animal, I'm all for it, but not closing businesses, blocking the construction of hydroelectric dams that are sorely needed, shackling our petroleum industry and hamstringing the mining industry or destroying the logging business.

The myth that the greenies harp on is the terrible damage we do to the environment. Logging denudes the hillsides, miners dump acid into our mountain streams, and so forth. To support their accusations they flash ghastly images on TV of filth in the water and other natural abominations. Their intent is to have us think that these atrocities are the norm, rather than the exception.

I know otherwise, from personal experience. They're lying, pure and simple. But what could be the environmentalist's motive for persecuting man, denying our rights, taking our land, throttling our economy? If it's not to protect wild creatures and wilderness, as they contend, then why?

The answer to this puzzle was a shocker for me, I'll admit. But once I discovered it, the pieces of the puzzle fit snugly into place.

The one motive that I had never considered was religion.

It wasn't until I began my research for this book that I ran across the answer to the question of motive. Suddenly, it all made a horrible sense. Even then, it was some time before I was convinced that I should include this chapter in this book. Why? Because the sheer magnitude of the delusion that would engender such actions is incredible, almost comical. It hardly seemed to warrant serious consideration. When I first ran into it, I considered it must be an isolated case of a few select members of the environmental crowd with highly unorthodox beliefs. But I was dead wrong.

As I continued my research, the continuous thread of spiritual overtones became more and more dominant, to the point where I realized that the quasi-religious aspect of the environmentalists' beliefs is not merely a lame idea that a very few of them toss around, but a concept that thrives at the very heart and soul of their obsession.

I am referring to the official eco-religion, the worship of Gaia, a.k.a. "Mother Earth." This chapter will inform the reader of the facts regarding the Gaia cult and its connection to the environmental movement.

To substantiate the connection between Gaia and environmentalism to my own satisfaction, I ran an Internet search using "mother earth" as the key words. Altavista came up with 1,072,000 hits. In other words, there are well over one million references to "mother earth" in the data that the search engine processed, and that covers only a tiny fraction of the millions of websites on the net.

Obviously, I didn't follow down every reference, but an overwhelming majority of those I did investigate were either on environmentally-oriented websites or related to environmentalist literature. I also ran a search for "Gaia" and got 179,719 hits. Many of these revealed that the updated term for this pagan religion is "New Age Spiritualism." A search for "New Age" yielded 756,763 hits.

These results established, beyond any doubt, that the worship of Gaia is far from isolated, and the connection to the environmental movement is also beyond question. Anyone who doubts that can run these searches and investigate on his own. I have included in this documentary only a mere fragment of the entire mosaic.

I'll begin by offering a brief introduction to one man's* version of Gaia, and the tenets of Gaia worship (from the website of M. Alan Kazlan, http://www.kheper.auz.com/gaia/consciousness/eco-spiritual.htm):

> Gaia Nation
> We hold these truths to be self evident: That all species are created different but equal; That they are endowed, each one, with certain inalienable rights; That among them are Freedom to Live, Freedom to Grow, and Freedom to pursue Happiness in their own style;
> That to protect these God-given rights, social structures naturally emerge, basing their authority on the principles of love of God and respect for all forms of life;
> That whenever any form of government becomes destructive of life, liberty, and harmony, it is the organic duty of the young members of that species to mutate, to drop out, to initiate a new social structure, laying its foundations on such principles and organizing its power in such form as seems likely to produce the safety, happiness, and harmony of all sentient beings.

This is an excerpt from Mr. Kazlan's theory of the origin of the universe:

> Now, don't get me wrong. I am as much against rigid reductionistic materialism as I am against fundamentalistic religion! I would actually consider myself a "Creationist" in that I derive the cosmos ultimately (via a process of emanation) from a transcendent Godhead or Absolute Reality. But I am not a "creation scientist" in that I do not seek to reconcile, or to deny, my evolutionary beliefs according to the dictates of a particular scripture.

What, exactly, does this mean?

The Gaia ground rules give an elevated status to the lower animal kingdom, those creatures that Kazlan calls "sentient," defined as possessing "unstructured consciousness," "feelings." In other words, Gaia proponents believe that all living things (including plants and even bacteria) have equal rights.

Voilà! The question of motive begins to come into focus, but this simple treatment of a complex and many times contradictory concept is far from sufficient to fully explain where the green movement is coming from.

The following excerpt is from the writings of the guru of Gaia worship, a man named Lovelock.

Lovelock's Gaia Hypothesis (an excerpt):

> The name of the living planet, Gaia, is not a synonym for the biosphere — that part of the Earth where living things are seen normally to exist. Still less is Gaia the same as the biota, which is simply the collection of all individual living organisms. The biota and the biosphere taken together form a part but not all of Gaia.
>
> Just as the shell is part of the snail, so the rocks, the air, and the oceans are part of Gaia. Gaia, as we shall see, has continuity with the past back to the origins of life, and in the future as long as life persists. Gaia, as a total planetary being, has properties that are not necessarily discernible by just knowing individual species or populations of organisms living together . . . Specifically, the Gaia hypothesis says that the temperature, oxidation, state, acidity, and certain aspects of the rocks and waters are kept constant, and that this homeostasis is maintained by active feedback processes operated automatically and unconsciously by the biota."
>
> "You may find it hard to swallow the notion that anything as large and apparently inanimate as the Earth is alive. Surely, you may say, the Earth is almost wholly rock, and nearly all incandescent with heat.
>
> "The difficulty can be lessened if you let the image of a giant redwood tree enter your mind. The tree undoubtedly is alive, yet 99% of it is dead. The great tree is an ancient spire of dead wood, made of linin and cellulose by the ancestors of the thin layer of living cells which constitute its bark. How like the Earth, and more so when we realize that many of the atoms of the rocks far down into the magma were once part of the ancestral life of which we all have come."

The connection between Gaia and environmentalism is clear, but one can only speculate what the underlying motive is to adopt this credo as the "official faith" of the eco-movement. Perhaps to legitimize and lend direction to their convictions? Or perhaps the human need to attach a sublime dimension to our obsessions? Regardless of the reason, it appears that this passionate belief in earth as a deity is, for many, a driving force.

These people have the right to worship whatever deity they wish. But I take adamant exception to any group that seeks to impose its religious beliefs on others. Shaping public policy and tyrannical legislation on the basis of a religious dogma is a clear violation of the separation clause in our Constitution.

I should distinguish between that happy-go-lucky segment of our society that ride mountain bikes and sip exotic coffees, and the hard core eco-activists.

The former are nature lovers who support the eco-movement for their own reasons, well meaning at best and naive at worst. These are not the dictators of eco-policy. By contrast the icons of the eco-movement, the prime movers, have been given the name "deep ecologists" by professionals in earth sciences and journalism that are most informed on their policies and tactics. The former group shares some responsibility, however, for they blindly support the dictums of the elitists.

Based upon the material I have presented above, and the following articles, there is a strong legal case for challenging almost every environmental law passed by the government in the past twenty years as a violation of the separation of church and state. The expressed purpose of this prohibition was to prevent the insinuation of any religious dogma into the laws of the United States. Whether or not all eco-activists have identical beliefs is not relevant. The fact is that the concept of equal rights for all living things is the core tenet of this ancient pagan faith, and the correlation with documented environmentalist dogma, are reason enough to bring this issue under close scrutiny.

The Endangered Species Act, and the abuses that have come of it, are prime examples of the conflict that our Founding Fathers attempted to avoid in the separation clause of our Constitution. There is no environmental argument that can overcome the clear evidence that the tenor of this act establishes the rights of animals as transcendent to the rights of mankind, and this proposition is a fundamental concept of Gaia worship.

Regardless of what spin you put on this law, it is hostile to the interests and future of humanity.

No belief, regardless of its origin, or the fancy words you use to explain it, is a valid reason to deny us the wherewithal we require to make a better life, promote prosperity, and establish a norm which provides opportunity to grow and prosper for all of our citizens.

An historical perspective certainly supports my view of Constitutional impropriety. The complexion of religious tyranny has always been consistent with the kinds of abuses we see in our society at the hands of the Gaia crowd. One doesn't have to be a man of letters to recognize the irrational acts of man, or to identify the litany of atrocities that are always associated with a government that exercises religious doctrine as the law. Torquemada's Spanish Inquisition is a prime example.

Their hostility to mankind, and the extremes to which these fanatics carry it (see the chapter on "Eco-Terrorism"), most certainly foment in a cauldron of spiritual misgivings.

"Battle For Sustainable Freedom" (excerpt) *The New American*, April 29, 1996:

> In her address to the conference, Representative Helen Chenoweth pointed out that the concept of "sustainable development" is inspired by a religious worldview — "a cloudy mixture of earth worship, pagan mysticism, and folklore." That worldview was endorsed by Interior Secretary Bruce Babbitt during a November 21st address to the National Religious Partnership for the Environment, in which he condemned traditional Christianity and exalted pagan nature worship as the basis for a new social "covenant." Chenoweth noted that Babbitt "really believes nature and the natural landscape are literally holy and that anything we do on the landscape is sacrilegious — that we're disturbing his temple."

Babbitt is not unique in his devotion to eco-paganism. Vice President Al Gore's soporific opus *Earth in the Balance* dismisses Christianity and other monotheistic religions as inadequate for the needs of contemporary society and urges the enshrinement of a "pan-religious perspective" as the basis of a world spiritual tradition.

Furthermore, the UN Environmental Programme's Global Biodiversity Assessment (GBA), a 1,140-page document which provides the theoretical and conceptual basis for the world body's environmental agenda, maintains that sustainable development will require the abolition of biblical civilization and the adoption of the values of pre-Christian pagan societies.

Excerpt from "Goddess Earth, Exposing the Pagan Agenda in the Environmental Movement" by Samantha Smith

> Private property ownership is impossible; free enterprise is exploitation; technology is an abomination against nature; Western Culture is the root of all evil. These are some of the teachings of what is little more than the bastardized products of Eastern mysticism. Now called New Age religion, it culminates in deep ecology, eco-feminism and the worship of an ancient Greek God called Gaia — Mother Earth.
>
> Gaia teaches that man has damaged or destroyed the fragile balance of nature. Disciples of Gaia believe that all living things on earth are interconnected (except man) and to damage or destroy even a tiny insect is to damage

whole ecological systems. Such a premise was the basis for Vice President Al Gore's book, "Earth in the Balance."

Gaia worship is at the very heart of today's environmental policy. The Endangered Species Act, the United Nation's Biodiversity Treaty and the Presidents Council on Sustainable Development are all offspring of the Gaia hypothesis of saving "Mother Earth."

One of the prime spokesmen for the Gaia earth religion is Father Thomas Berry, a dissident Catholic priest and a leader of the Temple of Understanding, located in New York City. Father Berry contends that Christianity promotes "deep cultural pathology of human greed and addiction." He advocates that the earth is disintegrating and that Christianity is mostly to blame.

Father Berry believes that we are now entering an era of "earth consciousness" and he heralds a new era he calls the "Ecozoic Age" that will transcend God. Father Berry suggests that we will have to remove the idea that only humans are created in the likeness of God.

Father Berry says that "the world is being called to a new post-denominational, even post Christian, belief system that sees the earth as a living being — mythologically, as Gaia, Mother Earth — with mankind as her consciousness. Such worship of the universe is called "cosmolatry."

The Gaia Hypothesis, repopularized by James Lovelock and Lynn Margulis (formerly the wife of Carl Sagan), is an ancient idea presented in scientific-sounding language that makes it politically correct for the new age. The idea itself pre-dates the Christian era and even Greek mythology, from which the name Gaia was taken. The idea is rooted in ancient cultures and, until Lovelock, was generally known as "paganism."

There are three principles of paganism:

• Animism — the belief that everything is imbued with a soul;

• Polytheism — the belief that many gods exist and each one has a function to preside over various aspects of nature and life;

• Pantheism — the belief that all things, animate and inanimate, including the earth and humans, are manifestations of God, that God is ALL: the universe is totally God.

The Cathedral of St. John the Divine, in New York City, is the seat of a bishop in the Anglican Church, one of the largest religious denominations in the world. From that spot the Dean of the Cathedral, the Very Rev. James Parks Morton, is translating Thomas Berry's "cosmology" into specific programs, rituals and institutions in order to spread the Gaia theology into mainstream Christianity.

One of those rituals is the "Feast of St. Francis," where elephants and camels and other animals are paraded down the aisle to the altar for a blessing, as others present bowls filled with compost and worms. Vice President Al Gore delivers a sermon in which he tells the congregation, "God is not separate from the Earth."

Such rituals are not limited to the New York Cathedral. The Episcopal Diocese of Kansas and the Stewardship Office of the Episcopal Church sponsored a celebration of Earth Day in April, 1995 that featured, among others, James Parks Morton, Thomas Berry, and Paul Winter, official musician of the Cathedral of St. John the Divine. Samantha Smith, author of *Goddess Earth*, attended the affair and offered the following report:

> The gathering held at the Westin Crown Center Hotel included a North American Native Indian praying to God, then praying to the Grandfather Spirit and to spirits of the Four Directions to bless the earth and oversee the conference. California Senator Tom Hayden offered an Earth Day prayer, claiming the earth was speaking through him: "On this Earth Day let us say an earth prayer and make an earth pledge."
>
> "In the Bible, 'ruah' means both wind and spirit, so let us take time to breathe with the universe, connect with the earth and remember what we need to know and do. Celebrate that ancient spirits are born again in us, spirits of eagle vision, of coyote craft, of bear stewardship, of buffalo wisdom, of ancient goddesses, of druids, of native people, of Thoreau and Sitting Bull — born again and over again in John Muir and Rachel Carson and David Brower and Alice Walker." Hayden then asked us to "commit ourselves to carry the written word of Al Gore into official deeds." Thomas Berry offered a prayer for the healing of the earth.
>
> Gaia musician Paul Winter then entertained with his saxophone. He explained that he had gone into the Superior Forest and taped exchanges of howls between his saxophone and a wolf. With his sax, he demonstrated the sound. He then asked the audience to join him in a "Howl-le-lu-ia Chorus." He made a wolf sound, and nearly 200 Episcopalians from Kansas howled back, expressing their oneness with the wolf.
>
> This is the theology — or cosmology — which underlies the National Religious Partnership for the Environment. These are the people who conceived the NREP, and these are the people who are creating the material that is being delivered to 67,300 churches in America — in an envelope labeled from the National Council of Churches.

One of the several tenets of Gaia worship that are inimical to the existence of mankind is "voluntary extinction." There following commentary is from www.vhemt.org, a website dedicated to this insane objective as a means of sparing nature.

> [T]he hopeful alternative to the extinction of millions, possibly billions, of species of plants and animals is the voluntary extinction of one species: Homo sapiens . . . us. Each time another one of us decides to not add another one of us to the burgeoning billions already squatting on this ravaged planet, another ray of hope shines through the gloom. When every human chooses to stop breeding, Earth's biosphere will be allowed to return to its former glory . . . Good health will be restored to the Earth's ecology . . . to the life form known by many as Gaia. It's going to take all of us going.
> — Washington Times' "Culture, et cetera," March 3, 1999.

For obvious reasons, those who follow Gaia are hostile to Christianity. When they advocate persecution of Christians or anyone else, they abuse the license to worship freely in this country. The following article suggests some of the Gaia cult's practices.

The Pagan Roots of Environmentalism — Update On The Worship Of Gaia

In 1985, a friend of mine went to a meeting in Boulder (Colorado), called by Jose Arguelles (leader of PAN and New Age Transformation). It was attended by over 200 people, who "found their own space" and began by meditating and resonating (using vibrating sounds, something like locusts, he said). Participants were presented with "a new idea," that of seeing the earth as a living, spiritual being that could feel pain.

The group was asked to tune in to the crystal matrix frequency (Mother Earth's heartbeat) and to relax. Many went into trance-like states. As people felt they were being filled with the Earth's energy, they became vocal, with sounds rising and falling rhythmically. Some swayed and some fell down on the ground and began writhing. They were then "brought to silence."

Arguelles told the audience to concentrate on a cloud floating overhead, just drifting, and then told them to invite the cloud in to fill the empty spirit, the empty soul. He said to invite "PAN" in, accepting him as the leader and guide for their lives.

Jose explained that Pan was the first son of Mother Earth and used to live close to his mother in the primeval forest with his brothers and sisters, who went out and founded the temple-building societies (Aztecs, Egyptians, etc,). When Pan refused to join his siblings in the cities, they called him evil and Satan. They invented their own selfish religion, Christianity, which must be removed because it includes a vision of an Apocalypse.

The Boulder audience was told that "right now Mother Earth is bringing Pan[1] back to save us and lead us into the New Age. We can help by surrendering to him, tuning into the crystal matrix frequencies and carrying out the directions received while tuned in." Arguelles explained this might include the physical removal of Christians, because they are the biggest obstacle to transformation.

The following article presents the insights of Joseph Farah, Editor of the *Whistle Blower Magazine* on NetWorldDaily.com and an unabashed Christian into the influence of Gaia in our society.

A New World Religion

This "new" religious worldview is sugar-coated with high-minded and universal ideals of environmental protection and species preservation, but the ultimate agenda behind the movement is much darker.

The ultimate purpose of "green religion" is to convince the people of the world to embrace world governance — which for a free nation like America represents a massive loss of national sovereignty and personal freedom — for the supposed sake of Mother Earth ("gaia") and the environment. After all, it is a lot easier to administer world government if all people believe it represents their salvation, rather than tyranny.

How is this to be accomplished? To begin with, assign new names to old demons. What once was called "paganism" has been renamed and assigned a new respectability as the "gaia hypothesis." The once-hated idea of world government has been renamed "global governance." The concept of national sovereignty is eroding and transmuting into the concept of "sovereign equality."

"The vanguard of this movement," explains Henry Lamb in *The rise of global green religion*, "people like James Parks Morton, James Lovelock, Robert Muller, Al Gore, Timothy Wirth and many, many others, have been 'enlightened' through their biocentric belief in gaia" — the belief that the earth itself is a conscious, living organism — "and therefore they know what is best for the planet.

"They also know that the only way to protect the sacred gaia is to control the people who are degrading her. The only way to control the people is through an omnipotent government that is, at this moment, consolidating its power into an ever-growing bureaucracy, now stretching around the globe, extending its tentacles into every corner of human life, creating de facto global governance.

---

1. Pan, a cloven-hoofed half man/half beast, is one of the infernal names given to Satan in Anton LaVey's Satanic Bible.)

"And guess what? Not only has this new 'enlightened' worldview permeated Western schools and governments, but America's Christian churches themselves also are rapidly being converted to this new religious paradigm."

Few people realize how Gaia worship has invaded the churches of America. Apparently, many denominations see no conflict between the worship of God and the pagan tenets of the Gaia cult. The U.S. Constitution gives them full right to their pagan beliefs, but we are all guaranteed the right to practice our religious beliefs without interference from government or society. The hostile nature of their customs and their policies attack our freedoms. Any dogma that even suggests the "physical removal of Christians," or violent actions toward any person or persons, is spiritual piracy. Will the Gaia crowd eventually drive us all to use violence to promote harmony?

CHAPTER 3.
CONDITIONING OUR CHILDREN

We send our kids to school to be trained in life skills, but an elitist few fanatics, with the enthusiastic cooperation of the U.S. government, have successfully engineered the invasion of our public schools and integrated their dogma into every subject our children learn. Environmentalist propaganda is encountered in almost every textbook, even in math.

Children should be taught respect for our environment. But exposing them to one side's radical views, which may be in direct conflict with what the parents believe, is quite another thing.

What are some of the objectionable specifics?

Anti-capitalism, for beginners. There are balanced ways to inculcate an appreciation for the benefits of the free enterprise system while also teaching students that there are shortcomings in man's activities. That comes with the territory. Should schools be promoting the notion that businesses are necessarily evil, greedy, a curse on society, rather than a source of prosperity?

Worshiping the earth as a deity is another. It is up to parents to give their children spiritual guidance.

Advocating the concept of global government is a third. The U.S. was founded with a heartfelt distrust of "entangling alliances," and we still enjoy the benefits of being more self-sufficient than many other countries. If we are to relinquish any of our rights to self-determination, protecting the environment would not be the most compelling reason.

Our children are being programmed, right under our noses, to accept tyrannical measures that reduce individual (and national) liberty as ordinary and acceptable.

Most children are much more emotional than adults. There is little relativity in a child's mental processes: issues are black and white. Add to this predilection the child's vivid imagination and you have a volatile combination.

In the chapter on "Eco-Terrorism" I have documented some of the atrocities that have been committed in the name of environmental protection. The majority of people arrested for these crimes are mere teenagers, and most of them were excellent students.

The dominant role of the Department of Education in our schools precludes any possibility of changing the curriculum, at least in the short term. In my family, we compensate for the environmentalist intrusion by making an issue of these principles and giving my kids the right spin on things. It works. For now, I suppose that's the best we can do.

Had I been aware of the basis for eco-dogma earlier, I would have forbidden my children from watching many of the programs on television. Having investigated the nature and content of these shows, I realize that children are effectively brainwashed in all things environmental at an early age. The articles below (from the *Wall Street Journal*, April 14, 1993 p. A14:3) illustrate the problem.

Mr. Jonathan Alder is a senior analyst for the Competitive Enterprise Institute and his concerns run along these same lines.

The Greening of America's Youth
[By Jonathan H. Adler. Environmental Policy Analyst, Competitive Enterprise Institute]

On Friday [16 April], children from around the world will meet in Orlando, Fla., for the first annual Kids World Council, a meeting designed to promote children's involvement in environmental politics.

Nickelodeon, a cable channel aimed at children, has run a series of advertisements entitled "Plant It for the Planet!" to promote the council, which it intends to cover. One of the Nickelodeon advertisements talks about the dangers posed by aerosols, refrigerators and those "little white cups" made from polystyrene. All these products, the ad warns, contain chlorofluoro-carbons (CFCs) and are therefore bad for the environment.

There is only one problem. Like so much of the environmental "information" that is being directed at children these days, the ad is wrong.

In fact, those little white cups have been manufactured without the use of CFCs for more than three years. Aerosol cans, pictured in the ad with a skull and crossbones, have not contained CFCs since 1978. That is when the use of CFCs in aerosols was banned by Congress. Nickelodeon's attempt to raise environmental consciousness is actually promoting environmental ignorance.

Nickelodeon is not the only one. The error about CFCs in aerosol cans can be found nearly everywhere one looks. It is contained in the Teenage Mutant Ninja Turtles' children's book "ABC's for a Better Planet," as well as the popular cartoon television series "G.I. Joe." The fallacy hit prime time this year when it was spouted by a character on CBS's award-winning series "Northern Exposure."

Indeed, if one examines any sampling of green materials for children, one finds that they are filled with similar errors, or half-truths. The March 29 issue of *Newsweek* included a "Just for Kids" pull-out section titled "Saving the Earth." In listing the "10 Biggest Challenges" facing the planet, the supplement revives scares of declining agricultural production and resource depletion.

The Newsweek supplement ignores the fact that non-U.S. grain production has been out pacing population increases for the last three decades. Moreover, the prospect of running out of important resources, from precious minerals to oil, is no longer imminent. Proven oil reserves are greater than at any point in history. Should these reserves begin to dwindle, oil prices will again increase, restoring the price competitiveness of other energy sources. Despite what Newsweek claims, there is little prospect of running out.

If that were not bad enough, the pullout includes an "Ask Al Gore" section where kids ask the vice president about environmental problems. One child asks if ozone depletion will turn the earth into a desert. Rather than clarify this child's misunderstanding of the risks posed by ozone depletion and point out that, even if the direst predictions are true, it will mean an ultraviolet-B radiation increase equivalent to moving from Washington to Richmond, Va. (100 miles south), Mr. Gore merely reiterates the need to act now to save the ozone layer.

When asked, "What are we going to do about burning fossil fuels?" Mr. Gore responds by saying, "fossil fuels, such as oil" need to be displaced by "alternative fuels, like clean-burning natural gas." Yet natural gas is a fossil fuel, too.

The Environmental Protection Agency has also gotten into the act. The EPA produces "a student's first sourcebook" on acid rain that is anything but fair-minded. It completely ignores, for example, the conclusions of the National Acid Precipitation Assessment Program — a half-billion-dollar, 10-year government study — which found that significant environmental damage cannot be attributed to acid rain. The EPA's list of environmental materials for classroom use lists publications from every imaginable activist group, ranging form the Environmental Action Coalition to Zero Population Growth.

Thirty states have formal programs of environmental education, and more are on the way. But they won't do much to improve the situation — if the "proposed plan of action" developed by the New Jersey Environmental Education Commission offers any indication. One of this program's mandates is to "develop" the "values" needed to protect the environment. What are these values? Well, they include the fact that "environmental issues have a moral and spiritual dimension" and that the "diversity of culture" should be considered in environmental policies. Does this sound like education, or indoctrination?

Too often environmental education merely proselytizes and promotes pet causes. Newsweek tells children to buy rain-forest nuts and not to purchase products in plastic bottles.

The Teenage Mutant Ninja Turtles tell children to "write to your government leaders at every level — city, county, state, and federal." A "Save the Earth Action Pack" distributed by the Turner Broadcasting System even tells children "to increase the amount of time and money" they give to environmental organizations and to urge "governments to support the work of these organizations." Were this done with any other political matter, parents would be up in arms — and rightly so.

Clearly, environmental lobbyists have decided that one way of advancing their political objectives is to reach the hearts and minds of children who will not only pester their parents but will themselves grow up to be activists and voters.

Other would-be instructors of children are merely trying to act "responsibly," apparently without understanding that there may be more than one answer to any environmental question and that the "green" version of things can be extremely simplistic and misleading. Unfortunately, the creators of environmental books and toys rarely know much about the subject that they are promoting.

Environmental education would do better simply teaching about scientific matters, including hydrology, ecosystems and the weather. As children get older, the pros and cons of various environmental policies can be discussed in a fair and balanced manner. Right now, the environmental science pushed to children is more political than factual.

* *

My five-year-old daughter is being bombarded with the kinds of half-truths and outright lies Mr. Adler cites. Clearly, Nickelodeon is the biggest offender, with the Disney Channel running a close second. The barrage of environmentalist propaganda, much of it in the form of public service announcements (PSAs) produced by environmental advocacy groups, is so pervasive on Nickelodeon that channel is now completely off-limits to my daughter.

Consistent with Mr. Adler's contention that our children are being consciously targeted with this propaganda, no one who watches Nick at Night, Nickelodeon's adult-oriented programming, would get any indication that this propagandizing goes on. The PSAs and the messages about global warming and recycling suddenly disappear once the evening programming begins.

I encourage all parents who are concerned about what their children are seeing on television to question the validity of the messages being conveyed about the environment. Most of the information is not coming from scientific journals and legitimate research, but from special interest groups whose level of financial contributions depends on the perception [sic] that an environ-mental crisis exists.

Roy E. Cordato, Gaithersburg, Md.

* *

It's also revealing to look at why environmentalists are typically so successful at winning children over to their ideas.

Part of the reason, of course, is that few alternative voices exist for children to hear. Most of the industrial world feels contempt for industry as such, and has come to accept as gospel almost any environmentalist claim.

Journalists often uncritically accept hypotheses of politically biased scientists who are living on government grants; teachers and parents in turn often uncritically accept the hype of the media; and children, who rely on adults to teach them the art of critical thinking, are often left defenseless in the face of alleged "facts" and "environmental emergencies."

When adults feed children these daily doses of poisonous falsehoods (such as the idea that CFCs, which are heavier than air, rise to and destroy the ozone layer), children have little recourse to find an antidote or to even know that an antidote is needed.

But children are highly susceptible to environmentalist ideas for another reason: Children, like environmentalists, typically don't hold production in much esteem. Rational adults know that to live they must produce — that is, they know that they must refashion their environment to meet their needs. Children often don't fully grasp this connection because parents (properly) see to it that their needs are met for them. As a result, children often don't recognize how much of a sacrifice it is to close a factory for the sake of a snail darter.

Given environmentalists' low esteem of human life, it's not surprising that they feel no qualms about filling children's minds with falsehoods and playing them like pawns in a political game those children don't understand.

Erik Laughlin, Chicago, Illinois

* *

Environmental activists cloak themselves with moral superiority and therefore excuse small lapses of fact for the greater good of inculcating the laudable value of spiritual connection between humans and the environment.

They should be scolded for blatantly abusing their power as adults over children. The adult-child relationship is the definition of a power relationship. Children have almost no defenses against massive distortions perpetuated against them by powerful adults. Misleading children with made-up facts and imposing simplistic answers breaks trust, destroys respect and backfires.

Laura Childs Martisius, Denver, Colorado

Many websites target children, enlisting them as activists in the environmentalist campaign to tear down our American culture and rebuild it to comply with their fanatic vision. Much of the content on these sites is couched in simplified vocabulary that will appeal to a child. Their message, on the other hand, is anything but juvenile.

One site encouraged kids to compose hard-ball letters to their Congressmen demanding environmental reform. The text of the letter was also printed for them to copy.

Several others followed the same formula, posing a hypothetical problem and recommending an eco-elitist solution. The consistent thread of anti-capitalist cant invariably casts the business owner as an evil intruder intent on killing Bambis and Freddy the Skunk.

As an avid outdoorsman, I have no objection if our schools teach my children reasonable conservation measures, or provide a course that teaches them factual scientific data. But many of these radical views strike me as anti-American, in that they aim to unduly limit our freedoms as individuals, and thus are a gross violation of the mandate of public education.

CHAPTER 4.
TARGETING OUR ECONOMY

> Isn't the only hope for the planet that the industrialized civilizations collapse? Isn't it our responsibility to bring that about? [Maurice Strong, Chairman of the 1992 Earth Summit in Rio de Janeiro, Chief Aide to U.N. Secretary-General Kofi Annan]

> We already have too much economic growth in the United States. Economic growth in rich countries like ours is the disease, not the cure. [Paul Elhrich, Stanford University biologist and Advisor to Vice President Albert Gore]

> I think if we don't overthrow capitalism, we don't have a chance of saving the world ecologically. I think it is possible to have an ecological society under socialism. I don't think it's possible under capitalism. [Judd Bar, of Earth First? quoted by Walter Williams, columnists with Heritage Features (Syndicate, State Journal Register, June 25, 1992)]

> The immediate source of ecological crisis is capitalism...Capitalism is a cancer in the biosphere....I believe the color of radicalism today is not red, but green. [Steve Chase, ed., Defending the Earth: A Dialogue Between Murray Bookchin and Dave Foreman (Boston South End Press, 1991, p 57-59)]

Humanity has flirted, and even gone all the way, with any number of asinine views in the course of history. But holding misguided notions is one thing; orchestrating an aggressive campaign to accomplish insane objectives is different. Yet that is precisely what the environmental establishment is doing. In fact, they have already achieved spectacular success. I know. I was raised in a region of the United States that has languished under the oppressive hand of the EPA for decades: the towns of Troy and Libby in northern Montana.

The Northern Spotted Owl is the unfortunate fowl that the eco-mafia chose to serve as the mascot for their attack on the logging industry. I say "unfortunate fowl" because I can assure you, if one of these birds ever strays into Montana or any other outpost of civilization along the northern corridor, it won't survive 24 hours.

It's not that folks in that neck of the woods are spiteful, or negligent in their stewardship of the wilderness, but this owl now symbolizes the terrible suffering brought to millions of Americans along the Canadian border in the northwest. The EPA, at the behest of the enviro-elite, has brought on this dilemma. The Spotted Owl was unlucky enough to be chosen as the "endangered species" that led to the dismantling of the thriving logging activity in that region of the country.

When I was a strapping young lad in the north woods, the Kootenai National Forest, in the Troy-Libby-Eureka area of Lincoln County, like the entire northwestern region that stretches from the Dakotas to the West Coast, was a hotbed of logging activity. The majority of my friends were in families that depended on the logging industry for a livelihood.

We're not talking only about the men who actually cut down trees, but also those who owned and operated logging trucks, worked in saw mills, pole yards, paper plants, plywood plants and many other occupations that harvested and processed a large portion of the wood products sold in America.

All of the residents in that region depended on the revenues generated by the logging business: police officers, clerks, dentists, plumbers, salesmen, grocery checkers. . . They depended on the tax revenues that were invested in schools, streets, public buildings, law enforcement, and every other public service, and on logging dollars that prospered local businesses, paid the tuition for college, made it possible for people to get ahead a little bit every year, even put some hard earned money away in savings.

Not any longer.

When the Clinton Administration listed the Spotted Owl as an endangered species, it was the death knell for thousands of jobs. The economy of that entire region took a nose dive, and to this day the residents of the Northwest United States struggle to survive in a staggering economic malaise. Oregon is leading the nation in unemployment.

I moved back to Montana eight years ago and settled near my parents in the Gallatin Valley, near Bozeman. Even though that area, and a handful of other metropolitan areas, are far more prosperous than the remainder of the state, the average wage hovered somewhere around $8.50 an hour! It would be pointless to estimate the average pay in the rural areas and small towns. There are no jobs, period.

After two years of determined effort, with our bills in arrears and no prospect for better wages, I moved my family to the Omaha, Nebraska vicinity.

Five years ago I visited Troy and Libby, where I went to high school. The contrast to my youth was startling. The bustling mountain hamlets where I grew up were in a sorry state. Tourism has replaced logging as the primary industry, but revenues aren't sufficient to support the working population adequately. Most of the businesses that used to thrive along main street in Libby are closed, or replaced by one of the scores of casinos. My wife and I also noted the absence of young people. Almost every graduate of high school and college is forced to find employment in more affluent regions of the country.

My hat is off to those hardy souls who doggedly refuse to leave their beloved Montana. The price they pay to stay there is astronomical, not in dollars alone, but in the mental anguish that is born of oppression and injustice. Their futures and dreams have been hijacked by the eco-loonies and the goons in our bureaucracy who enthusiastically carry out the environmentalist agenda.

Even so, with these pitiful conditions to their credit, the eco-mafia smile and brag about their conquest. I have several quotes to the effect that the Spotted Owl was an enormous victory for the eco-left. They turn a blind eye to the suffering they have caused. If anything, their efforts to subject far more of the Midwest to the same tyranny have escalated. The logging industry is just the tip of the iceberg. The environmentalist assault on America's economy knows no bounds. Using their pantheon of weapons: the endangered species act, wetlands, pollution, wilderness conservation, ozone depletion, urban sprawl, and "sustainable development," they use our courts to hamstring and disrupt any business that comes into their cross hairs.

Successful lobbying and relentless litigation have also had a devastating effect on the mining industry. The states of New Mexico, Arizona, Nevada, Wyoming, Colorado and Montana have been the hardest hit, particularly the arid region in the Mohave Desert, whose natural resources are limited to coal and ore. The economies in most of these states are not diversified and depend heavily upon the mining industry for employment and tax revenue.

A third sector of the economy under virulent attack is agriculture: farming and livestock production. Because most ranchers across the Midwest rely on grazing lands controlled by the Bureau of Land Management (BLM), they are vulnerable to governmental fiat; and because the environmentalist domination of those agencies that manage natural resources is almost total, the onslaught of new legislation and continuous litigation has successfully bankrupted hundreds of family operations across the West.[2]

Those who are able to survive continue to fight the attempts of their antagonists to deny them access to federal lands and waterways. Because ranchers extract no raw materials from the earth, nor harvest the timber, the strategy of the eco-mafia has been to use endangered species and degradation of grasslands to cripple their industry.

Every endangered species is allocated a habitat which is placed under federal control, even though it may be private property. By law, this habitat cannot be altered in any way, which precludes any new structures to protect cattle in harsh weather, road building, or any other improvement. Of course, the wildlife that is listed as endangered in the open country is not abundant enough to disrupt ranching to the satisfaction of the greenies, so they turn to plants and flowers too, even bugs and viruses. The Clean Water Act is another popular weapon.

---

2. According to the USDA Agricultural Fact Book, 1998, 9 out of 10 farms are owned by individuals. The large number of "corporate" operations is deceptive in that 79% of them are family entities in which the ownership remains with blood relatives. As for tax dollars; the enormous cost of land management is attributed to the huge bureaucracies in Washington, and much of that is spent on environmental programs. The Spotted Owl, alone, will cost us 46 billion.

Much of the micro-management these entities waste money on is unnecessary. Ranchers and farmers are far better qualified to manage the land. Most of them have been on their properties for generations, and they have a vested interest in conservation in as much as their livelihoods are at stake. The alarmist propaganda that grazing is destroying rangeland overlooks the fact that BLM and USDI, and other agencies, confine ranchers to just a very small allotment of grazing land which leads to overgrazing. There are vast tracts of land which could be opened to grazing that would completely eliminate the problems that environmentalists blame on ranchers and farmers. Individual liberty, again, is at stake. The number of people ranching, or any other consideration, is secondary to the guarantee of freedom that each American has been given in our Constitution. However, as a matter of record, if we removed every farm and ranch tomorrow the money we spend for environmental programs would remain high. In fact, without the rural populace the cost would increase, as they are instrumental in preventing many destructive effects of nature, such as erosion. Bureaucracies have a bad habit of inventing innovative ways to justify their existence, and in the case of environmental agencies, they have the added incentive of draining the American economy by every ploy they can seize upon.

A fourth vital sector of the economy that is under the thumb of environmentalist tyranny is oil and gas production. Their crusade to block access to the Arctic National Wildlife Refuge is ongoing, even now. Yet the resources there would strengthen the U.S. considerably. Quoting Andrew Bernstein, Senior Fellow at Ayn Rand Institute:

> [The refuge] is an area so abundant in oil that Senator Frank Murkowski of Alaska, chairman of the Senate Committee on Energy and Natural Resources, states that it could produce oil for decades, adding as much as $325 billion to the U.S. economy and reducing imports by well over one million barrels per day.

This is just one instance of obstruction that seriously hampers our domestic oil and gas production. Natural gas is currently being vented into the atmosphere (burned) in Alaska around the clock — enough to supply every household in America for a long, long time (just how long would, of course, depend on weather conditions). Millions of dollars worth of this valuable natural resource is destroyed because environmentalist litigation has successfully stalled any hope of building a pipeline to transport it to the lower 48 states.

How much the American public would save in the price they pay for natural gas can be estimated in various ways, but any savings at all would be a welcome change.

What potential hazard does a pipeline pose for the environment? These lines are managed with meticulous care, constantly monitored, patrolled, and upgraded before any serious mishaps come to pass. The possibility of a leak is remote, but even if one did occur it would be repaired immediately and the impact on the environment would be negligible.

Apart from environmentalist propaganda and scare tactics, the self-appointed champions of the environment can offer no valid reason why we shouldn't begin to tap the rich petroleum deposits on the North Slope and build a second pipeline for natural gas. Their warnings of catastrophic damage to the environment are no more than rhetorical nonsense, with no basis in fact. What's more, given their habit of playing fast and loose with the facts, and relying on "scientific data" that is refuted by every creditable institution and scientist in this country, it is reasonable to doubt their veracity and the accuracy of their doomsday predictions.

Since exploration and drilling began on the portion of the North Slope where it is permitted, the caribou have increased in number from 2,000 to 23,000. Environmentalists' claims regarding the scars that man would leave on that unspoiled wilderness is also hooey. Trucks and equipment travel over ice, and every spring their tracks are obliterated.

The estimated revenues from expanded drilling and extraction would be $325 billion a year and over 700,000 jobs would be created. An added benefit, and a huge one, is that North Slope oil could replace the crude we purchase from Saudi Arabia — there's enough to cover us for 36 years.

Just as critical as the economic considerations is our dependence on foreign oil. We have suffered the consequences of OPEC manipulation in the past, which created astronomical prices at the gas pump, and nothing has changed. The Middle Eastern states are not natural allies of the United States, and they can play the oil card at any critical moment. The possible consequences are unthinkable. And yet, we have it within our means to free ourselves from this hazardous dependency.

The obstructionist tactics of the eco-lobby and agencies in Washington D.C. are not only a grievous drain on our economy, but a policy that places us in great peril, affecting even our ability to defend ourselves militarily.

It may not sit well with many readers, but my personal opinion is that some things are more important than the perpetuation of a certain species of frog, or wild flower. We need a balanced policy in environmental law that gives due consideration to human needs and priorities as opposed to the needs of an animal or plant.

Environmentalist doctrine is inflexible, with no allowance for variables, and is extremely biased against man. If an acre of ground has a rare plant on it, it is declared sacred ground. You can't drive across it, graze cattle on it, build on it. But there is no way to be sure that the plant will not become extinct anyway, even if we leave things as they are — certainly not adequate cause to deny a hard-working family an income. It would appear to be a reasonable alternative to dig the plant up and transplant it somewhere in the millions of acres of undisturbed wilderness where it can thrive without persecuting human beings.

Unfortunately, this isn't how environmentalists think. Their approach is that the plant must remain where nature put it. Who cares how much suffering it causes to impose oppressive regulations to protect it?

Case after case illustrate the fact that the vast majority of court actions which deny citizens their rights of property ownership are based on trumped up charges and false allegations, supposition, and worse — outright lies. They adamantly refuse to consider any reasonable course of action that would spare human suffering.

Yet another industry that has come under environmentalist attack is power generation. Quoting Mr. Bernstein again:

> Green activists have worked for decades to stop the construction of major power plants in California — and have succeeded. As a result, California generates less power per resident than any other state, and "imports" about one quarter of the energy it consumes. Since 1985 only minor power plants have been built in California, adding only 6,000 megawatts to the state's supply — hardly enough to meet an increased demand for 10,000 megawatts. If plants generating an additional 4,000 megawatts had been built in the last decade, there would be no energy crisis today. By preventing entrepreneurs from building power plants, environmentalists choked the supply of power and set the stage for crises like the current one.

When brown-outs crippled California during the summer of 2002, I was working for Enron. I recall that Jeff Skilling, the CEO, was jeered at a speech he gave in the Sunshine State and had a pie thrown in his face. Enron (now Northern Natural Gas) is a gas transmission operation. They don't drill and refine petroleum, nor do they charge the consumer for gas. They offer a service to the producer, moving the product from one place to another.

Attacking Jeff Skilling was ludicrous. He had nothing to do with the availability or, rather, the lack of power resources, but this is just what you might expect of the eco-gang. It has been their lobbying and litigation that has denied the citizens of California adequate energy. Every time a power company tried to build a nuclear plant, they litigated them to death. Those that did finally prevail are so heavily regulated, and over budget, that they can't provide energy at a reasonable price.

When the shortage hit the West Coast, the suppliers were forced to buy power on the spot market to meet demand. The price they paid was high, as it always is in that situation. The energy had to be brought up from Texas, which added to the cost. And what did Californians do? They lambasted Texas for taking advantage of them! But perhaps the Texans would have preferred to have fewer energy plants, too; only they had been realistic enough to know that if they wanted the power, they'd have to accept the building of power plants.

Instead of finding solutions, environmental groups throw up spooky visions of disaster that turn public opinion against legitimate businesses. All the while, it is they who support irresponsible laws and legal actions that cause the problem.

It is man's unhampered ingenuity that assures our future, and the future of our environment. The key to our well-being and health is the fertile inventiveness of the human mind and the freedom to implement possible new solutions as we devise them. The most advanced and effective methods of protecting the environment are only possible in nations with the prosperity to afford them. A robust economy helps make a healthy environment possible.

See Appendix A — "Economy," for additional documentation.

CHAPTER 5.
OUR PROPERTY RIGHTS UNDER ATTACK

The Fifth Amendment to the United States Constitution guarantees that no person shall "be deprived of life, liberty, or property, without due process of law; nor shall private property be taken for public use without just compensation."

The original intent of this provision was to safeguard the citizen's property from illegal seizure for use as a public amenity: streets, parks, sewers, utilities — any use to benefit the public.

But the environmental flim-flam artists have successfully circumvented our rights by using wetlands and endangered species as the linchpin of their assault on private property. Although they do not actually take the property for public use, as such, when a parcel of land is designated a wetland or an endangered species habitat, the property is rendered commercially worthless and any activity that alters the terrain or poses a threat to the plants or indigenous wildlife is prohibited.

Since, in a sense, the land has not been taken away from its owner, they argue that no compensation is due him.

This kind of brazen attack on our rights as American citizens is not an isolated incident. Every year thousands of Americans suffer the loss of their property value, and their right to use their land as they see fit, at the hands of environmental organizations, or the U.S. Government, or both.

Billions of dollars in grant money and private contributions enable the eco-establishment to retain legions of sharp attorneys, who are experts at using our own legal system against us. Even the most egregious cases are rarely won by the private citizen, either because they cannot afford the extravagant sums it takes to hire legal counsel, or simply by attrition. Using injunctions, and other legal instruments, the eco-law-dogs can delay a decision in a case for years. By then, many families and businesses, having been prevented from the just enjoyment of the value of their property, are insolvent. For while the haggling goes on, citizens are unable to sell their property (unless they are willing to accept a small fraction of its worth) and cannot make improvements. Farmers and ranchers cannot cultivate their own land, or graze their livestock. The high percentage of victory in the courts has resulted in contempt of our rights and interests.

President John Adams said:

> The moment the idea is admitted into society that property is not as sacred as the Laws of God, and that there is not a force of law and public justice to protect it, anarchy and tyranny commence. Property must be sacred or liberty cannot exist.

The Honorable Mr. Adams was not speaking from the standpoint of theory alone. It was the tyrannical rule of the English throne, especially where it impinged on a man's ability to earn a living, that inspired our ancestors to risk life and limb and leave behind their homes and all that they knew to brave a harsh wilderness to establish a new society.

It was not until the English throne continued the flagrant abuse of citizen's rights in the colonies that the American people resorted to the only recourse they had left, force of arms. Their deep love for liberty, born of suffering and degradation, drove them to put everything on the line for the chance to live free.

That commitment to the principles of self-determination and inalienable rights is woven into every sentence of our founding documents, the Declaration of Independence and The Constitution of the United States of America.

The abuse of property rights was singled out by President Adams as a critical factor in turning a just government into a form of tyranny. At this moment in Americas' short history, this very process us taking shape. Excessive taxation, distortion of the law to solve social ills, gun control, and the subject of this documentary, environmental extremism, are among the prominent symptoms of growing tyranny, the subjugation of a people to the totalitarian rule of massive government.

In America tyranny has taken on a humanitarian facade, masqueraded as the quest for equal rights and protecting life and the environment. It is difficult to recognize despotism when it assumes the guise of noble causes, but the usurpation of freedom has the same catastrophic effect regardless of how seemingly benign is the instrument of its destruction.

There is a growing tidal wave of outrage across the entire United States. Grassroots citizens' groups have sprung up in every state. The litany of abuse has touched so many thousands that the environmental madness is no longer isolated to areas like the Northwest, or the plains of the Midwest.

When the rule of law, which was intended to protect our rights, becomes diluted, and a people cannot trust the state to protect their rights any longer, they do what our ancestors did: they fight. The passions that this kind of abuse gives rise to don't subside over time. If anything, they burn hotter; and when the afflicted become so numerous that they form a huge network of the dispossessed, their cause gains momentum. That is precisely what is happening at this moment in America.

In his article, "States Rights Rebellion" (7-23-94) Patrick Buchanan noted:

> In Catron County, N.M., rhetoric about "taking back America" has taken on real meaning. When the Forest Service curbed timber harvests to protect the habitat of the Mexican spotted owl, and started reviewing whether cattle grazing was endangering the range land, county officials drew up their own plan for managing the land.
>
> Forest rangers who tried to cut ranchers' livestock grazing permits were threatened with arrest. "The Forest Service has been run off at gunpoint," says Susan Schock, a silver City, N.M., environmentalist. "They've turned the forest over to the county."
>
> "If we didn't have the plan, there would have been bloodshed," says rancher Dick Manning. "Things have gotten to that point."
>
> Interior Secretary Bruce Babbitt, who is prosecuting Mr. Clinton's "War against the West," chuckles at the "sovereign nation of Catron County." But Catron's defiance has inspired a nationwide "county movement," enlisting county and state governments in the battle against environmental regulators.

Environmentalism is by far the most dangerous form of tyranny in our society, for it is not a gradual loss of our autonomy, as by over- taxation, but a sudden, abrupt intrusion. In a matter of weeks, or months, it sweeps away all a family has worked for, their future and their dreams, often leaving them destitute. Thousands of Americans are beginning to do more than just speak their mind.

Mr. Scott Sonner, of the Associated Press, filed this report:

RENO, Nev. — Western ranchers and farmers who have clashed with the government over fish protection are leading a new call to arms, heading to Florida with a giant shovel and bucket in tow.

The cross-country convoy by the Klamath Bucket Brigade of Klamath Falls, Ore., and the Jarbidge Shovel Brigade of Elko, Nev., is meant to rally support for the cause the groups share with Florida farmers: property rights. All three groups say the government is trampling their rights in order to protect endangered species.

"We want to spread the message about how property rights are being assaulted all across the U.S. — how the Endangered Species Act is being used by environmentalists and government groups to run people off their land," Bill Ransom, a third-generation rancher and logger from Klamath Falls, said during a stop Tuesday in Reno.

The groups left Oregon on Saturday for the 3,000-mile, 22-day drive to Homestead, Fla., towing the 13-foot silver bucket and 30-foot green-and-yellow shovel behind.

The two brigades hope to raise money for Florida farmers who oppose raising water levels that they say will flood their fields to help an endangered sparrow in the Everglades — an effort environmentalists have worked for years to support.

Oregon's Klamath Basin farmers have been in conflict with the federal government since it cut off irrigation water to benefit salmon and other fish 14 months ago. Last summer, farmers desperate for water confronted federal marshals, pried open irrigation gates and formed a bucket brigade to dump water into irrigation ditches.

"When you put a fly or a small animal above a human life and human good, there is something wrong with that," Ransom said.

A new U.S. Bureau of Reclamation strategy redirected water from salmon to farmers at the upper end of the river. But environmentalists and tribal groups blamed the policy for the deaths of at least 12,000 adult salmon.

Officials said last week that they would redirect more water to the salmon without curtailing water deliveries to farmers nearing the end of their season.

In Nevada, just south of the Idaho border, the Shovel Brigade has been battling the Forest Service and U.S. Fish and Wildlife Service for five years over the agencies' refusal to rebuild a washed-out road along a stream that is home to the threatened bull trout. The group's symbolic shovel illustrates their determination to rebuild the road with hand tools if necessary.

Meanwhile, farmers in Florida's Miami-Dade County have organized a "Sawgrass Rebellion" against the planned Everglades flooding, named for the preferred nesting ground of the endangered Cape Sable Seaside Sparrow. They say the flooding is unnecessary to save the sparrow and would destroy their private farms of citrus fruit, avocados, mangoes, winter tomatoes and other crops.

But environmentalists say opponents of the Everglades project are part of a small minority, many of them extremists. They said the government intends to buy out any farms that would be flooded.

"We've pulled together a strong coalition of agricultural interests, water supply interests, conservation interests and national park interests to get this Everglades restoration plan through Congress and get it kick started," said Mark Kraus, deputy director of the National Audubon Society's Florida office.

"We really have a very mainstream project here with broad support. . . . The Sawgrass Rebellion is one of those groups that aren't willing to work within the compromise system we are using to get the Everglades restored."

A core group of about a dozen people from the two brigades are making the entire journey to Florida, with other activists joining and dropping off along the route that will pass through Utah, Colorado, New Mexico, Oklahoma, Texas, Louisiana, Mississippi and Alabama, before ending with a Florida rally Oct. 19.

"The miners, loggers, farmers and ranchers are making a united front," said Rocky Dippel of Mesquite, Nev., who said he's been at odds with the government since his mining claims were pulled in Alaska 20 years ago.

What is striking about Mr. Sonner's article is the environmentalist's complete lack of compassion for the people they hurt, as is made clear in the statement by Mark Kraus, deputy director of the National Audubon Society's Florida office.

Mr. Kraus labeled anyone who resists having his own farmland flooded an "extremist." What is "extreme" in objecting to the loss of your farm, land you have toiled on, nurtured, and depended on for income, to raise a family, put food on the table?

He further stated that the government intends to buy out any flooded farms.

What if the owners don't want to sell? That's the issue here, the rights of an individual to use or dispose of his property as he chooses, not at the whim of an organization or government agency with absolutely no concern for his welfare.

Mr. Kraus also made reference to the coalition of "agricultural interests, water supply interests. . . " as justification to ride roughshod over the objections of land owners. Those "interests," as he puts it, are other environmentalist factions and state agencies, not neutral parties.

The 5th Amendment clause that stipulates no private land shall be taken for public use without due process and compensation does not make allowance for a bird, nor fish, nor any animal, fowl, or any other creature. Can environmental concerns correctly be defined as "public interest" at all, when they do not constitute a hazard to public health?

What portion of the population is enriched, or otherwise served, by the draconian measures the environmentalists are so well known for? Land owners are "the public," and their interests are certainly not served. The issue of property rights is addressed in the Constitution to protect property rights, not to provide any special interest groups the legal means to violate those rights.

There is another category of property rights that have come under an virulent attack: the right of the American people to enjoy our wilderness areas. To people who cherish the solitude and beauty of nature, this is a sensitive issue.

Over 400 millions acres of "federal lands" have been essentially closed to those who enjoy escaping from civilization for a time, camping in the unspoiled wilderness, fishing, hunting or simply reveling in the magnificent splendor of the American frontier.

Environmental groups, in collusion with federal agencies, have been successful in their attempts to restrict access to the wilderness by motor vehicles, to ban road building, limit hunting and fishing, and restrict prospecting and placer mining by individual enthusiasts.

Their idea of "protecting the environment" is keeping man out.

The theory that motor vehicles cause damage is ridiculous. The amounts of exhaust released into the air by the relatively small number of enthusiasts that venture into the wilderness are infinitesimal. Carbon dioxide is healthy for plant life, in fact, and even the other components of exhaust do not kill all the plants in America's. Another weak argument is that the sound of an engine scares wildlife. Most wild animals will flee from anything they perceive as a danger, even other animals. However, they are far more adaptable to changing surroundings than we generally give them credit for. Many visitors to Yellowstone National Park find that animals are an outright nuisance, standing in the road and begging for handouts.

"Tracks in the ground?" Even when you travel across muddy ground and leave deep ruts, the ceaseless renewing of the natural order erases any signs of man in a very short time. Nature is not so delicate that it is easily despoiled by man's presence (by large-scale pollution, yes, but I am not referring to industrial waste, here). #There are reasonable compromises that will have to be made from both sides of the question. On the environmentalist side, the public has the right to access remote wilderness, and that demands adequate roads. On the sportsman's side, people should be willing to confine their travel to the road and refrain from off-road travel. This restriction, however, has nothing to do with leaving tracks in the timber, but with the right of other hikers or fishermen to enjoy the solitude of nature. We must all acknowledge the freedoms of others as well. In the case of heavily populated areas, this is a reality we have to accept. People have the right to enjoy the splendor of nature, and if anyone requires more privacy he will simply have to travel farther to find it.

Consider the fact that nature recovers from catastrophic events like volcanoes, hurricanes, tornados, floods, droughts, earthquakes, and fires. Natural phenomena in the last hundred years have been vastly more destructive than all the effects of human impact. [3]

Environmental propaganda uses junk science, fright-mongering and outright lies to gain the support of the public. The following statements were extracted from speeches or literature from environmental groups.

[W]e have to offer up scary scenarios, make simplified, dramatic statements, and make little mention of any doubts we may have. Each of us has to decide what's the right balance is between being effective and being honest.
— Stephen Schneider, proponent of the theory that CFCs are depleting the ozone

Now, in a widening sphere of decisions, the costs of error are so exorbitant that we need to act on theory alone, which is to say on prediction alone. It follows that the reputation of scientific prediction needs to be enhanced. But that can happen, paradoxically, only if scientists disavow the certainty and precision that they normally insist on.
Above all, we need to learn to act decisively to forestall predicted perils, even while knowing that they may never materialize. We must take action, in a manner of speaking, to preserve our ignorance. There are perils that we can be certain of avoiding only at the cost of never knowing with certainty that they were real.
— Jonathan Schell, author of *Our Fragile Earth*

A global climate treaty must be implemented even if there is no scientific evidence to back the greenhouse effect.
— Richard Benedict, an employee for the State Department working on assignment for the Conservation Foundation

3. According to the USDA report "Acres of Forestland Converted to Developed Land (1982-1997)," a total of 10,229,200 acres were developed. By contrast, the United Nations Forest Fire Statistics (ECE/TIM/BULL/52/4) reports that 91,000,000 acres of forest land burned between 1989 and 1998, a 6 year differential. At an average of 10.15 million acres a year that would add 61 million acres, a total of 152 million acres.

These statements, and many more like them, shine a garish light on all that these organizations do and say. If they have no moral or ethical standard of conduct, then what can we believe?

Clearly, not every member of the environmental movement is dishonest. Many thousands of men and women who are concerned about preserving the environment adhere to a high ethical standard in their lives. However, if they willingly associate themselves with organizations that promote such views, and support them with contributions, then they compromise their personal honor to some extent. The organizations they support are not lifted to a higher standard by their participation; rather, the opposite is true: they are tainted by the tawdry practices they advocate.

It is obvious that the eco-elite have a false sense of security. They feel that they are at liberty to use any ploy, no matter how low, to have their way. They cloak their actions in a pretense of superiority. Fueled by broad public financial support, by the press, by their active membership, and by their cabal entrenched in the most powerful agencies in our government, they confront the average citizen with arrogant self-assurance.

The litany of half-truths, junk science and veiled threats is a continuous thread that runs through the entire spectrum of environmentalist strategy. An example of misleading and deceptive propaganda is the argument against placer mining by private citizens. The average placer is a portable device with an engine about the size that a lawn mower uses. It can be carried into a remote location on a man's back. This simple device is used to process gravel in a stream bed to filter out the gold. Environmentalists play on the ignorance of the public at large with their claims that placers damage the habitat, leave ugly scars, and endanger fish and other aquatic life.

This is not true.

When a prospector discovers "color," he finds a nearby bend in the stream, because gold is the heaviest metal element and it settles in pockets at the inside of a bend where the water tends to eddy, or on sandbars during spring "run off" when the water level is high. The "suction line" is a flexible tube about 4" in diameter, with which he sucks gravel into the dredge where it is discharged onto a small ramp. A fabric with a deep nap, similar to outdoor carpeting, covers the bed of the ramp and, as the sand and gravel pass over it, the gold settles and is trapped in the rough fabric.

The remainder of the "aggregate" flows down the ramp, back into the stream. Any evidence that a man has been there will be obliterated in the next spring run off, when high water carries tons of particulate matter downstream and distributes it in low spots, or builds new sand bars. In most cases, however, the prospector dredges only aggregate from under water and there is no sign that he has been there an hour after he leaves.

As for endangering aquatic life, the dredge releases millions of tiny plankton that thrive in the finer sand under the gravel. These tiny creatures are the food that fry (baby fish) feed on. Consequently, dredging actually contributes to the health of the fish population. Further, if the ludicrous claim that muddy water hurts the fish were true, every living creature in every watercourse in America would be wiped out in one spring. During high water the loose gravel, sand and smaller particles in the stream and river beds is carried along in huge quantities for several weeks, even months.

Why would the eco-mafia support the abolishment of recreational placer mining? It leaves no unsightly damage and actually contributes to healthy fish. What's the problem?

The answer to that question is that eco-extremists want us all locked out, forbidden to trespass on our own public domain. Their cause has nothing to do with protecting anything, only usurping individual freedom.

The ban on road building is another farce. Details are provided in the chapter "Let it Burn," but the gist of it bears repeating.

Good roads serve several valuable ends. They provide the sportsman, camper, picnicker, or sight seer with a safe and easy means of driving miles off the well-traveled main roads in order to enjoy wonderful solitude. Equally important, they are needed for the work of fire control and timber management. Good roads make it possible for fire fighters to reach a burn quickly, and in most cases where there are roads they can extinguish the blaze in hours, before it grows out of control. At this point in time, the only access to America's more remote areas is by helicopters or smoke jumpers who parachute in. Once on the ground, however, there are no routes of supply, nor are there passable escape routes in case the fire gets out of control. If emergency workers are injured, there is no efficient means to rescue them — only helicopters; and many times the fire or other factors make it impossible for helicopters to land, or even hover, near a raging wildfire.

One article in the Documentation Section recounts the death of four young fire fighters because Forest Service officials refused to allow helicopters to dip water from a river because it was endangered steel head salmon habitat. They burned to death because eco-maniacs wouldn't risk disturbing a fish.

The public uses roads to hunt and fish, gather berries in season, pick morel mushrooms in the spring, camp, or just get away for a day. They also rely on the roads as emergency routes when there is an injury or death. It is the right of citizens to have this convenience at their disposal so they can derive optimum enjoyment of *their land*. It doesn't belong to the government, but to the people.

In closing this chapter, I want to touch on an obscure principle at work in the management of our public lands by the federal Government that can easily become a threat to our peaceful society.

Wealth is inextricably tied to our natural resources. There is no industry that does not depend on materials that come from nature. Even such "clean" industries as computer technology and insurance companies depend, indirectly, on the wealth we extract from the land because they rely on industries that do use natural resources or the incomes of Americans that work in these industries.

Government regulation of our resources is a very subtle form of creeping socialism. If government has absolute control of the source of wealth, then they have absolute control of capital. The fact that businesses may still be owned by private individuals, or corporations, is a meaningless technicality that supports the illusion of a private sector.

That government owns most of the land in the United States is, on a larger scale, the same malpractice as that which leaves the ownership of private land in the hands of the individual, but denies him the free use thereof. Ownership without autonomy is merely a very clever device to placate the masses by providing them the facade of freedom.

While it may smack of melodrama, the inevitable outcome of this attack on the framework of our liberty will eventually result in bloodshed. The usurpation of our freedom is occurring at such an alarming rate that totalitarian rule will come about during the lifetime of millions of Americans who have believed they were living in freedom. It is already happening.

The demise of freedom is hardly evident in an apathetic society; it is more clear in a nation of citizens who are sensitive to the issues of self-determination. The Sawgrass Rebellion and the shovel and bucket brigade drive this point home. Already the rural population of the United States, who are traditionally independent in their lifestyle and attitudes, are joining forces, forming alliances across the breadth of America with others like themselves who have suffered the scourge of tyranny. Sooner or later their frustration and anger will erupt in violence, perhaps even a full scale civil war.

The interdiction of county and state officials in New Mexico, with the enthusiastic support of the citizens, against federal hegemony is not an incident that we would be wise to view as insignificant, nor is it an isolated phenomenon of no importance. Local governments and law enforcement personnel are also members of their local communities, and their interests naturally coincide with that of their fellow citizens. When the leaders of our far flung rural citizenry feel justified to take such extreme measures, it bespeaks an undercurrent of desperation, social agitation beyond the normal range of discontent we might expect, complaints about high taxes and the like.

These developments are quietly fermenting beneath the surface, largely unnoticed, ignored by the press; and unless we use our votes and freedom of speech and assembly to right this grievous wrong, an explosive reaction can be expected.

See Appendix B — "Regulatory Abuse," for additional documentation on the abuse of property rights.

See Appendix C — "Fraud," for additional documentation on the use of lies and propaganda by environmental organizations and federal agencies.

CHAPTER 6.
CAMPAIGN AGAINST FARMERS AND RANCHERS

Americans who live in metropolitan communities, those who are not familiar with their rural neighbors, may have little idea of the character of the citizens who are the victims of these terrible injustices. I would like to dispel the notion that ranchers and farmers are arrogant and ungrateful in their use of public lands to graze their livestock. I've read petty comments that insinuate that these folks call it "their land," and demand the right to use it.

Mike Hudak, director of Public Lands Without Livestock, a project of Social and Environmental Entrepreneurs of Binghamton, NY., has stated: "This is a national issue; taxpayer dollars are being used to prop up the private exploitation of our public lands to the detriment of the nation's wildlife. Animals and plants by the hundreds are being pushed onto threatened and endangered lists by livestock production."

This kind of inflammatory rhetoric is typical of the environmental propagandists, and is without basis in fact, for the most part. It is doubtful that Mr. Hudak has ever spent so much as a day on a ranch, or spoken to the owners, or rolled up his sleeves and worked beside a rancher for an afternoon. He has no idea whatsoever what he's talking about, but he does make a strong impression!

First let me address the issue of "exploitation." The word can mean the appropriate development of a resource in order to extract value, but in common parlance it is more often used to mean "victimization," or "mistreatment," "abuse"; and Mr. Hudak plays on that meaning, stirring the public's fear of being had.

When Mr. Hudak says "exploitation," he insinuates that ranchers are taking advantage of the tax paying public — that *they* are being exploited. However, grazing permits are not free. Now, any environmentalist or BLM official will tell you the fee ranchers pay doesn't even cover the cost of land management; but perhaps what is wrong with the equation is their heavy bureaucracy that drives up the expense end of the accounting, not the fees charged. It is not at all a given that the high cost of land management has to be so high.

Of course, banning ranchers in the West from BLM-managed land would not reduce the cost, anyway. Bureaucrats have a habit of stretching the parameters of their official duties in order to justify their salaries and benefits. One can always find reasons to micro-manage things; but that does not necessarily mean that the work being done is needed or useful.

It should also be noted that ranchers are not exactly on the dole. Their average day entails back-breaking, sweaty labor. They don't sit indoors when the winter wind is howling outside, either. Raising livestock is a demanding job that requires them to endure freezing cold, rain, wind, deep snow and burning heat. The truth of the matter is that rural Americans have a deep love for the land; not a textbook exposure to the environment, but hands on experience in dealing with storms, drought, freezes, floods, and every other feature of the unruly power of the elements. Most of them have been caring for the land for generations, and it couldn't be in better hands.

Livestock does not have an adverse effect on wildlife; in fact, in a hard winter you will find thousands of deer eating hay next to cattle. Likewise, geese and ducks land in the corn and wheat fields and glean the grain on the ground. Certainly, there may be conditions that result in some minimal damage, at times, but mother nature, itself, is many times more destructive. Drought, rain and wind do the majority of the damage to range lands.

Most ranchers are confined to grazing on a lease that is inadequate, which causes overgrazing. If the BLM opened up the vast rangelands that are available, then the impact of grazing would be well within federal guidelines. Just a fragile fence line stretches across the vast face of the terrain, their land on one side, and public lands on the other. If they call it all "their land," it isn't because they are disdainful of the public's interest; to the contrary. It is far more accurate to consider them responsible caretakers of our public lands than interlopers.

Their children go to college to earn degrees in agriculture or animal husbandry. They aren't the bumpkins that alarmists like Hudak portray. Today, the majority of farmers and ranchers employ sophisticated systems that they, themselves, many times have helped to develop. Their kids are members of 4H, where they learn every aspect of ranching, land management and care for animals from an early age. They take their responsibilities toward the environment seriously. They rely on the land to live. Nobody, certainly not a nature-lover from the big city or a bureaucrat in Washington D.C., is more dedicated to caring for the land and protecting it than our rural neighbors.

So much for "exploitation."

I've never known kinder, more compassionate people anywhere. If a neighbor suffers a death in the family, casseroles and pies, baked goods and jellies magically appear on the porch, or at the mailbox. Men show up unannounced to help with the chores. When someone suffers hardship, their neighbors are there, dozens of them, to supply food and clothing, even transportation, and what small amounts of money they can afford. City dwellers may find this difficult to imagine, given that we don't usually know the people on the next block over.

But as gentle and kind as those folks are, they are fiercely independent. The harsh country they live in demands it. After a heavy snowfall, they start the tractor and plow their own roads. When their vehicles break down, they fix them on the spot. They gather wood during the summer to burn during the winter. The women can vegetables and fruits, make jellies, and freeze a side of beef at a time. They don't wait for someone to help; they do it themselves.

It may occur to a city dweller that this is a brutal life, and it is in many respects, but there is no feeling in the world so glorious as the sense of freedom those people enjoy. Just so, they respect the rights and freedoms of others and ask nothing more than the right to live their lives without interference. But when outsiders import their attorneys and case workers and start making demands, taking their land from them, shutting them out of the country they dearly love, they will reach a limit and take matters into their own hands.

I don't think that time is far off.

The best way to find out what is going on in the open spaces of Wyoming, Arizona, New Mexico, the Dakotas, Montana, or anywhere in rural America, is to turn off the highway and drive up to a ranch house, get out of your car and knock on the door. You don't need an invitation. You'll probably be invited to the table. Come right out and tell the family what's on your mind: that you'd like to learn something about their ranch or farm. That you've heard a lot of talk and you want their side of the story. I'll bet a month's wages that they will take you in tow and show you what ranching is all about. They'll answer your questions about alleged damage to the environment, and the dangers to wildlife, to your complete satisfaction. If you really are concerned about the alarming claims of eco-propaganda, and you want the truth, go to the source. Find out for yourself.

The spectacular success of the Spotted Owl initiative, and hundreds of subsequent court actions using wetlands and endangered species as the basis for environmental litigation, have given the eco-mafia's confidence a turbo-boost. They have good reason to be confident. They rarely lose a major case.

In the past, the strategists of the environmental establishment have followed the doctrine "divide and conquer." They typically isolate a small region and set up local offices, recruit volunteers from the vicinity, send in their well-funded spin doctors, and kick off an organized campaign to accomplish their objective. In this way only a relatively small number of citizens are affected, which reduces the possibility of armed resistance or massive retaliation in the courts or the election booth.

The Klamath Basin is a textbook example of their tactics.

The Wilderness Society and eleven other national, regional, and local conservation organizations sued the Department of the Interior, charging mismanagement of two national wildlife refuges in the Klamath Basin of northern California and southern Oregon.

Until 2001, this region was one of the most fertile and productive farming and ranching areas in the United States. The terrain is semi-arid, in its natural state, so the U.S. Government granted rights to an irrigation system after World War II that would pump water from the Iron Gate Dam on the Klamath River.

Environmentalists claim that irrigation of farmland and pesticides have killed thousands of Coho Salmon and driven them to the point of extinction. The facts present a radically different picture:

In recent years, the water levels in the Klamath have been higher than water levels during the preceding decade. There was no significant loss of salmon in those years, even when water levels were lower than they have been recently — suggesting that factors other than water flow levels may be responsible for the disease that is killing the salmon.

Environmentalists point out that there was a fish kill of 33,000 Chinook salmon 200 miles from the Klamath Basin recently. Even though 100,000 healthy fish are currently returning to upstream hatcheries and spawning areas (the third highest level since records were begun in 1961), they have pressed their lawsuit demanding that the 1,500 families in the Basin be denied the water to irrigate their farms and have their cattle shut out of their grazing lands.

They were successful. The water was shut off in 2001.

The Klamath Project only represents 2% of the entire Klamath River watershed. Project releases from Iron Gate Dam represent just one of over one hundred downstream "tributaries" to the Klamath River mainstream.

A study conducted by The National Academy of Science found no benefits of raising the lake levels for endangered fish, and said that the 2001 water shut-off was unnecessary. In fact, increasing flows will almost certainly cause great harm to the federal and private wildlife refuges, as well as Klamath Basin communities that need this water to support the agricultural economy.

Dr. Robert McLandress, Ph.D. in ecology, University of California, reports that the farms and wetlands supply the food for 200 million waterfowl, in all over 300 species. Their consumption is estimated at 70 million pounds of food a year — and over half of that is produced by farming.

The ironic twist to this dilemma is that the eco-planners have offered a plan for watershed management that calls for the creation of wetlands (marshes) where the thousands of acres of farmland now lie. The required water to create and maintain these wetlands would be many times the amount used for irrigation. There is apparently a serious flaw in their rationale, but not if you know their hidden agenda: an enormous undertaking called The Wildlands Project.

There have also been some startling facts reported of late that explain the fish-kill cited above. Law enforcement authorities have discovered several large methamphetamine operations in the Klamath region, and they have evidence that proves the toxic materials used to make *meth* have been dumped into the Klamath River, often in sizable quantities. Biologists have confirmed that those chemicals would certainly kill any fish they came in contact with.

At the time of this writing, the battle for the Klamath Basin rages on. Thousands of hard-working Americans have lost their jobs. Many have lost the farms that have been in their families for generations. Local communities have been plunged into a depression, but the environmentalist juggernaut rolls on.

Several other isolated regions have suffered similar fates at the hands of eco-zealots. But their continued victories have given rise to their most ambitious campaign ever, The Wildlands Project, which will return 50% of the land mass in the United States to its pristine state.

To accomplish this incredible program, they will have to remove hundreds of thousands of citizens from their farms and ranches and force evacuation en masse from the hundreds of small rural communities that depend almost entirely upon agriculture in their economies. A group of people has decided, without consulting the voters at large (much les the people directly affected), to return half our country to what they consider to have been its natural state; and they are clearly unconcerned about the suffering and anguish they have caused, and will cause in the future, to the rural population that represents, in itself, a species of American that deserves a little habitat protection of its own.

Environmentalists are sophisticated in their use of the courts, and they have deep pockets. Rural families can hardly compete fair and square. While I surely do not advocate violence, I predict that many are facing such dire situations that they may be ready to break a few rules to make their point.

And what, exactly, are our rural neighbors so upset about? Let me quote from Mr. John Davis, editor of the Wildlands Project journal, *Wild Earth*. He writes:

> Wilderness recovery must start now but continue indefinitely — expanding wilderness until the matrix, not just the nexus, is wild . . . Does [this] mean that Wild Earth and the Wildlands Project advocate the end of industrial civilization? Most assuredly. Everything civilized must go.

This outrageous statement is not the view of a fringe cult, but the objective of every deep ecologist in every major environmental group and federal agency in our government. It isn't enough to have the wilderness areas, as they exist today; they advocate removing every human being, every farm, every town, and every home in the vast West.

This very process is underway at this moment and it has been very successful thus far.

In his book *Green Gestapo*, Jarret Wollstein writes:

> Absurd, anti-human environmental laws are part of a much larger Green Gestapo agenda for your future. Their blueprint is the UN's 1,140-page UN Environmental Programme's Global Bio-diversity Assessment (GBA), which Clinton has urged the Senate to ratify.
>
> Called the "Wildlands Project," this scheme would convert at least half of the continental US into an "eco-park" devoid of industry and private property...
>
> Although the Biodiversity Treaty has not been ratified, implementation has already begun in several states. In Chicago, a coalition of 34 federal agencies,

cultural organizations, and environmental groups has created the Chicago Region Biodiversity Council, which the Chicago Tribune calls,

"[A]n ambitious and unprecedented effort to restore what nature created, not piece-by-piece, but on a regional scale . . . . The idea is to create a network of native natural areas not just in [Illinois] forest preserves but in city and suburban neighborhoods and on corporate campuses. Lawns and parkways could be replaced by fields of prairies, wildflowers, and boring detention ponds could be replaced by living wetlands."

J. Zane Walley, of the Paragon Foundation, a watchdog group monitoring the environmentalist campaign to implement the Wildlands Project, filed the following report:

In a November meeting, eighteen environmental activist groups from the eleven western states, several other states and Canada, gathered in Reno, Nevada to plan a program intended to force some 20,000 BLM permit holders from federal lands.

"They are a mean spirited bunch," said C.J. Hadley, Publisher of *Range Magazine*, who attended RangeNet 2000. "They fully intend to shut down all grazing on public lands," she angrily noted. "The ugly part is they are really organized."

Hadley further explained that the environmental groups attending the Reno greeno summit are for the large part the same groups that shut down logging on public lands. "They learned how to be effective in the spotted owl wars and now they aim to use the same tactics against ranchers."

Attorney Marl Salvo, of the Oregon-based American Lands, spoke at the meeting and explained how to use the Endangered Species Act to end ranching on public lands.

Salvo said, "Conservationists must address the symptoms of degraded ecosystems through the Endangered Species Act. While sage grouse are considered a good candidate for protection, federal biologists have admitted that any number of other sagebrush obligate species could also be successfully petitioned for listing." Salvo referred to the sage grouse as the "Spotted Owl Of The Desert." He concluded that it can be used to force ranchers from desert grazing lands as the spotted owl was used to destroy logging industry.

University of Wyoming Law Professor Debra Donahue, author of "The Western Range Revisited: Removing Livestock from Public Lands to Conserve Native Biodiversity," explained how The Taylor Grazing Act could be used against ranchers. She stated, "Grazing on arid BLM lands is inconsistent with the governing laws, specifically the Taylor Grazing Act, which authorizes grazing only on lands 'chiefly valuable for grazing and raising forage crops,' and the Federal Land Policy and Management Act, which prohibits land uses causing 'unnecessary or undue degradation' of the lands."

Donahue also claimed that driving ranchers from BLM land would affect less than two percent of the nation's livestock products and fewer than 20,000 permittees. She also indicated that BLM Managers possess the authority under current law to end livestock grazing on these range lands.

Other conspicuous attendees at the RangeNet 2000 Symposium were Martin Taylor of The Center for Biological Diversity, John Horning of Forest Guardians and Jon Marvel, founder of Idaho Watersheds Project.

The strategy laid out at the gathering involves listing more endangered species indigenous to the pubic lands which the greens believe should be "cleansed of livestock." The listing of species will be followed with dozens of lawsuits clamoring for huge spaces of restricted habitat.

Other lawsuits against federal land authorities, especially BLM, will try to make the agencies interpret current regulations by the standards of the environmental groups. The lawsuits and the ESA listings will be accompanied by a polished media campaign.

C.J. Hadley of Range stated emphatically, "If there has ever been a time for ranchers to pull together, it is now! If we don't, we'll lose this one."

The first question to ignite in this brush fire has to do with the cool statement that their plan will affect "fewer than 20,000 permittees." Is it alright to plot the disruption of "just" 19,999 families? Of course, the number of people this campaign will affect, if it meets their goals, is far greater. That is only the number of ranchers and farmers whose names appear on the lease documents. How about their families? How about the people who work for these folks? How about the businesses that supply seed, equipment, veterinary services, fuel, equipment repair, tires and feed?

A figure closer to 700,000 sounds more realistic. But even if it was just 20,000 — have we become so insular in America that we can sit quietly by and allow even 20 American citizens to suffer at the hands of these fanatics?

Are we so blind to reality that we fail to see the handwriting on the wall? The eco-zealots have no more compassion for city folks than they do rural folks.

Yale Lewis, a reporter from Pocatello, Idaho, wrote that in 1994 the U.S. Fish and Wildlife Service revoked grazing privileges at two national wildlife refuges in eastern Idaho and is poised to do the same at two others in the state.

"Annual permits to run cattle in the Grays Lake and Camas national wildlife refuges will not be re-issued next year," says Chuck Peck, regional wildlife manager with the Fish and Wildlife Service in Pocatello. The agency will also soon decide when to terminate grazing at the Minidoka and Bear Lake refuges, Peck says. Hay-cutting privileges on the refuges will be restricted in the future as well, he says.

The decision is the direct result of the Interior Department's settlement of a lawsuit brought by environmental groups over incompatible uses at nine refuges, including seven in the West (HCN, 11/15/93). Under the settlement, the agency has a year to modify, eliminate or justify all secondary uses that harm wildlife, as identified by the agency in a 1990 survey.

But the 25 ranchers who have grazed cattle on the refuges since the 1960s say some will be forced into bankruptcy. Many feel betrayed, since they sold their land to the Fish and Wildlife Service to help create the refuges.

"I finally sold them 400 acres," says Reed Humphrey, a rancher from Grays Lake. "They promised we'd have grazing and haying rights on these lands forever." Humphrey, who has been running cattle on his ranch since 1950, says he'll lose 90 percent of his summer pasture and be forced out of business if he can't graze the refuge.

I lived around cattle in the wild for all of my childhood, and I never saw a conflict between cows and wild birds. Cattle stick to the open ground, and rarely get into the brush where wild fowl would build a nest.

Those grazing lands are sorely needed. It is the birds who must accommodate the human values at issue here, not vice versa. Wildlife is far more versatile and adaptable than the environmentalist gives them credit for. Are they really so convinced that grazing will cause problems? I suspect that the alleged fragility of wild animals is merely an excuse, for the sake of public consumption, to impose their true agenda.

There isn't even the slimmest pretext in this controversy to justify the persecution of Idaho ranchers. The vague suggestions that cattle may trample bird nests, or disturb the privacy of the fragile fowl, are wholly inadequate grounds for causing irreparable damage to the lives of American ranchers. And if, from time to time, the cattle did disrupt the duck's routine, there are millions of acres in the wilderness where cattle cannot graze — remote mountain lakes and waterways that are far beyond their reach — but not beyond the ducks' reach.

What year do they want to turn us back to? Has anybody asked America if we want this? Millions of buffalo roamed the Great Plains just 150 years ago. The cattle that graze there now are, by comparison, extremely few. How did the ducks and other wildlife survive amidst that sea of roving bison? After a herd of buffalo passed through, the ground was churned to mulch and every sprig of vegetation for miles was decimated; yet abundant wildlife survives to this day.

It stretches the boundaries of credibility that a comparative handful of domestic cattle could pose such a virulent threat to the habitat.

In closing this chapter, I want to redirect the focus of the reader on the true agenda of the environmentalist movement. Alarmist propaganda, mostly rhetoric that is unsupported by the facts, is disseminated throughout our society in the news media, schools, magazines, newspapers, Internet sites and by speakers at public meetings, politicians, and a host of other effective strategies. But a close examination of the facts reveals that there is no real danger to our environment. It is these organizations' objective to cripple our economy and displace millions of citizens in order to "rewild" rural America.

See Appendix D — "Farming and Ranching," for additional documentation.

CHAPTER 7.
THE WETLANDS TRAVESTY

Robert J. Pierce, who helped write the 1989 EPA wetlands standard, bluntly states: "Ecologically speaking, the term 'wetland' has no meaning. . . For regulatory purposes, a wetland is whatever we decide it is." — National Wetlands Newsletter, Nov/Dec 1991, pp. 12.

The law is allegedly the instrument of justice in our society, and as such must be explicit, precise, and well defined. With this in mind, the outright admission of Mr. Pierce is nothing less than an abomination, for he is saying, in effect, that the government has ordained a body of laws that are vague by design in order to give the state unlimited power over the fate of the accused, to virtually invent crimes at their discretion, on the spur of the moment, to accomplish their ends.

The case of John Posgai is an excellent illustration of the calamity that can befall an unfortunate citizen at the hands of arrogant bureaucrats. Mr. Posgai fled Hungary at the close of World War II to start a new life in America. He purchased a parcel of land that had once been a junkyard. Most of the rubbish had been removed, but some remained, and Posgai set about collecting the unsightly trash. There were 41 old tire casings scattered about, and he disposed of them.

Imagine his astonishment when federal marshals arrested him and locked him up to await trial for violating the Clean Water Act! His land was bone dry.

John was found guilty on 41 counts, imprisoned in a federal penitentiary for three years, and fined $202,000.

What crime was trumped up to persecute this old man?

The tire casings had stagnant rain water standing in them which supported aquatic life: mosquitoes. According to the Environmental Protection Agency, the water in the tires qualified as a federally protected wetland. As Robert Pierce said, "a wetland is whatever we decide it is." Need I add that, with the growing concern over exotic mosquito-borne diseases, in some areas of the U.S. citizens are *required* to dispose of tires that might harbor stagnant water?

John Posgai's words, as they led him away to prison; "I thought this was a free country?"

Lest the reader get the idea that such outrageous conduct is a rarity, an aberration, I have included several other accounts below. These are a mere sampling of the hundreds of accounts I have encountered in my research.

> Louise and Frederic Williams of Little Compton, Rhode Island, bought five acres for a new home. When their home was already partially constructed, they received a letter from state environmental officials ordering them to tear it down. Although there was little water on the property, eco-bureaucrats had declared their property to be a wetland. The EPA also ordered them to plant trees and tend them for a full year at their own expense. The value of the Williams' property plummeted from $260,000 to less than $30,000.
> — National Wetlands Newsletter, Nov/Dec 1991, pp. 12.

Frank LaDue lost the right to use 29 of his 30 acres of land — or 96.7% of it — when the Washington Department of Ecology [DOE) designated most of it a wetland.

> LaDue's troubles began when he filled four acres of his land with waste wood to build a garden and wooded area. The DOE charged that the wood dried up a wetland, seriously damaging the ecosystem. In response, LaDue removed the waste wood, pulling it towards his house. But because he failed to recover wood that had already decomposed into the soil, the DOE argued that he had not returned the wetlands to their original state and fined him $5,000.
> But that wasn't the end of LaDue's ordeal. A specialist from another section of DOE determined that removing the waste wood could do more harm than good. So they instructed LaDue to make hummocks (elevated tracts of land) of the fill and place it all on one acre.
> LaDue was allowed to use that one acre for his garden, his house, and other uses. The remainder has been designated a wetland.
> — Citizens for Property Rights

Maryland Developer James J. Wilson has been sentenced to 21 months in prison, fined $1 million personally, and his company fined $3 million after he created lakes and open spaces on a 50-acre wetlands site he was developing in St. Charles, Maryland.

The government is pursuing this action against Wilson even though it agrees that his actions "had no adverse environmental impact." In fact, in 1979 the Army Corps of Engineers approved Wilson's original master plan and environmental impact statement he filed as required by law. But in 1990, the Corps changed its mind and ordered him to stop development on one parcel. Wilson halted construction and promptly filed a lawsuit against the Corps for expropriating his land without compensation.

Then, in 1995, the Corps charged Wilson for criminally violating the Clean Water Act. After a seven-week trial, he was found guilty of four felony counts of violating the Act.

Wilson is currently preparing a sweeping challenge to the constitutionality of the government's wetlands regulation. The Corps maintains that it can regulate as a wetland any land that is ever wet, which can be anything from a swamp to a temporary mud puddle. The wetland that Wilson was developing in St. Charles was actually dry for most of the year.

— Max Boot, "The Wetlands Gestapo," *Wall Street Journal*, March, 1997

When I was a boy, we had another name for "wetlands." They were called "swamps," and we avoided them whenever possible because of mosquito infestation, poisonous snakes, quick sand and other dangers posed by stagnant water. But the environmental community holds the sanctity of swamps above human rights and health.

Of course, there are legitimate issues that involve our rivers, lakes and marshes, but the aggressive advance of environmentalism has far exceeded those reasonable interests.

The primary concern that dominates the issue of wetland management is the draconian measures that deep ecologists bring to bear on free Americans under the guise of "wetland management." If they confined their meddling to regulating standing bodies of water there would be far less for the American citizen to be concerned about.

In the fashion so characteristic of the eco-mafia, the environmental establishment has seized upon the wetland as an instrument of their zealous effort to discourage construction of new homes (what they call "urban sprawl") and throw even more obstacles in the path of ranchers and farmers.

As Mr. Pierce pointed out, by definition, a "wetland" isn't necessarily wet!

As these crimes against our 5th Amendment rights so clearly point out, the notion of "wetlands," in the strategy of deep ecologists, is not, as they claim, to protect aquatic life, but to serve as another weapon to limit human activity and suppress rural communities.

Wetlands serve another sinister purpose.

When I was working in the civil engineering field, designing subdivisions, the company I was working for built a road across a parcel of land for dump trucks and heavy machinery. It was a shock to all of us to learn that a small portion of the parcel, less than an acre, was a designated wetland. Although it was bone dry during most of the year, probably ten months, in the rainy season it held water for a short time.

My company was advised that we had violated a wetland and we were summoned to a meeting with EPA officials. According to the allegations, we had committed a crime and the company's permit to operate could be revoked. But the EPA folks are a kind and loving bunch. They told us that if we created another wetland, three times larger, we would only get a warning.

We complied, of course.

Preparing a subdivision site requires grading, digging trenches for sewer pipe, water lines, concrete work, and surveying, and once the parcel is ready, the home builder, landscaper and paver. All of these activities require different contractors. They have millions of dollars invested in heavy equipment and hundreds of men on their payrolls. When a shutdown occurs, the costs can spiral into the tens of thousands of dollars per day. The same holds true when building roads and bridges, municipal structures, commercial sites and airports, sports complexes, shopping malls.

Every construction specialty has a national organization which represents their interests in Washington, D.C. Lobbyists for these industries work tirelessly to influence legislation that impacts these businesses.

Of course, any state or federal entity which has the power to suspend a multi-million dollar project, or cause expensive delays, can expect to be wooed by these business interests and the politician who solves bureaucratic problems will receive generous contributions to his re-election campaign.

Farming is another major industry that is severely impacted by ridiculous wetland laws, as demonstrated in the following reports.

Turf Fight Between Two Federal Agencies Deprives California Farmer Use Of Property

[Source: Pacific Legal Foundation]

Dave Pechan, a farmer near Linden, California, wanted to convert 40 acres of his land into a vineyard. In accordance with the law, Pechan asked the United States Soil and Conservation Service (USCS) to evaluate his property for possible wetlands.

The USCS is one of the federal agencies charged with enforcing wetlands regulations. After inspecting Pechan's land on two occasions, the USCS determined that only a 0.3 acre swathe could be considered a wetland.

He was instructed to go ahead with his vineyard plans as long as he plowed around the tiny wetland. That seemed to settle the matter until one week later, when Pechan saw representatives from the Army Corps of Engineers and United States Fish and Wildlife Service on his property taking pictures.

They told Pechan that he may be violating the law by farming in wetlands. When Pechan produced documentation from the USCS showing that he was in compliance with regulations, the agents rudely rejected the claim.

It seems that the Corps of Engineers and USCS are locked in a bureaucratic turf fight over which agency should have the lead role in enforcing wetland law. In 1994, the Corps of Engineers signed a Memorandum of Agreement that ostensibly recognized the USCS as the lead federal agency.

However, the Corps of Engineers reneged on the agreement because they refuse to give up any power over wetland enforcement. The end result is that Dave Pechan is snared in the middle of a bureaucratic turf fight. The Corps has told him that regardless of what the USCS has determined, he will be subjected to civil and criminal penalties if he continues to work his land. He is now in limbo while the Corps conducts its own wetlands evaluation of his property.

Kansas Farm Ruined by U.S. Soil and Conservation Service
[Source: National Center for Public Policy Research]
In 1988, Kansas farmer David Worth purchased 320 acres of land. At the time, the United States Soil and Conservation Service (USCS) determined that there were nine relatively small wetlands on the property which could not be farmed.

In 1993, a severe flood washed away the alfalfa crop which Worth used as a covering crop to protect his land against erosion. The next year Worth needed to replant a new covering crop, so he asked the USCS to come to his property and tell him where the wetlands were located (it was hard to remember the location of the wetlands on such a large tract of land).

However, the USCS initially refused the request. When they finally came out in October to flag the wetlands, Worth had already lost a whole growing season at a cost of $25,000. Even worse, though, was that the USCS increased the number of wetlands it believed was on the property to 19, for a total of 25 scattered across the land.

Worth was angered that the wetlands were not only growing in number but were also changing location. Even more ridiculous, only three or four of the original nine matched up with the 19. He filed an appeal on the USCS's new determination.

In the meantime, Worth had to knock over the flags indicating the location of the wetlands as part of the normal process of maintaining the land, a practice which doesn't violate wetland regulations. In the spring of 1995, he once more sought to plant a covering crop and needed the USCS to come back out and reflag the wetlands.

Again, it was difficult to remember the precise location of the wetlands. The USCS district manager told Worth they wouldn't reflag the land until he dropped his appeal over their wetland ruling.

Not interested in responding to this blackmail, Worth got the United States Department of Agriculture to order the USCS to do the markings. Again, it wasn't until October 1995 that the Service marked the land, costing Worth another growing season.

Incredibly, when they remarked Worth's land, the number of wetlands had increased to 26. And once again, they had changed location. Worth continued to appeal the USCS's questionable wetlands designations.

Then, in April 1996, a severe storm blew away a foot and a half of the topsoil, virtually ruining the land for farming. This was directly due to the USCS preventing Worth from planting covering crops for two consecutive years. Worth has been trying to sell the land ever since but has few takers due to the wetlands designations. Ironically, in 1997 the USCS cited Worth's rutted farm as an example of what bad farming does to the land. Worth estimates that the dispute has cost him approximately $300,000.

No one need remind these unfortunate victims of a system gone berserk that "a wetland is whatever we say it is."

See Appendix G — "Wetlands," for additional documentation.

CHAPTER 8.
ENDANGERED SPECIES VS. FREEDOM

The Endangered Species Act of 1973 (ESA) began as legislation to protect a handful of animal species; it's safe to say that Richard Nixon didn't have the faintest idea what a can of worms he was opening.

As it turned out this law, in the hands of unscrupulous fanatics, has become one of the most destructive elements in America's history, and the possibilities for even greater abuses of our property rights are limitless.

The ESA has been expanded to potentially include every living organism. At present we know of a mere fraction of all species, a few million — but it is estimated that there are in excess of 100 million species in the United States alone.

The latitude that the courts have been willing to give the eco-spin doctors will enable them to list as endangered an entire species, if one variation of the species appears to be limited in number. That really opens Pandora's box.

When any organization or government enters onto our land, or into our home, and wrests control of that which we own, they are not only violating our 5th Amendment rights, they are invading our privacy. Under such conditions, there is no freedom. We are vulnerable to any whim, any ridiculous demand that they may make on our time, our finances, even our mobility.

How far the eco-fanatics are willing to stretch the law, what encumbrances they are willing to burden us with, apparently know no ends. Consider the case of the Delhi Sands Fly.

According to a report compiled by the National Center for Policy Analysis, the day before San Bernadino and Riverside counties in California were to break ground for a new hospital, the United States Fish and Wildlife Service (USFWS) listed the Delhi Sands flower-loving fly as endangered. Eight Delhi flies were found on the hospital site and the (USFWS) threatened to prosecute the counties if they built the hospital as planned. According to Ike Sugg, a wildlife specialist at the Competitive Enterprise Institute, while the counties and the USFWS have been negotiating hospital construction has been delayed for more than a year.

The counties have spent more than $4.5 million — more than half a million per fly, and they may have to spend millions more to buy land to establish a fly preserve.

As if it weren't enough to deny local residents nearby medical facilities, and further, to drive the cost of service even higher than the astronomical price we now pay, one USFWS official made the outrageous demand that Interstate 10, an eight-lane freeway adjacent to the hospital site, be shut down or slowed to 15 miles an hour during the two months of the fly's above-ground lifespan! It almost appears that these people are competing to impose the most ridiculous, petty restrictions on society.

There is more to this morbid tale. The town of Colton, California was declared part of the habitat of this fly, a distinction that virtually shut down any and all construction. City streets could not be repaired. Sewers could not be repaired or upgraded. Property values were reduced to a tiny fraction, a few cents on the dollar, and the economy is staggering under the weight of these regulations.

* Update: After the federal government designated the Delhi Sands fly an endangered species, San Bernardino County, California had to spend $10 million to build a special 10-acre "preserve" for the bugs. In 1999, the Interior Department demanded an additional 2,200 acres be set aside for the fly — land that cost more than $200 million. To date, the cost to the taxpayer to protect fewer than 100 flies has been in excess of $300 million, and the total is still climbing.

Is it worth it, America? This is a question we will all be required to answer sooner or later. The voracious appetite of the environmentalist juggernaut will not be sated by its advances in rural America. The economy is their target, as well as development and farming. Any opportunity to burden our society with astronomical costs is quickly exploited.

We are already paying a high price, in freedom and in dollars; and we're not getting results.

Following a speech by Clinton's Secretary of Interior, Bruce Babbitt, in which he declared "The Endangered Species law works!" the National Center for Policy Analysis filed Brief No. 276, prepared by NCPA policy analysts Sterling Burnett and Bryon Allen, Koch Foundation intern at the NCPA:

> [Babbitt] announced that within the next two years the United States Fish and Wildlife Service (USFWS) will remove (delist) 33 species from the endangered species list. His claim comes as the ESA is being considered for renewal — the law authorizing it having lapsed in 1992. These 33 delistings will mean that a total of 60 species have been removed from the endangered species list.
>
> Should Secretary Babbitt brag about the success of the act, or apologize for its failure? Suppose a federal education program for high-risk students enrolled 1,139 U.S. children and 565 foreign children but graduated only 60 in 26 years, at a cost of billions. This is the record of the ESA.
>
> Measured by any reasonable standard, the ESA has failed.
>
> Even counting all the delistings as "successes," they account for only 3.5 percent of the species listed in the 26 years since the ESA was enacted. A more careful examination of the facts shows that of the 60 species delisted:
>
> - 12 were delisted due to extinction.
> - 24 were delisted because of "data errors" — they either were under-counted when added to the list or were later determined not to be distinct species.
> - exist solely on federal lands and are therefore federally protected without the ESA.
> - were decimated by a pesticide, DDT, and recovered largely due to the DDT ban in 1972.
> - 12 remaining species are conserved by state agencies or private organizations, with only minimal contributions by the federal government.

Not a single delisting was attributable to ESA protection!

The true cost of the ESA is hard to estimate because, in addition to billions in federal spending, state governments and the private sector have spent additional tens of billions for this program with no common accounting system.

The government has estimated that to recover all currently known endangered species would cost more than $4.6 billion. This estimate is seriously misleading, because it refers to recovery costs alone; whereas for every dollar thus far spent on recovery, federal agencies have spent more than $2.26

consulting with scientists and stakeholders and developing the species list. That bumps the cost to $14.9 billion.

Even the recovery cost estimate is low, since dozens of species on which much more money has been spent have not been delisted. Millions of dollars have been spent on species that were wrongly listed — like the Tumamoc globeberry, a gourd in southern Arizona. And estimates for the recovery of the Northern spotted owl alone range from $21 billion to $46 billion, depending on which recovery plan is finally selected. These are only the direct costs.

That estimate could explode to $200 billion after we factor in lost jobs, forgone wages, delayed and halted development, increased construction costs, losses on investments and difficult-to-measure social costs — such as community disruption, increased suicide and divorce rates, higher crime rates, drug addiction and alcoholism.

The true costs should be measured in houses, homeless shelters and hospitals not built or significantly delayed; medical and technological discoveries not advanced; and funds not available for education, crime control and other health, safety and environmental matters — including species lost or still declining. Then there is perhaps the greatest cost of all: the destruction of the dreams and aspirations of thousands upon thousands of Americans. For them there is only bitterness and failure, a future without hope of an improved lifestyle.

Just being more careful with the allotted monies would improve species protection. The government spends an average of $107,000 satisfying paperwork and reporting requirements to list and delist, exclusive of the costs of monitoring species and developing or implementing habitat conservation plans. Thus, the species that were wrongly listed cost us more than $3.9 million.

Based upon its record of costly failure, the best policy might be to end the federal government's role in endangered species protection entirely. Since in the current legislative environment this is unlikely, perhaps the best policy is to minimize the damage the current act causes.

Causes of Failure: Perverse Incentives

One problem with the ESA is that it creates perverse incentives to destroy species and their habitat. Over 75 percent of the listed species depend on private land for all or part of their habitat requirements. Yet if people provide suitable habitat for an endangered species, their land becomes subject to severe regulation, if not confiscation.

As a former USFWS official stated: "The incentives are wrong here. If I have a rare metal on my property, its value goes up. But if a rare bird occupies the land, its value disappears. We've got to turn it around to make the landowner want to have the bird on his property."

Even Michael Bean of the Environmental Defense Fund recently acknowledged that:

> [I]ncreasing evidence suggests that at least some private land owners are actively managing their land so as to avoid potential endangered species problems...by avoiding having endangered species on their property. [Mr. Bean admitted that this was not the result of a desire to harm the species or the environment but, rather, a rational response to the incentives in the current act.]
>
> The success of the ESA depends upon making allies of landowners. The Fifth Amendment to the Constitution prohibits the taking of private property for any public purpose without the payment of "just compensation."

When the government imposes land use restrictions on private property to preserve species habitat and the land loses value, a "taking" has occurred and the property owner should be compensated. The government also is constitutionally obligated to compensate people who must "house" protected species. The fear of uncompensated takings leaves an owner three options: to kill an endangered species member, destroy species habitat (before it is declared as such), or lose the value of his land. Honoring the Fifth Amendment would shield the landowner from choosing between his welfare and that of the endangered species.

For the first 26 years of the ESA, the federal government has used the threat of fines, imprisonment and federal management to force state and local officials and property owners to protect species. This produced the "shoot, shovel and shut up" syndrome, the opposite of its intended effect. Clinging to this approach will guarantee continued failure.

The survival of many endangered species literally rests with American property owners. At a minimum, to improve the chances of species recovery, the government needs to swear an environmental Hippocratic oath to "do no harm." This entails assuring that landowners who protect a species valued by the public will be compensated by the public. Other ESA problems will remain, but this is a good first step.

~ ~ ~

However, the likelihood that landowners will be compensated is almost non-existent. In the many pages of legislative precedents and Supreme Court findings relating to these issues, the courts consistently deny property owners just compensation, based primarily on the premise that imposing environmental restrictions on land use does not constitute a "taking" because the land, itself, is not the focus of the sanctions.

This song and dance is merely a technicality that our judges use to assuage their conscience, or so it would appear. Those jurists who have no qualms in upholding such findings are guilty of gross neglect to honor the Constitution of the United States of America, a duty they are sworn to carry out.

Any arbitrary action of a government which deprives landowners of the use of their property, or which lowers its value, is an intrusion on property rights, whether it can be technically called a "taking" or not.

The following articles demonstrate the kind of atrocities that are ongoing in America:

> For more than 17 years, Patty and Findley Ricard ran a flourishing nursery business on Big Pine Key in the Florida Keys. In order to protect their property from the ravenous Key Deer, the Ricards built a fence around a three-acre tract. The fence was properly built. "All of a sudden," says Patty, "the state's Department of Community Affairs said that we weren't allowed to have a fence and we had to tear it down." When the Ricards asked why, officials responded that the fence blocked the unfettered movement of the Key Deer and caused increased auto traffic on the adjoining road.
>
> Eventually, the Ricards were asked by the state to move to a less environ-mentally-sensitive location. But due to the excessive land regulation in the Keys, it was impossible for the Ricards to find a buyer for their property.
>
> Protracted negotiations and threats of condemnation of their property ensued. After Findley had a heart attack, the Ricards gave up and sold their property to the state "for half of what we paid for it," says Patty. Ironically, the United States Fish and Wildlife Service took over their property and left the fence standing.
>
> — "Almost Paradise," by Sean Paige (*Insight*, April 6-13, 1998, p. 10)

The Mountain States Legal Foundation, a stalwart defender of our rights as free Americans, cited the following account.

The United States Fish and Wildlife Service (USFWS) has threatened to fine a Utah man $15,000 for farming his land and allegedly posing a risk to the Utah Prairie Dog, a protected species. The only problem is that there are no Utah Prairie Dogs on his property.

Originally, the USFWS told the man that he should hire an outside expert to determine if any Utah Prairie Dogs were present. The expert prepared a report which indicated that there were no Utah Prairie Dogs, so the farmer proceeded to work his land. But the USFWS told him that they will fine him anyway. The USFWS reasons that since it is theoretically possible for Utah Prairie Dogs in the surrounding area to migrate onto the property, they have the right to issue a fine for harming a potential habitat.

— William Perry Pendley, President of Mountain States Legal Foundation

The following article by Katie Cobb, Fox News, was published on 1/30/01.

SIERRA VISTA, Ariz. — Steve Lindsey and his family have raised cattle in eastern Arizona for more than a century. But now, he says, his way of life is threatened. Environmental groups want his land in their quest to return some of the West's farm and ranch land to the wild. And Lindsey fears the federal government is on their side.

"We've been in this country since 1860," he said from his more than 600-acre ranch outside the small town of Sierra Vista last week. "We are environmental stewards."

Lindsey, a husband and father of nine, never had trouble until the U.S. Fish & Wildlife Service found "Spiranthes Delitescens" on his property. The herb, more commonly known as the "Canelo Hills Ladies' Tresses," grows only in four mountainous areas of southeast Arizona. It can reach to 19 inches tall, and its stalk contains as many as 40 small, white flowers.

Fish & Wildlife officials offered him a conservation agreement to protect the plant, Lindsay said, and told him if he didn't sign it they would list the species as endangered.

"I said, 'That is extortion, and this is America,'" he said. "They said, 'Watch me.'"

The species first became endangered Jan. 6, 1997. It not only restricted his ability to graze his cattle on leased federal land, something his family had been doing for generations, it also gave ammunition to environmental groups that want his land as a nature preserve.

One such group is the Tucson-based Wildlands Project, a group that aims to reclaim and connect wildlife corridors throughout the entire North

American continent. Its founder, Dave Foreman, ends his public speeches with a wolf's howl in support of endangered species.

Foreman lectured at the University of Arizona last week about his plan to "rewild" 10.5 million acres in Arizona, New Mexico and Mexico.

"You live in a world of wounds, a world infected by us human beings," he told the gathering.

The group's Web site insists an "audacious" plan is needed for the survival of the North American environment. In essence, that includes acquiring Lindsay's land.

In an interview with Fox News Channel, Foreman said the wolf needs to become "functionally present" from Canada to Mexico through the Rocky Mountains.

"By functionally present I mean not there in some sort of open-air zoo," he said.

For the Wildlands Project to work, it needs more than just land owned by the federal government." And some, like Lindsey, have no intention of giving it up.

"It's more reaching out and grabbing of the property rights of the people," Lindsey said.

Because the government's Endangered Species Act prohibits Lindsey from grazing cattle on federally protected land, Lindsey says his only choice is to sell the farm or go broke.

"We're backed into a corner," he said.

Barbara Mossman wrote this article about the spotted owl fiasco.

[RuralCleansing.com, *Horror Stories Of Regulation Madness*, 1992]

In 1979, Barbara and Dick Mossman mortgaged their farm to buy a new International logging truck to start their own logging business in the Pacific Northwest.

Initially, the Mossmans experienced hard times, losing virtually everything except their truck and a few other goods during the 1980-1981 recession. In 1986, however, they landed a good job hauling logs in Forks, Washington — at the time the logging capital of the world. Things gradually improved for the Mossmans. They got rid of their debt, restored a good credit rating, started a modest savings account and bought a four-acre farm.

Then in June 1990, the United States Fish and Wildlife Service (USFWS) declared the Northern Spotted Owl an endangered species. Since the owl was found virtually anywhere there was logging, the timber industry collapsed.

The Mossmans' business was no exception. In 1990 alone, their revenue dropped by 33%. By October of 1991, less than 18 months after the USFWS ruling, the Mossmans went out of business. Because they were self-employed, they could not apply for unemployment benefits.

As a result, the Mossmans had to sell their boat, trailer, welder, tools and motorcycles to get the cash they needed just to make ends meet. That was not enough, though. In the spring of 1992, they received a foreclosure notice on their farm. The electricity was turned off, leaving the couple without heat, lights and water. The Mossmans were unable to respond to collection notices and deputies began knocking on the door with lawsuits in hand. However, Barbara says the most degrading thing of all "was being forced to walk into a public assistance agency, after 13 years as independent truckers, and ask for a voucher for food, because we were hungry."

Barbara has since become a spokeswoman for the thousands of other families whose lives were ruined by this reckless application of the Endangered Species Act. "I am not interested in pointing a finger of blame," says Barbara. "What I am interested in is a commitment from the Members of Congress that they will change this cruel and vicious law, so that no other families, no other community will have to endure the pain we in the timber community have been forced to endure."

See Appendix H — "Endangered Species," for additional documentation.

CHAPTER 9.
THE GLOBAL WARMING MYTH

The unscrupulous prey on the ignorance of others, and there is no issue that demonstrates this principle more clearly than the global warming controversy.

The strategists that guide the gargantuan environmental movement are adept at seizing upon issues that conform to a consistent pattern. They choose an issue that has widespread appeal based upon a compelling argument, usually moral or humanitarian in nature, such as protecting helpless animals, preserving our wilderness, cleaning up our environment, and in the case of global warming, preventing a worldwide catastrophe.

Fear is the motivation that garners public support in this case.

Few of us, mainstream Americans, are qualified, by way of education or training, to analyze the complex scientific questions raised by the global warming theory, and environmentalists have exploited our naivety with great success.

Fortunately, the men and women of the earth sciences community, distinguished scholars and practitioners of this diverse field, have come forth en masse to refute the ridiculous claims that they are uniquely qualified to recognize as false. It is a lamentable fact that the mainstream press has ignored their protestations in favor of eco-propaganda, which is why the public are not well informed.

Speaking of well informed, recent discoveries that have revealed valuable data have just come to light in the last few months.

In September of 2002, U.S. scientists based at the Amundsen-Scott South Pole Station announced that they successfully measured the temperature of the atmosphere 18 to 68 miles over the pole. They found it to be 68 to 86 degrees (Fahrenheit) colder than the data used by computer models to predict global warming.

"Since 1988, when global warming first was introduced as a potential problem, we the taxpayers have spent some $18 billion for researchers to study this theory. The preponderance of the evidence show that there has been no appreciable warming since 1940 — before the widespread use of the combustion engine — which indicates that we humans have had very little, if any, effect on the climate at all." [NetWorldDaily.com, September, 2002.]

The reaction in the scientific community to alarming predictions of global disaster, first publicized in 1988, were immediate, yet very little accurate information reached the American public through the media. Just four years after the debut of global warming in 1988, the following statement was delivered to the Congress in February, 1992:

"As independent scientists, researching atmospheric and climate problems, we are concerned by the agenda for UNCED, the United Nations Conference on Environment and Development, being developed by environmental activist groups and certain political leaders. This so-called Earth Summit is scheduled to convene in Brazil in June 1992 and aims to impose a system of global environmental regulations, including onerous taxes on energy fuels, on the population of the United States and other industrialized nations.

"Such policy initiatives derive from highly uncertain scientific theories. They are based on the unsupported assumption that catastrophic global warming follows from the burning of fossil fuels and requires immediate action. We do not agree.

"A survey of U.S. atmospheric scientists, conducted in the summer of 1991, confirms that there is no consensus about the cause of the slight warming observed during the past century. A recently published research paper even suggests that sunspot variability, rather than a rise in greenhouse gases, is responsible for the global temperature increases and decreases recorded since about 1880.

"Furthermore, the majority of scientific participants in the survey agreed that the theoretical climate models used to predict a future warming cannot be relied upon and are not validated by the existing climate record. Yet all predictions are based on such theoretical models.

"Finally, agriculturists generally agree that any increase in carbon dioxide levels from fossil fuel burning has beneficial effects on most crops and on world food supply.

"We are disturbed that activists, anxious to stop energy and economic growth, are pushing ahead with drastic policies without taking notice of recent changes in the underlying science. We fear that the rush to impose global regulations will have catastrophic impacts on the world economy, on jobs, standards of living, and health care, with the most severe consequences falling upon developing countries and the poor."

SIGNATORIES:

David G. Aubrey, Ph.D., Senior Scientist, Woods Hole Oceanographic Institute

Nathaniel B. Guttman, Ph.D., Research Physical Scientist, National Climatic Data Center

Hugh W. Ellsaesser, Ph.D., Meteorologist, Lawrence Livermore National Laboratory

Richard Lindzen, Ph.D., Center for Meteorology and Physical Meteorology, M.I.T.

Robert C. Balling, Ph.D., Director, Laboratory of Climatology, Arizona State University

Patrick Michaels, Ph.D., Assoc. Professor of Environmental Sciences, University of Virginia

Roger Pielke, Ph.D., Professor of Atmospheric Science, Colorado State University

Michael Garstang, Ph.D., Professor of Meteorology, University of Virginia

Sherwood B. Idso, Ph.D., Research Physicist, U.S. Water Conservation Laboratory

Lev S. Gandin, Ph.D., UCAR Scientist, National Meteorological Center

John A. McGinley, Chief, Forecast Research Group, Forecast Systems Laboratory, NOAA

H. Jean Thiebaux, Ph.D., Research Scientist, National Meteorological Center, National Weather Service, NOM

Kenneth V. Beard, Ph.D., Professor of Atmospheric Physics, University of Illinois

Paul W. Mielke, Jr., Ph.D., Professor, Dept. of Statistics, Colorado State University

Thomas Lockhart, Meteorologist, Meteorological Standards Institute

Peter F. Giddings, Meteorologist, Weather Service Director

Hazen A. Bedke, Meteorologist, Former Regional Director, National Weather Service

Gabriel T. Csanady, Ph.D., Eminent Professor, Old Dominion University

Roy Leep, Executive Weather Director, Gillett Weather Data Services

Terrance J. Clark, Meteorologist, U.S. Air Force

Neil L Frank, Ph.D., Meteorologist

Michael S. Uhart, Ph.D., Meteorologist, National Weather Service

Bruce A. Boe, Ph.D., Director, North Dakota Atmospheric Resource Board

Andrew Detwiler, Ph.D., Assoc. Prof., Institute of Atmospheric Sciences, S. Dakota School of Mines & Technology

Robert M. Cunningham, Consulting Meteorologist, Fellow, American Meteorological Society

Steven R. Hanna, Ph.D., Sigma Research Corporation

Elliot Abrams, Meteorologist, Senior Vice President, AccuWeather, Inc.

William E. Reifenyder, Ph.D., Consulting Meteorologist, Professor Emeritus, Forest Meteorology, Yale University

David W. Reynolds, Research Meteorologist

Jerry A. Williams, Meteorologist, President, Oceanroutes, Inc.

Lee W. Eddington, Meteorologist, Geophysics Division, Pacific Missile Test Center

Werner A. Baum, Ph.D., former Dean, College of Arts & Sciences, Florida State University

David P. Rogers, Ph.D., Assoc. Professor of Research Oceanography, Scripps Institution of Oceanography

Brian Fiedler, Ph.D., Asst. Professor of Meteorology, School of Meteorology, University of Oklahoma

Edward A. Brandes, Meteorologist Melvyn Shapiro, Chief of Meteorological Research, Wave Propagation Laboratory, NOM

Joseph Zabransky, Jr., Associate Professor of Meteorology, Plymouth State College

James A. Moore, Project Manager, Research Applications Program, National Center for Atmospheric Research Daniel

J. McNaughton, ENSR Consulting and Engineering

Brian Sussman, Meteorologist Robert D. Elliott, Meteorologist, Fellow, American Meteorological Society

H. Read McGrath, Ph.D., Meteorologist

Earl G. Droessler, Ph.D., North Carolina State University

Robert E. Zabrecky, Meteorologist

William M. Porch, Ph.D., Atmospheric Physicist, Los Alamos National Laboratory

Earle R. Williams, Ph.D, Assoc. Prof. of Meteorology, Massachusetts Institute of Technology

S. Fred Singer, Ph.D., Atmospheric Physicist, Univ. of Virginia, President, Science & Environmental Policy Project

This was only the opening volley.

Dr. Fredrick Seitz, past President of the National Academy of Sciences, and President Emeritus, Rockefeller University, is now with the Oregon Institute of Science and Medicine. He initiated a Petition Project that accepted no outside funds or political affiliation. Every scientist that participated paid their own expenses. His project attracted 19,200 scientists who signed the petition, 75 of which were Nobel Prize recipients. The full text of the petition, and a partial list of signatories, can be found in Appendix E — "Global Warming".

Another document was prepared, long before the aforementioned petition, titled "The Heidelberg Appeal." It was released at the 1992 Earth Summit in Rio de Janeiro. 425 scientists signed it. Since then more than 4,000 signatories, 72 of which are Nobel Prize winners, from 106 countries have signed it. The Appeal is also documented in Appendix E.

The global warming issue poses a far more ominous threat to our country than even the gross negligence of our bureaucracy in the violation of our 5th Amendment rights. The reason? Because according to environmentalist propaganda the adverse effect of greenhouse gases will cause catastrophic changes in climate, affect agriculture worldwide, and raise the level of the oceans, which will result in worldwide flooding and destruction of shoreline cities and communities. Thus, global warming is an international issue, and activists propose to surrender American sovereignty to a world tribunal in order to prevent it.

The international impact, say the eco-alarmists, is justification for imposing the rule of international law on all nations, which would give the power to a global police force to prosecute American businesses and individuals for breaking international law. We would be stripped of our Constitutional rights, brought before a world court, and subject to fines and imprisonment without due process.

The Greenhouse laws would also lay waste to our economy, posing stringent regulations on industry and individuals, and all at the whim of an international court. The immediate effect would be increased taxes on all fossil fuels, as much a 100%, which would double the price of gasoline, propane, natural gas, diesel oil and motor oil.

Massive reductions in motor vehicle use would deprive millions of Americans the unrestricted use of their automobiles, farmers would need permits to operate their tractors and combines, limits would be placed on airline travel, the trucking industry would be severly impacted, and the cost of electricity would likely sky rocket as well, as most power generation facilities burn coal.

The prices of goods and services would escalate 100%-300% as a result of the heavy regulation of the industries that transport and manufacture almost every product we buy and use. The simultaneous loss of millions of jobs, estimated at 3-5 million, and the astronomical rise of taxes to pay for regulatory costs, would plunge our nation into an unemployment crisis, coupled with such prohibitive increases in the cost of living that even wealthy Americans would lose their luxurious lifestyle.

The total cost to our economy is estimated to be $300 billion.

I sincerely hope that no single reader will fail to recognize the undisputable truth that we needn't suffer any of these debilitating effects, regardless how great or small, because the global warming theory is completely false, even comical.

Needless to say, an international treaty on greenhouse gas regulation would make America the prime target of every nation in the world, not only to drain our treasuries to support this tyranny, but to weaken us as the world's largest exporter, thus creating a vacuum for our competitor nations to fill. In effect, this is a blatant attempt to impose international socialism, and redistribute our wealth on a scale never dreamed of before. We, the people of America, being the most affluent of all nations, would be the ones having our wealth plundered and distributed to the poor nations of the world.

Bill Clinton signed the Kyoto Protocol without the consent of Congress, but he left office before he was able to push for approval of the treaty. President Bush has already given a resounding thumbs down to the pact, which predictably brought him under heavy fire from the eco-mafia crowd.

This is an issue that should be scrutinized very carefully in future elections, for if another of the supporters of Kyoto are elected, such as Hillary Clinton or Albert Gore, the rule of international law will become the law the of the land, if they are successful in their attempts to ratify the Kyoto Protocol.

The new Clean Skies proposals by President Bush gives equal priority to health without sacrificing prosperity, a proposition that infuriates the eco-gestapo. Their methods call for our citizens to sacrifice whatever we must to meet their radical agenda, an agenda which is clearly inimical to American interests at home and abroad.

As stated on several occasions earlier, scare tactics are a favorite strategy of the eco-left, and a very effective one. But their frightening "Chicken Little" scenarios, as one gentlemen phrased it, are supported by junk science at best, and outright fabrication at worst, neither of which is a justifiable cause for the widespread concern about so called "global warming" and the ozone layer.

Professor Glenn Shaw, a noted atmospheric scientist, caught my attention with the following article. [Global Warming News and Views, on www.sitewave.net/news.]

> Global warming is a "name brand fashion" with just enough of a whiff of scientific legitimacy and Old Testament apocalypse to make it attractive to the populace at large. The issue is quite much like Camel Cigarettes advertisements in the 1940. And buying into greenhouse warming is just as dangerous as smoking Camels!
>
> Make no mistake about it, "global warming" is a political instrument of the left wing. It's the favorite scare tactic of environmentalists. Its being employed with vigor to bridle what Europeans are fond of calling a "cowboy economy" and to rein in a country thought of by competitors as being "out of control".
>
> Greenhouse warming is one of the most massively overstated issues ever to hit.
>
> Trying to cow the US by hurting the nation's economy with greenhouse gas scare tactics is France attempting to bully Germany with crippling reparation

payments in the Versailles treaty at the end of World War I. This basically unenlightened policy resulted in many unexpected consequences, including the rise of Hitler!

The Greenhouse Warming issue, unless somebody starts to speak some sense and defuse the issue, is likely to cause a major conflict on the scale of a World War. I think this is real strategic political business with serious consequences and not a playing around thing.

What about the science? Is global warming scientific? The answer is a qualified yes. Indeed carbon dioxide is "building up." This effect, all by itself, would force a small planetary scale warming. That's the physics.

But everything poops out fast after that. The greenhouse forcing is at most like stringing a few quite dim Christmas tree lights around on the planet. Predictions of climate change for the greenhouse warming next century or next decade are much like computer models of the weather change next month: basically meaningless or at least quite inaccurate. I can make rational and intelligent arguments that global cooling by other effects such as the "Twomey Effect" is in the cards for the future. Moreover, cloud and water vapor feed backs are pathetically incorporated in climate models, yet they are among the most important drivers of future climate.

Scaring people about the warming on a basis of such flawed science and proposing massive social engineering in which the United States comes out the loser is asking for real trouble. For one thing, it would be relatively simple to engineer a way out of any global warming, if it ever wound up getting big enough to document. I reckon it would be on the scale of constructing the great hydro plants in the western United States. Whatever the net effect will prove to be, it will be less than most home thermometers can resolve and pretty unimportant on global economic and human health and welfare scales of events.

Don't swallow global warming. Its political hot air with a lot of bravado. It's a Stamp Act! It's an overblown issue that could well end up causing grave harm to this nation's economy and well being. Don't buy it.

Environmental extremism enjoyed a quantum boost during the Clinton Administration. Albert "Global Warming" Gore, the man who claims he invented the Internet, blamed every hiccup in the range of natural disasters on this ludicrous theory.

Hundreds of hard-core eco-fanatics were appointed and hired to staff our federal agencies that regulate and manage all things environmental. The success of the Spotted Owl fiasco was one of their landmark victories, a measure that Clinton claimed, at the time, would take "only" 10,000 jobs. He was only short by approximately 1,000,000. The infamous owl caused a major disruption in the lumber and wood products industry, gave rise to astronomical price increases, diminished American exports, increased lumber imports, and set the stage for the turf wars that are now in progress: the U.S. Government vs. The American People.

See Appendix E — "Global Warming" for additional documentation.

CHAPTER 10.
LET IT BURN

The environmentalist policy regarding forest fire is "Let it burn!" Of all the myriad issues tied to environmental protection, this one is, in my opinion, the most significant, for it not only reveals the twisted logic that drives this movement but it also exposes the bogus nature of their alleged commitment to protect the environment, the one issue that they depend upon more than any other for public support.

The deep ecologist's devotion to their god, Gaia, is at the heart of this ludicrous position. It is their belief that nature is the domain of Goddess Earth, and any interference from man is an abomination to their pagan deity.

Nature, in their view, is a living entity that is capable of maintaining itself. The source of the prescient faculty that governs this process is a mystery to me, and I suspect to them as well. Regardless, they cling to the notion that the primordial intellect of some formidable power is in control of the natural order.

Even if this theory were true it is clear that "The Power" is hostile to mankind and oblivious to the requirements for our survival. Either that, or "it" doesn't give a damn about the welfare of man! Either way, we are bound to this planet by the force of gravity and we have little choice in the matter. If we are going to survive and prosper then nature is going to have to accommodate us. In return, we will protect nature from herself, as it appears that Gaia has a masochistic side.

Even the environmentalists that are not Gaia worshipers support the "let it burn" theory as an effective strategy in wilderness management.

One may find many articles citing the Yellowstone burn as an example of nature's way of renewing itself: the forest floor, enriched with the ashes of burned trees, is soon lush with grasses and wild flowers. This is a common argument among the eco-"experts."

But nature's ability to recover from catastrophic wildfire is yet another argument in favor of human use of the environment, whether in logging and mining, or snowmobiling and skiing. What damage we may inflict is swallowed up in the ongoing process of renewal that has been going on for millions of years. If, as they maintain, nature has such extraordinary powers of recovery, then man's negligible impact should be no problem whatsoever.

Man has a brain, and the environment is far better off when we take intelligent measures to prevent catastrophe, or limit it. Logging accomplishes that objective, and is usually conducted in a way that leaves behind a generous stand of trees. Letting fires burn out of control makes no sense.

Another environmentalist claim is that drought is the major cause of fire. This is certainly a contributing factor, but hardly the primary cause. The presence of abundant fuel on the ground, and stands of "dog hair" pine, are the factors that create hazardous fire conditions, and those are factors that have developed as a result of environmentalist policies.

I also want to address the subtle strategy, adopted by eco-organizations of late, that we should focus on the conditions near inhabited areas to protect life and property. I suggest that the advocates of this policy, which sounds reasonable enough to me, discuss their concerns with fellow environmentalists! The following excerpt from Jarret Wolstein's *Green Gestapo* leaves me with serious doubts that eco-groups know what "common sense" is:

> In Riverside, California, 76,000 acres — much of it privately owned and occupied, was declared a preserve for the kangaroo rat. Kangaroo rats are common throughout California, and for centuries have been regarded as destructive vermin. However, homeowners were repeatedly threatened with prison sentences and fines of up to $100,000 if they cleared overgrown brush from their own property.
>
> On October 26, 1993, wildfires swept through the area. Fire quickly leapt from brush to homes. As homeowner Yshmael Garcia explains:
>
> My home was destroyed by a bunch of bureaucrats in suits and so-called environmentalists who say animals are more important than people.
>
> In fact, the ban on clearing brush also killed the kangaroo rats, who burned along with the homes.

We should indeed improve hazardous conditions near populated areas, but the tangle of environmental regulations is the greatest obstacle to accomplishing any such measures. Every time anyone proposes any project involving the environment, regardless the purpose, the eco-mafia shift into high gear: filing injunctions, orchestrating propaganda campaigns, and even staging demonstrations to prevent any tampering with the environment. In most cases, such as clearing brush near a residential neighborhood, the residents would probably do the work themselves, and gladly, to protect their homes; but if they did, they would end up in a federal pen and be fined $150,000.

The following statement was copied from Forest.org, an environmentalist website.

> It is well known scientifically that "commercial logging actually increases fire severity by removing large, fire-resistant trees and leaving behind very small trees and flammable "slash debris" — branches, twigs and needles from felled trees.
>
> The removal of mature trees also decreases the forest canopy, creating hotter, drier conditions on the ground. The additional sun exposure encourages the growth of flammable brush and weeds. Reduction of flammable underbrush can reduce fire severity, and environmental groups have encouraged such projects. However, the Bush Administration has grossly misused the funds that Congress appropriated for brush reduction near homes.
>
> In Sierra Nevada national forests last year, more than 90% of these funds were instead earmarked for preparation of large timber sales focused on the removal of mature and old-growth trees miles from the nearest town.

Here we have a classic example of environmentalist misinformation and outright lies. Once again, science comes into play, a ploy that is used to lend credibility to their nonsense.

This claim is neither "well known" nor "scientific." In fact, the opposite is true. By what stretch of the imagination are we to believe that "removing large, fire-resistant trees" contributes to fire hazard? It's true that large trees many times survive a forest fire, but that does not mean that removing them increases the likelihood of a fire.

Destroying the forest canopy does, indeed, contribute to drier conditions on the ground, but Forest.com fails to mention that timber management practices regulate the removal of old-growth trees. Before the logging contractor ever sets foot on the land, the USFS "cruises" the timber and designates which trees are not to be harvested.

It is true that "reduction of flammable underbrush can reduce fire severity," but the claim that "environmental groups have encouraged such projects" is not true. Environmentalists oppose any and all intrusion by man into the sanctuary of our wilderness timberlands.

The closing comment of the Forest.com diatribe reveals their true objective: attacking the Bush Administration for promoting logging in national forests. But as I have already stated, USFS management policies restrict the harvesting of old-growth trees.

As for the statement that "more than 90% of these funds were instead earmarked for preparation of large timber sales," one wonders what "preparation" is meant? The logging contractor pays to log an area, not the government. The public treasury is enriched by selling timber, not drained.

It may also occur to a rational observer that the President is intent upon removing the ground cover "miles from any home" so as to prevent fires in the first place, and make them easier to control in the second, to protect homes "miles away."

These comments are the customary subterfuge that environmentalists use to cloud the issues while they attempt to discredit their adversaries, a mingling of half-truths, lies and "hot button" issues that appear to be in the public interest. Meanwhile, their intent it to attack sane management policies.

Removing the forest canopy does make conditions on the ground drier, but there are other, complex factors at work. Two researchers at Colorado State University's Natural Resources Ecology Laboratory have found fire suppression is a factor in the decline of quality habitat and food supply for mule deer on the Western Slope of Colorado.

The study was funded by the Colorado Division of Wildlife and conducted by Daniel Manier, a postdoctoral research associate, and senior research scientist Tom Hobbs. According to Manier and Hobbs:

> [Lack of fire is part of a] complex combination of ecologic changes that might be contributing to the declining growth of mule deer populations.
> Mule deer prefer plants that are close to the ground. They eat grasses and wildflowers in addition to many shrubs. When trees and dense shrubs become overgrown, they compete with plants that deer prefer to eat, eventually changing the composition of plants in important deer habitat. In the past,

natural fires have cleared deer habitat of trees and shrubs, which are replaced with new vegetation, thus creating a beneficial and plentiful food source.

Deer have evolved over thousands of years with natural disturbances of the landscape, and when fire is removed, habitat conditions change in ways that are detrimental to deer.

Manier and Hobbs also found that fire suppression, which led to a gradual increase in forested areas in the region, caused an acceleration in canopy coverage in the area that was studied. The increase in tree cover caused a reduction in grazing areas.

"The lack of fire caused an initial encroachment on the habitat, but there have been conservation efforts to increase the quality of the deer environment," Manier said. "The question is, have those efforts been enough to begin to increase the population?"

There seems to be a clash in ideology here. It's advisable to let fire remove the canopy, but logging is unacceptable. Who gets to decide what is enough, or too much, canopy? Why do the eco-extremists get to decide how the canopy is to be removed? The one common thread in these statements is the anti-human cant that characterizes the pronouncements of the eco-crowd. Ground cover creates fire hazard and encroaches upon deer habitat; but both problems could be alleviated by controlled logging.

Jonathan Alder, in his article on the folly of federal land management during the Clinton Administration, had this to say about fire suppression policies:

> And how are the federal eco-saviors performing? The truth is chilling. They have created ecological disasters of near-apocalyptic proportions. Tens of millions of acres of once-beautiful forest land have been transformed into charred moonscapes and dying, bug-infested, overgrown tinderboxes set to explode into blazing infernos. Likewise, millions of acres of verdant grasslands have been ravaged by wildfires and turned into weed-choked wastelands. Wildlife habitats and watersheds have been destroyed on a massive scale, while the economic, aesthetic, and recreational values of vast areas of the West have been devastated.

Lost Livelihoods

Just how devastating federal negligence and mismanagement have been to people and the ecosystem was the subject of a July 10th congressional hearing in John Day, Oregon. Nearly 500 local residents turned out for the hearing of the House Resource Subcommittee on Forests and Forest Health chaired by Representative Helen Chenoweth (R-ID).

Tom Partin, the mayor of John Day, testified that due to Forest Service policies, his small community of 2,000 people is facing record-high unemployment, empty storefronts, bankruptcies, and plummeting property values. "We are in trouble," he said, "because our National Forests that have been a partner with us since their formation have managers that are turning their backs on rural America.

"This is happening not by accident, but rather by design of our current administration (Clinton)." Mayor Partin is also a partner in the local Malheur Lumber Company, which employs 100 people in its mill and another 75 in the woods and related trucking jobs.

In 1983 his company invested $15 million to build the mill, based on the Malheur National Forest Plan that called for 210 million board feet of annual timber harvest. But that harvest has been arbitrarily cut to less than 50 million board feet annually, even though the Malheur National Forest, like virtually all of the federal western forests, is overstocked and badly in need of thinning.

"Our county has only two industries, timber and cattle," Ralph Goodwin, president/CEO of the Grant-Baker Federal Credit Union in John Day, told the subcommittee. "When someone loses their job in the county, they cannot go down the street and pick up a job in some sort of emerging industry.

"During 1997 and 1998, Grant County had the unfortunate distinction of having the highest unemployment in the state for 14 of those 24 months. . . .Why are our mills desperate for saw logs? We are in the middle of one of the largest stands of ponderosa pine in the world and yet our three mills are on the verge of closing. The people of this county are hard-working people who are not looking for handouts, only the opportunity to remain here and raise their families."

The availability of logs is not in dispute. According to a detailed report issued by the U.S. General Accounting Office (GAO) this past April, entitled Catastrophic Wildfire Threats, "39 million acres on national forests in the interior West are at high risk of catastrophic wildfire" due to unnatural and excessive tree density, massive buildup of undergrowth, disease and insect infestation.

Don Johnson, the scrappy owner and president of Prairie Wood Products and Grant Western Lumber Company, couldn't understand why he should be lacking logs when, by the Forest Service's own figures, the Malheur Forest alone was experiencing tree "mortality at over 200 million board feet per year." "That is more than 50,000 truck loads of trees dying on this forest."

When I was growing up in northern Montana, my Dad was a Fire Dispatcher with the U.S. Forest Service. I learned timber management first hand, at the knee of a professional.

In those days fire crews were stationed at every ranger station and men were posted on the lookout towers. Every spring Dad took the fire crews out to clear the fire trails; it was a process that took all season. The crews would load mules with supplies and follow each trail, clearing downed trees and debris so that, if a fire broke out, they would be able to get to it quickly. Dad would be gone for days at a time; he and his men camped in the mountains until all the trails were clear.

One of the most exciting experiences for me was an electrical storm. Dad and I would climb into the barn loft and he would establish contact with the lookouts via the Motorola. As reports of lightning strikes came in, my father would grid them on his maps, marking each location.

Most strikes were either extinguished by rain or never amounted to much, but some flared and started to burn. Even those usually dwindled to nothing, but when a flare began to spread, Dad swung into action. Within the hour he would muster his crew at The Upper Ford, the ranger station closest to our home, and set out immediately for the fire location.

Over the years I remember only one fire that got out of control. Dozens of them were put out before they got out of hand. Today, the USFS has no dispatcher, nor fire crews. Neither do they maintain fire trails any longer. Today the standard procedure is to import smoke jumpers and fire fighters, but by the time they respond to a fire it is already out of control.

The old system was efficient; now, the new age eco-managers have employed "prescribed burns" to clear off the ground cover. However, the low priority placed on fire suppression does not provide adequate funds to deal with the buildup of combustible fuels on the millions of acres that the U.S. Government controls.

Consequently, the number of workers is grossly inadequate, and using fire to fight fire, this way, is dangerous. If a wind kicks up, a fire can grow to an uncontrollable size in minutes. Two of the wildfires in the summer of 2002 were caused by USFS personnel. One started as a prescribed burn.

Contrary to the environmentalists' claims, logging is the best system for timber management. Rather than address their claims one by one, I will summarize the procedure I watched my Father follow many times. After a sale was awarded to a contractor, a ranger or one of his assignees would "cruise" the entire site. All ranked USFS personnel were involved in timber management. A member of the contractor's management staff would accompany him. It was the ranger's job to mark the trees that could not be harvested and note terrain features that would require special attention. Everything was documented and filed in a report for review prior to the onset of the actual logging operation.

Once approved, the contractor first built roads into the site and established a "landing," the large area where logs would be skidded and loaded on trucks. Even these features were prescribed and monitored by USFS personnel. Roads had to be built according to rigid guidelines that took into consideration terrain features such as streams and precipitous slopes in order to protect wildlife and avoid erosion.

When the work was completed, the contractor was responsible to 'doze the debris into "slash piles," and incidental to that activity, any large stands of small "trash trees," called "dog hair" pine, were cleared, along with dead fall and heavy concentrations of brush and standing stumps.

The site was inspected after cleanup to insure it was done properly, and also note such features as bridges and road grading. The slash piles would be burned in the wet months.

Much of the slash consisted of tree tops and large limbs, as well as dead fall, which could be sold to pulp mills. A "gypo logger" was given the contract to redeem any usable wood, bringing additional revenues into USFS coffers and further reducing slash.

The final phase would take place the next spring, when crews would plant saplings in any open areas.

Not only were old growth trees left standing, but a belt of timber along public roadways was left undisturbed to preserve aesthetic beauty for the sake of tourists and local residents. Two years after a site was logged, it was hardly noticeable that human activity had taken place at all.

The benefits of logging were many; the economy of the local communities was vigorous, there were plenty of jobs, and businesses that depended on logging-industry pay checks thrived. Communities were enriched by tax revenues as well, which provided public services and utilities.

Contrary to alarmist propaganda, the habitat benefited as well. The heavy ground cover was removed, reducing fire hazard to almost nil, and the forest floor was renewed. New vegetation had no competition from weeds and dog hair pine, and the canopy was thinned enough to allow adequate sun to bathe the forest floor.

Roads served several valuable purposes. Fire crews could be moved into the most remote areas by vehicle within hours. Fires would be extinguished easily and safely. The dangerous method of fighting fire by airborne jumpers was not necessary; supplies and equipment were on hand as they were needed during the operation; and injured personnel were evacuated quickly. If a fire did get out of hand, there was a means of evacuating fire crews to a safe location.

In addition, the public was provided a means of access into the wilderness areas. Hunters used them in season, fishermen drove into remote lakes and rivers, or picnickers could escape the well-traveled roads and enjoy an undisturbed outing in nature's bosom. In the fall we would drive up to the higher elevations and pick huckleberries, and in the spring we hunted morel mushrooms. Many of these recreational activities would not have been possible without well made, safe roads. I can remember how much we enjoyed our drives into the remote regions. The logging industry made our lives better in every respect, and wood products that we import from Canada and Japan today, at a dear price, were available in abundance at an affordable cost.

The environmentalist opposition to logging is illogical and extremely dangerous. Whatever claims they make to the effect that they are only interested in protecting the wilderness is a sham. More than once, after new fire management policies were put into practice, logging crews volunteered to contribute men and equipment to the fire fighting effort — but USFS officials refused to allow them to help.

The Fisher River fire that destroyed one of the most magnificent stands of ancient Tamarac in Montana, between Kalispell and Libby, could have been avoided had logging crews been given permission to help. There was a logging contractor just miles from the fire with adequate manpower and heavy equipment to stop the fire in the early stages.

Here is a case where both man and the environment are well served, but obstructionist tactics have contributed to perilous conditions, deprived thousands of people of their jobs, plunged local communities into near poverty conditions, and taken away the opportunity to enjoy the beauty and solitude of our public lands.

One other issue is a popular myth about the infamous clear cut. Eco-propaganda flashes images of hillsides that have been denuded of all timber and their loud cries of outrage inform the public that this is a standard practice in the logging industry.

This is a bald-faced lie.

The Forest Service never allows a healthy forest to be clear cut. This extreme measure is only used to eradicate pine beetle infestation, a blight on timber that cannot be stopped any other way. Unless infected areas are clear cut, the beetle will spread and kill thousands of acres.

A private land owner can also allow a logger to clear cut, usually because he wants the land cleared for building or cultivation.

The only other instance of clear cutting is an old burn. When thousands of dead snags are left standing, it is not only an ideal environment for pine beetle, but a fire hazard. These snags can be harvested and the revenues used to reforest — but environmentalists won't allow it.

In all my years in the Montana wilderness, I only saw two clear cuts: one for beetle infestation, and the old burn on Caribou Mountain at the east end of the Yaak River Valley.

In closing this chapter I have a sad tale to tell, a tragedy that took the lives of four young people in a fire in the Okanogan National Forest. These three accounts give stark evidence that ecologists are placing the welfare of fish above that of human beings.

Four Fire Fighters Die Because of Endangered Fish
[William LaJeunnesse and Robin Wallace, Fox News, Tuesday, July 31, 2001]

Fire fighters struggling to contain a blaze in central Washington State that ultimately killed four of their own were hampered in their efforts by a federal policy to protect endangered fish, Fox News has learned.

Fire fighters were unable to douse the deadly fire in Okanogan National Forest in Winthrop, Wash., in July because of delays in granting permission for fire-fighting helicopters to use water from nearby streams and rivers protected by the Endangered Species Act, according to sources close to the fire.

Fire fighters Tom L. Craven, 30, Karen L. Fitzpatrick, 18, Devin A Weaver, 21, and Jessica L. Johnson, 19, burned to death while cowering under protective tents near the Chewuch River, home to protected species salmon and trout. Seventeen other fire fighters survived the ordeal.

Forest Service policy in the Northwest requires that special permission be obtained before fire helicopters can dip into certain restricted rivers, lakes and streams. The fear is that the dippers could accidentally scoop up protected species of fish.

A 17-member team from the Forest Service and other federal agencies is now investigating whether the four fire fighters died as a result of the policy.

Rep. Scott McInnis, R-Colo., chairman of the House Subcommittee on Forests & Forest Health, said the committee is also looking into allegations that environmental policy and bureaucracy were factors in the deaths.

The Thirty Mile Fire Burns in the Okanogan-Wenatchee National Forest [Associated Press July 13, 2001]

Testifying before the committee Tuesday, USFS Fire Chief Dale Bosworth said that under standard procedure, fire fighters would have used the Chewuch water to fight the fire and addressed any environmental violations or restrictions after the fire was extinguished. He said he was investigating why dispatch waited for approval before sending the helicopters.

"We get the water where we can get it and ask questions later," Bosworth said.

Forest Service District Commander John Newcom told Fox News last week that the Chewuch River's population of salmon, steelhead trout and bull trout are all considered when fighting fires, but insisted helicopter permission was never delayed or denied because of the policy.

But the USFS reversed that position Tuesday with the release of a timeline of events that depicts the harrowing plight of a band of very young, inexperienced fire fighters waiting desperately for helicopter relief that never came.

According to the timeline, the first team of fire fighters, an elite crew called "Hot Shots," had contained what came to be known as the "30-mile fire" by the very early morning and requested a helicopter water drop at 5:30 a.m. However, they were told one would not be available until 10 a.m.

At 9 a.m., the Hot Shots were replaced with a young "mop-up" crew expecting helicopter relief to arrive within the hour. When the mop-up crew inquired about the missing helicopter just after noon, the dispatch office told the crew field boss that helicopters could not be used in the area because the Chewuch River contained endangered fish.

A Team Investigates the Deaths of Four Fire Fighters in the Thirty Mile Fire. Final Permission to Use Chewuch Water Wasn't Granted Until 2 P.M. [Associated Press, July 12, 2001]

Jan Flatten, the environmental officer for the Okanogan and Wenatchee Natural forests, confirmed that environmental concerns caused crucial delays in dispatching the helicopter.

"At 12:08, the dispatch office ordered the helicopter," Flatten told Fox News. "However, because there are endangered species in the Chewuch River, they wanted to get permission from the district in order to dip into the river."

However, the dispatch office could not reach anyone at the district with the authority to approve the helicopter drop. Flatten said those authorities, Newcom, Fire Manager Peter Sodoquist and the Methow Valley biologist — were actually meeting during that time to approve an exemption to the policy.

"That time lag of about two hours was when they were trying to locate someone with the authority to tell them they could go ahead and take water out of the Chewuch River," Flatten said.

The USFS did not explain why the intra-agency team required to approve an exemption did not convene until 12 p.m., two hours after fire fighters had been told the helicopter would be available.

Two former USFS fire fighters familiar with the Thirty Mile Fire said getting permission to dip into the Chewuch caused the delays that led to the death of their colleagues.

"(The crew) were told that (the Chewuch River) was a protected water source and they needed to go through channels to use this water source," one of the former fire fighters told Fox News.

The first load of helicopter water was dumped on the fire around 3 p.m., but the fire was by then out of control. An hour later, air tankers had to be turned back and the ground crew fled on foot to the river where they deployed their survival tents. The crew was completely surrounded by the flames with no avenue for escape.

Knowing that lives were at stake, why didn't anyone in authority make the call to dip water from the Chewuch; why didn't the helicopter crew take it upon themselves to make the drop? Because disturbing the habitat of an endangered species is punishable by a one-year prison term and a $150,000 fine. Apparently, none of the people involved were willing to take that chance, and four people paid with their lives. The greatest share of the blame, however, must be shouldered by an oppressive bureaucracy that instills such fear of reprisal in its subordinates.

The people in these agencies are well aware of the consequences of offending a fish, or muddying a stream. They have been first-hand witnesses to the cold blooded, merciless treatment of innocent citizens who have made this grave error. The eco-mafia rules with fear.

CHAPTER 11.
ENVIRONMENTAL POLITICS

> "As a man is said to have a right to his property, he may be equally said to have property in his rights."
> James Madison

History teaches us that government is a "necessary evil" that is best controlled by limiting its powers. This limiting of powers was clearly the intent of our Founding Fathers, as reflected in the documents they authored and their personal observations. Their model for control was based upon the citizen's vote as the ultimate power of the people to determine their own destiny. An ingenious system of checks and balances were put in place to facilitate the reasonable application of governmental fiat.

However, man can foul up even a perfect system. The U.S. system as it is practiced at this hour is a terribly distorted effigy of the vision that became reality over 200 years ago. With each generation, there has been a gradual erosion of respect for our Constitution. Few adults and fewer children have more than a topical understanding of the liberties that this critical document guarantees (and those liberties are being wiped away fast by legislation that purports to defend us from terrorists — in fact, it exposes us to abuse by our own government). Anyway, most Americans' knowledge about their Constitutional rights is confined to the highly publicized activities of special interest groups.

The evolution of our political institutions also mirrors the lack of reverence for Constitutional law. Our elected officials today subscribe, in the majority, to the mechanics of expediency. Political parties in the U.S. now engage in an ongoing battle for dominance rather than fostering bipartisan or multi-partisan coalitions whose foremost priority would be the welfare of the people. Policies are shaped by the upcoming elections, a poll-driven ideology that ignores the mandates of public service.

No single issue is more indicative than that of environmental law and its enforcement. The rise to power of the environmental syndicate has resulted in abuses of our rights to property and privacy that are so onerous that they defy belief.

Bill Clinton's presidency spawned a subculture in the highest levels of government that are dedicated to anti-American, anti-Constitutional objectives. Led by Albert Gore, the despotic duo of Bruce Babbitt as Secretary of Interior and Carol Browner as Chief of the Environmental Protection Agency brought the formidable power of government to bear on thousands of individual Americans and communities.

The culmination of Clinton's eight-year rule was The Community Character Act (S.975), and its counterpart in the House of Representatives (H.R.1433). The vast majority of Americans have never heard of this bill; yet, if it is passed, it will drastically change the lives of every man, woman and child in this country.

Tom DeWeese, President of the prestigious American Policy Center, discusses the ramifications of this legislation in his article titled "The Back Room Deal To Destroy America" [www.sierratimes.com, June 3, 2002].

A group of U.S. Senators have conspired to destroy local zoning throughout the United States of America. They are trying to do it in secret. They don't want to hear from someone saying they are betraying the Constitution they swore to uphold.

Americans should take note of the names of these Senators: Former Republican turncoat Jim Jeffords; Republican Arlen Specter; Democrat Max Baucus; Democrat Harry Ried; Democrat Bob Graham; Democrat Joseph Lieberman; Democrat Barbara Boxer; Democrat Ron Wyden; Democrat Thomas Casper; Democrat Hillary Rodham Clinton; and Democrat Jon Corzine.

These U.S. Senators, members of the Senate Environment Committee, hold American liberty in such disdain that they conspired behind closed doors to railroad through a bill that would put faceless bureaucrats in Washington, DC, in charge of decisions that have always been made at the community level. The bill, S.975, also known as the "Community Character Act," authorizes the use of federal money so that un-elected environmentalists can advance their extreme-left political agenda.

Secrecy was needed because opposition has been growing as the harsh realities of S-975 are being revealed by property rights advocates. The Jeffords-led cabal knew fast action was required if the bill was to sneak past. S.975, and it's counterpart in the House (H.R. 1433) will turn all of Bill Clinton's land-grabbing Executive Orders into legislation. The Community Character Act will officially make the environmental goal of "sustainable development" the law of the land.

What is "sustainable development"? Imagine an America in which a single ruling principle is created to decide proper societal conduct for every citizen. That principle would be used to determine everything you eat, what you wear, the kind of home in which you live, the way you get to work, the way you dispose of waste, the number of children you may have, even your education and employment decisions. Imagine, too, that all of these decisions are called "voluntary" while the federal government uses its full power to induce —coerce — what it deems "correct behavior."

On June 29, 1993, former President Bill Clinton issued Executive Order #12852 to create the President's Council on Sustainable Development. Sustainable development calls for changing the concept of private property, protected by the Fifth Amendment to the Constitution, to nothing short of a national zoning system. Under such a system, the federal government, backed by an army of private, non-governmental organizations (NGOs) like the Sierra Club, Planned Parenthood, and the National Education Association will influence, if not dictate, property and other policies to the States and to local communities.

Locally elected officials will no longer be the single driving force in making decisions for their communities. Most decisions will be arrived at behind the scenes by non-elected "sustainability councils" armed with truckloads of federal regulations, guidelines and money. The power of citizen's votes would be nullified. This system is already in place with regard to the nation's education system, controlled entirely from Washington, DC. How much centralized bureaucracy is necessary to guarantee reasonable standards nationwide, and when does it morph into invasive control that negates the very notion of democracy?

The Community Character Act (S.975), and its counterpart in the House of Representatives (H.R.1433), is legislation that will legalize enforcement of "sustainable development" in every community in the nation. The bill requires local governments to implement land-management plans using guidelines outlined in a federal document called the "Smart Growth Legislative Guidebook." This publication was developed with $2 million provided by the Clinton Administration to "guide" counties, cities and towns on how to "update their local zoning."

The Community Character Act offers grants to communities that will pay up to 90% of the costs for localities to update their zoning, but only if they do it the way the federal government wants it done. Among other goals, the guide requires localities to "promote social equity." Communities will be required to establish social programs that will be paid for with new or increased taxes on businesses and industry. What better way to discourage business growth?

The Community Character Act requires localities to "conserve historic, scenic, natural and cultural resources." These are euphemisms that mean more land grabs and fewer places where humans can freely go about their daily lives. It means planned economies, restricted housing, diminished use of cars, and government control of property.

The Community Character Act demands that communities "integrate local land- use plans with federal land-use plans." That means local needs, local problems and local culture will be ignored as the entire nation is homogenized into one, unhappy, colorless, controlled Big Brotherhood.

The bill contains not a single mention of private-property rights protection. The federal government and states now own forty percent of the entire landmass of the nation. Under the Community Character Act, money would be provided to tender more land unavailable for any development or use.

This legislation must be stopped. If not, America will be unrecognizable to future generations. It is time for the Republicans in Congress to decide if they truly believe in the concept of limited government under which individual Americans are free to determine their destinies and achieve their dreams and goals, without intrusion and dictates. Under "sustainable development" there are no individual decisions, rights or actions. Virtually everything will come under the scrutiny of a Washington-sanctioned federal bureaucrat.

Senate Minority Leader Trent Lott and House Speaker Dennis Hastert must unite their party to stop this attack on one of the fundamental principles of the Constitution. If enacted, it will not "sustain" development. It will end it. It will destroy the machine that maintains our economy and insures its growth. A secret, backroom deal has set this in motion.

The encroachment of totalitarian power on the fundamental rights of the citizens of America reached a high point in Clinton's Administration. No political operative in recent decades has been guilty of misconduct on the scale of Carol Browner, head of the Clinton EPA. In her exhaustive investigation into the mismanagement of the Coeur d'Alene Superfund project, U.S. Rep. Helen Chenoweth-Hage (1st District of Idaho) made the following statements in her

Congressional Report of October 24, 2000 (due to the length of this document I have included only small portion).

> Furthermore, EPA's harassment and mistreatment of local mining companies is indefensible in light of the federal government's culpability in creating the problem in the first place. It was the War Department who demanded 24-hour a day operation of the mines during World War II — when the smelter at Kellogg was responsible for one-fifth to one-quarter of the United States' output of lead and zinc. It was the United States' Justice Department that allowed the flight of Gulf Resources — the company primarily responsible for the massive release of toxic lead particles. Through the EPA, the federal government now is holding responsible companies who had virtually no part in creating the current situation.
> Region X's abuse of federal law and the citizens of north Idaho is surpassed only by its attempts to evade and distort the truth. But the facts are clear — EPA has acted recklessly, treading on the rights of citizens, polluting the Basin, and aimlessly spending millions of taxpayer dollars.

Clearly, the agency has distorted the purpose of the emergency administrative order created by Congress in CERCLA, using it not only for convenience and to avoid dealing with the public on a compromise basis, but also as a means of coercion. To determine the full extent of EPA's usage of the UAO, the Request For Information Order, and other emergency powers of CERCLA, Rep. Chenoweth-Hage has written EPA Region X Acting Administrator Chuck Findley, asking for copies of every UAO or RFI issued in the Coeur d'Alene Basin. As expected, the agency's response was inadequate and Chenoweth-Hage is following up with additional requests.

Throughout the history of America, the use of force, and the ability to project force by any branch of government has been the single most closely-guarded, closely-regulated power of all.

Despite this foundational tenet of the American system of government, the EPA has shown a clear intent to use the force of the emergency administrative order on a widespread and common basis for purposes clearly outside of the scope of our Constitution, and in ways not intended by Congress.

The arrogant attitude of EPA officials culminated in a plan to dredge Lake Coeur d'Alene, a measure that would probably result in the bankruptcy of several local mining companies, and create an environmental crisis. Continuing with Rep. Chenoweth-Hage's report:

Among EPA and its co-complainants' plans in a $3.8 billion claim against the mining industry to dredge the bed of Coeur d'Alene Lake and tributaries, lifting lead-sulfide from its very stable chemical composition under water into exposure to the atmosphere, where it will by exposed to the air and fresh rainwater and could convert to lead-oxide, a highly bio available substance. Approximately one billion dollars are budgeted for such effort in a claim by The Coeur d'Alene Tribe.

EPA knows, or should know, that a similar dredging experiment conducted at Strathcona Lake on Vancouver Island, British Columbia, produced disastrous environmental results.

At edict of the provincial government's environmental agency, the inert mining sulfides — mine tailings — dredged from the lake bed were placed on the lake shore, where, oxidizing in the light and rainwater, they quickly flowed back down into the lake and killed a fish population — where before no aquatic biota problem previously existed.

In the Coeur d'Alene Basin, a 1993 U.S. Geological Survey report by Horowitz, et al. was partially responsible for bringing about the discussion of dredging.

The report alleged that sulfide metals in the bottom sediment of Lake Coeur d'Alene could, under the right trophic conditions, mobilize into the water column and become bioavailable. Although the Horowitz report remains gospel in EPA circles, it was not peer-reviewed.

Dr. Tom Pedersen, marine geochemist and Professor of Oceanography at the University of British Columbia, completely debunked the faulty theory in a peer-reviewed critique of the Horowitz study, saying Horowitz's modeling and sampling procedures both were flawed. Nevertheless, EPA continues to pursue dredging and other massive soil-moving projects in the lake through the lawsuit, and is expected to recommend such actions in its forthcoming cleanup plans.

When the actions of our own government become so destructive to our freedom, and further place our citizen's in peril by their myopic practices, it is time to demand accountability.

An ignorant society is a vulnerable society, a dictum that certainly applies to our people in regard to environmentalist plundering. But an informed society that fails to act decisively to protect its freedom is doomed by its own ineptitude.

President Bush II has taken concrete steps toward addressing many of the problems endemic in the government's environmental policies. He has announced sweeping changes in the longstanding forest management practices that resulted in the catastrophic wildfires of 2002 and announced plans to restore logging as a solution to the buildup of hazardous ground cover.

As of this writing, he has also indicated that he supports relaxing environmental restrictions on oil production on the North Slope of Alaska.

Bush's Clean Skies proposal is another refreshing departure from the Draconian rule of the past two decades. His stated objectives are realistic and achievable, but most importantly, they do not place an untenable burden on our business sector in the process of cleaning up the environmental and protecting our citizens from toxic hazards.

There is still much to do, and thousands of Americans who have suffered the lash of bureaucratic tyranny are watching intently to see what transpires in the future.

Our ranchers and farmers need relief. Clinton's "war on the West" has left deep scars, bitter resentment against our own government, and a sense of profound mistrust. Hopefully Gale Norton, appointed as Secretary of Interior by George Bush, will give a high priority to the needs of our rural population.

Instead of throwing billions of dollars away on counter-productive non-solutions, the U.S. should be awarding grants to the people who live on the land to fund conservation efforts. Make them partners in the process. They were stewards of the environment long before it became a politically correct obsession. With the scientific expertise our government can provide, and a spirit of willing cooperation, far more can be done to preserve our wilderness, and for much less money.

The same goes for the loggers and miners, fishermen and oil producers. These companies and individuals have a vested interest in our natural resources. The eco-mafia's demonization of resource-intensive industries is false and misleading. No business concern would willingly destroy the very source of its prosperity.

Given the right incentives, and reasonable laws to regulate industry, the future of our natural heritage is assured, our economy is enriched, new jobs are created, and most important: the rights of America's people are held sacred above all else.

See Appendix J — "Environmental Politics," for additional documentation.

CHAPTER 12.
URBAN SPRAWL — A NEW WEAPON

As growing cities such as Omaha, Nebraska attract new businesses, the need for housing and commercial enterprise grows accordingly. In the six years the author has lived in Omaha, there has been a dramatic change in this thriving metropolis. New subdivisions are added to the outskirts, with hospitals, schools, malls, boutiques, dining establishments, and all manner of businesses needed to serve the population.

If one prefers to look at it from an economic point of view, prosperity is breaking out everywhere. The economy is booming and there are jobs a-plenty.

In some cases, inner-city-dwellers have decided to move to a more laidback atmosphere and escape the traffic and bustle of the city. In other cases, young couples who grew up here and wish to remain here are starting new families. Yet other home buyers have been transferred here with an established business.

There are thousands of acres of cultivated land here, right up to the developed areas, that won't ever see a house or business. In the meantime there are improved highways, and more services and commodities to make life more enjoyable.

What's the furor all about?

As usual, we are hearing all the usual charges designed to sway public opinion, ploys that have been immensely successful in the past: degraded ecosystems, encroachment on endangered species. The same old stuff.

Perhaps, with global warming and ozone depletion pretty much disproven, they need another vehicle to continue their relentless campaign against prosperity and civilization.

There is also a glaring contradiction in their alleged concern for the loss of arable farmland: For decades the eco-crowd has been waging an ongoing war against the agricultural community. In the Klamath Basin, they have successfully denied farmers irrigation, forcing hundreds of families to file for bankruptcy. Throughout the West, deep ecologists have marshaled their legions to finance local offices from which they carry on their relentless propaganda campaign and use the courts to evict ranchers and farmers from public lands, denying them grazing and water rights.

Suddenly, the tender hearted eco-elite have developed a profound respect for the rights and welfare of the rural farming population? I don't think so! They have simply employed their time-proven technique of offering bogus issues to the vulnerable public in their drive to achieve their true agenda, the limiting of human use of the land. It's much easier to remove one farmer than an entire subdivision.

The following excerpt is from the website Trust for Public Land [www.tpl.org, June 2002].

> In the spring of 2003, TPL will publish "The Conservation Finance Handbook," a manual for communities seeking to raise funds for conservation. The book includes chapters on understanding greenprinting; researching demographics, financing options, and legal restraints; measuring public opinion; designing a winning conservation finance measure; and running a conservation campaign.

First off, the term "conservation," as they use it, can be interpreted as "restriction." The objectives of the environmentalists' urban sprawl initiatives are precisely the same as those of the many other campaign fronts they wage against the property rights and prosperity of American citizens.

"Conservation campaign" translates as "propaganda machine": recruiting volunteers for phone canvassing, posting placards and posters, packing town meetings with hundreds of "concerned citizens," mass mailing to local and state officials, contacting schools and churches, and so on.

What are they so upset about? Someone is going to build some beautiful new homes! Businesses are being established, new jobs and commerce will run rampant! Schools, hospitals, fire stations, all manner of public facilities will mar the landscape, and the poor bugs and fish and birds will have to relocate. How tragic!

Their alternative to "low density housing," which means houses with nice yards, spaced far enough apart to ensure each family a measure of privacy, is to add to existing neighborhoods, high rises and condominiums, and to convert old industrial areas to housing.

They paint a rosy picture, a utopian scene, of their projected plans for a metropolitan *valhalla*, but they conveniently neglect to mention that adding more people to existing residential areas and converting industrial locations to accommodate residential development will overburden the existing sewer systems, water resources and roadways. It brings even more automobiles onto already crowded streets and creates an untenable parking situation.

Many citizens won't want to be crowded into the inner city. However, far from according their fellow citizens the right to and the freedom to choose what kind of home they would like, these plans advise activists to familiarize themselves with "legal restraints." In other words, "use the law to cram it down their throats!"

The following articles offer some excellent insights into this issue.

Managing Suburban Growth. . . Destroying American's Freedom
by Joseph L. Bast Founder, The Heartland Institute (from the Libertarian Solutions website, March 1999)

Several times each year for the past 23 years, I've driven from Chicago to Appleton, Wisconsin, and back again. I've seen the fields and woodlands along Highways 94 and 41 gradually replaced by office parks, shopping malls, and residential developments. Over the years, the change has been dramatic.

Urban sprawl worries some people. They say it will lead to a shortage of agricultural land, deplete the planet's limited supplies of fossil fuels, and load the air we breathe with hazardous pollutants. Others worry that sprawl reinforces social inequalities by separating jobs from workers and encouraging race-and income-based isolation. Still others think sprawl is compromising our quality of life by taking away the intimacy, social connectivity, and sense of social identity that come from living in compact neighborhoods.

SPRAWL AND THE ENVIRONMENT

I have a difficult time taking seriously any of the concerns raised by the growth control crowd. What triggered my skepticism were the claims of environmental damage that so often accompany calls for growth management.

Urban expansion is, in fact, responsible for surprisingly little conversion of either forest or croplands into roads, houses, and parking lots. In 1945, according to the U.S. Department of Agriculture, urban land uses accounted for just 1% of the area of the U.S. By 1992, that figure had risen to 3%. Forests covered 32% of the U.S. in 1945 and a not-much- smaller 30% in 1992. Cropland stayed unchanged at 24%.

Urban sprawl is not correlated with a decline in air quality. Air quality in nearly all major American cities has dramatically improved during the past 20 years, even as suburban sprawl boomed. Concentrations of all six of the air pollutants tracked by the Environmental Protection Agency (EPA) fell dramatically between 1975 and 1991: Dust and airborne ash fell by 24%; sulfur dioxide by 50%; carbon monoxide, by 53%; ozone, by 25%; nitrogen dioxide, by 24%; and lead, by 94%.

Will the long commutes caused by sprawl lead to depletion of the world's petroleum supplies? Not in our lifetimes, and almost certainly not in our children's. During the past 20 years, estimates of oil reserves have increased nearly every year due to new discoveries and technological advances, even as we consume more gasoline with every passing year.

ECONOMIC DEVELOPMENT

Those who blame suburbs for luring industry and jobs away from cities, leaving behind many skilled but unemployed workers, have confused cause with effect.

As cities grow, property values in their central business districts rise, prompting businesses that require large amounts of space — typically manufacturers — to leave, and companies requiring less space — typically service providers — to enter. The new companies are less likely to impose nuisances upon their neighbors — noise, odors, and smoke — than the companies they replace.

While the migration of manufacturers and other space-intensive employers from central city locations is inevitable, the net loss of jobs by cities is not. New employers will take the place of businesses that leave, provided adequate crime protection, quality schools, reliable transportation, and other basic requirements of urban living are met.

When suburban expansion harms low-income families, it is usually due to government policies that inflate the cost of housing in suburban areas, making it more difficult for low- and moderate-income families to relocate closer to the new suburban job markets.

Many suburbs require large lot sizes, restrict the number of new developments, and act in other ways to prevent the construction of affordable and multiple-family homes. Rather than complain that the poor cannot travel to suburban jobs, advocates of growth management ought to campaign for the repeal of policies that unnecessarily restrict the supply, and increase the price, of housing.

ARE SUBURBS INEFFICIENT?

It is a myth that the cost of providing infrastructure and services is significantly higher for low-density suburban development than for high-density urban locations. Randal O'Toole says empirical investigations consistently find that lower operating costs in the suburbs more than offset the higher initial capital costs of installing new infrastructure.

One study of public service costs per housing unit in 247 counties found that "above 250 people per square mile (about one house for every eight acres) costs increase with higher densities."

Some say automobile owners don't pay enough in taxes and other fees to cover the full cost they impose on society, and that ending that subsidy would slow urban expansion. But a careful study of taxes paid by road users in 1992 found total revenues of $114 billion, while spending on roads that year (including law enforcement and administration) was just $76 billion. The difference, some $38 billion, was used to finance social services and other infrastructure needs.

Quality of Life

I lived in a small town for my first 18 years, then in Chicago for 16 years, and in a rather distant suburb of Chicago for the past six years. Reflecting on the benefits and disadvantages of all three locations, I find it impossible to say one is better than the other. Each, in fact, is best at delivering the quality of life most desired by those who choose it.

My life growing up in a small town could have come straight from a Norman Rockwell painting. In the mornings as I walked to school, I passed a steady stream of men carrying lunch buckets heading for a paper mill whose front gate was just two blocks from my home. Doors went unlocked and kids roamed the neighborhood almost unsupervised. During summer evenings we would play kick-the-can in the street under the branches of majestic oak trees while our parents sat on the front porch and talked with the neighbors.

At the age of 18, I decided work in a paper mill wasn't for me, so I headed to the Big City to attend college, get my first real job, and start a career in the think tank business. It may take a village to raise a child, but it requires a city to give birth to a school such as the University of Chicago and organizations such as The Heartland Institute.

By the age of 4, I had grown to dislike the noise, crime, and grit of city living. Diane and I left the city to those young enough or old enough to sleep through the nighttime police sirens, car alarms, and mysterious loud noises (gun shots? cars? backfiring? fireworks?). In suburbia we found peace, quiet, and access to amenities, such as tennis courts and walking paths, that we now value more than good restaurants and night clubs.

I am struck by how my lifestyle choices have determined the places I've lived, and how those places, in turn, have served the peculiar needs of each lifestyle. Why, I wonder, would anyone want to deny people the same choices I was able to make?

The growth management debate may sound arcane or of little interest to most people, but in fact it touches on an enormous range of public policies affecting virtually every aspect of our lives. Growth management policies aim to influence where we live and work, how we travel from place to place, whether elected officials or unelected bureaucrats will decide important planning issues, and the character of our local communities.

At the heart of the debate over growth management is not whether growth should be managed, but how it is managed and by whom. In most parts of the country, the path and nature of growth were traditionally left to the private sector. Individual home buyers, developers, and business executives drove most decisions about where new neighborhoods would be born and where a business would be located. Elected local officials participated in the process by using zoning powers, their control over the public infrastructure, and their power of eminent domain.

We should not assume that giving government more authority or resources is the solution to whatever problems are produced by urban growth and expansion. Indeed, the problems often attributed to unplanned growth are more often the result of prevailing government policies that distort market processes that would otherwise lead to win-win situations.

Editor's note: Joseph L. Bast is president of the Heartland Institute, which publishes *Intellectual Ammunition* bimonthly. This article by Samuel R. Staley first appeared in the September/October 1998 issue and was excerpted from: "The Sprawling of America: In Defense of the Dynamic City," Policy Study 251, Reason Public Policy Institute National Center For Policy Analysis, March 24, 1999.

The Truth About Urban Sprawl

Urban sprawl has sparked a national debate over land-use policy. At least 19 states have established either state growth-management laws or task forces to protect farmland and open space. Dozens of cities and counties have adopted urban growth boundaries to contain development in existing areas and prevent the spread of urbanization to outlying and rural areas. The Clinton administration has proposed to make urban sprawl a federal issue.

Although a clear definition of sprawl remains elusive, public debate over sprawl is driven primarily by general concerns that low-density residential development threatens farmland and open space, increases public service costs, encourages people and wealth to leave central cities and degrades the environment.

However, evidence suggests that suburbanization — which might be defined as urban-like development outside central urban areas — does not significantly threaten the quality of life for most people and that land development can be managed more effectively through real-estate markets than comprehensive land-use planning.

Are Open Spaces Threatened?
Historically, the most rapid rate of suburbanization occurred between 1920 and 1950. By the 1970s and 1980s, the trend was moderating, according to a study of more than 300 fast-growth rural counties. Despite widely cited reports

on the pace of urban growth, urban land remains a very small part of overall land use, and urban development does not threaten the nation's food supply.

Less than 5 percent of the nation's land is developed and three-quarters of the population lives on 3.5 percent of the land. Only about one-quarter of the farmland loss since 1945 is attributable to urbanization.

Predictions of future farmland loss based on past trends are misleading because farmland loss has been moderating since the 1960s, falling from a 6.2 percent decline in farmland per decade in the 1960s to a 2.7 percent decline in the 1990s. In addition, with dramatic increases in agricultural output, American farmers are producing almost 50 percent more food than in 1970, using less land.

Rural parks and wildlife areas have increased as dramatically as urbanized land. More than three-quarters of the states have more than 90 percent of their land in rural uses, including forests, cropland, pasture, wildlife reserves and parks. Acreage in protected wildlife areas and rural parks exceeds urbanized areas by 50 percent.

Does Suburban Growth Increase Public Service Costs?

Many studies of the cost of development exaggerate the effects of suburbanization on local government costs. Most costs are recovered through on-site improvements made by developers. Local governments often do make conscious policy decisions not to recover the full costs of development, when officials and voters decide for one reason or another to subsidize development through general revenues. The evidence is mixed on infrastructure costs and whether low-density development causes them to increase.

While some infrastructure costs (street maintenance, for example) fall as density increases, as a rule increases in density are accompanied by increases in population and in the level of general spending.

Is Suburban Growth Responsible For The Decline Of Cities?

Sprawl has been blamed for the decline of big cities and older, inner-ring suburbs. But while large cities have a number of features that attract businesses and people — roads, cultural activities, diverse and sometimes inexpensive housing opportunities and easy access to mass transit — many cities suffer from poorly functioning school systems, high tax rates, anticompetitive regulations and deteriorating housing stock.

Studies show that for many families, particularly working-class families, the poor quality of central city schools is the driving factor in their moves to the suburbs. Concerns about public safety in general and crime in particular also drive many people from cities.

Does Suburban Growth Damage The Environment?

Some critics of low-density residential development maintain that it means more pollution, more congestion and fewer preserved natural resources. They believe that higher-density compact development would mitigate those impacts. However, population density does little to alleviate auto-caused smog. Metropolitan areas with the lowest population densities have the fewest air pollution problems. Furthermore, population density or compactness has little relationship to how much commuters depend on automobiles.

More than 75 percent of commuter trips are by car in every area except New York — and more than 90 percent are by car in the vast majority of areas. Studies show that the number of vehicle miles traveled actually increases with population density in the United States.

Thus a policy strategy that attempts to increase population density could lead to more traffic congestion, exacerbating air pollution levels and potentially causing more areas to fail to meet federal clean air goals.

Another important environmental objection to suburbanization, the potential loss of open space, overlooks the fact that limiting development often accelerates the loss of open space inside urban areas. To overcome the shortage of land, developers eventually do projects on odd-shaped parcels and other lands that would ordinarily have remained vacant lots and the equivalent of mini-parks. In addition, plans to increase population density may call for the destruction of most farmland inside an area selected for high-density development, reducing urban open space still further.

CAN WE TRUST POLICY PLANNERS TO SEE THE FUTURE?

Policy recommendations using a 20-, 30- or 50-year vision for a state or community inevitably adopt top-down planning tools and government control of land to achieve state policy goals. However, there is little evidence that governments are better suited than real estate markets and private conservation efforts to provide the kinds of homes and communities people want. Indeed, many planners have acknowledged that "bad planning" (for example, large-lot zoning) was a significant contributor to the urban sprawl they now want to eliminate. Ironically, many reformers expect state and local governments to operate differently once the "right" urban planning reforms are in place.

My own spin on urban sprawl is that heaping more people on top of existing populations in the city is counter productive. But the most important issue continues to be our freedom. If people want to live in an urban community, then what's the problem? The preceding articles offer compelling evidence that urbanization is not the horrific destruction of the environment that eco-fanatics claim.

See Appendix K — "Urban Sprawl," for additional documentation.

CHAPTER 13.
THE BIG PICTURE

This chapter deals with two critical issues: "Who is bankrolling the environmental movement?" and "The One-World Agenda."

There is far more at stake here than the internal vitality of our society, although that is certainly a concern that deserves our attention. While our rights are being assaulted from within, a more ominous storm is building on the international horizon.

THE MONEY BEHIND THE MOVEMENT

There was a time, in the infancy of the eco-movement, that it was relatively benign, simplistic in its approach and seeking reasonable goals. Men such as Muir, Adams and Audubon had genuine concerns about the environment, and their focus was on protecting our wildlife and wilderness.

The support their message generated grew rapidly in an increasingly cosmopolitan society, so much so that someone recognized the issues they espoused as the perfect vehicle to accomplish their own objectives. Consequently, if the movement ever was truly grassroots, it didn't remain that way for long.

But there was more than the movement's public appeal that attracted the power brokers. Natural resources are the raw materials from which America's wealth is derived, and upon which our sovereignty depends to a significant degree. Simply put, those who control natural resources control the nation, and the facade of a noble cause, which would throw the weight of public opinion behind them, presented an ideal scenario.

Today the environmental organizations in the U.S. are immensely wealthy, raking in some $8 billion a year (and this is a figure based upon data compiled in the early 1990s). $8,000,000,000 is a formidable war chest by any standard.

The largest contributors to environmental organizations include some of the most prestigious institutions of the Eastern liberal establishment, centered around the New York Council on Foreign Relations and including the Trilateral Commission, the Aspen Institute, and a host of private family foundations such as Mellon, Rockefeller, Pillsbury, Kennedy, et al. The total of their gifts: $2 billion.

Another $3 billion was given by our own government to enviro-organizations and causes (as of 1991 figures; who knows how much that has grown to!). From these two sources, the combined total is over $5 billion.

Our largest corporations all give generously to the non-profit environmental sector, to the tune of approximately $2 billion annually. Among them is a list of major oil companies that reads like a Who's Who of the petroleum industry.

Private donations account for the smallest fraction, an estimated $1 billion. Since most of these figures are outdated, we can assume that revenues exceed $8 billion a year, and this is probably a very conservative figure.

Where does most of this money go? Lawsuits, advertising, salaries, buildings and land to house their offices and facilities, investments and acquisition of privately owned property. There is no accurate data to indicate how much of this vast sum is spent on remedial projects, or any other improvements to the environment; the absence of these records certainly suggests that very little, if any, is invested in our environment. I was not able to turn up *any*, in my research.[4]

---

4. I looked into the Nature Conservancy. According to their 2002 Annual Report their net income was less than 1 million. Of that amount there was land given to them which they sold for income, apparently. There were many references to multi-million dollar land purchases, but the NC only brokered the deals from what I can tell. They all spoke of "...in partnership with the State of Oregon....", or something similar. Apparently the funds for the tracts of land they "help" to buy come from Federal grants, Federal agencies, state agencies and private endowments, etc.

Since the aim of capitalist institutions is unapologetically to make money, this study of capitalist largesse toward a movement that demonizes industry leads to one profound conclusion. . . someone is making money this way!

I'm sure there are many individuals in corporate America who are genuinely concerned about environmental issues, but the obvious inconsistencies suggest that there is something more afoot. Why would industry, under constant fire from the eco-mafia, cast as the "bad guys" in a massive propaganda campaign, named in countless law suits that cost them millions, support their antagonists with huge contributions? I smell a rat, and as it turns out many astute individuals smell it, too.

[Mr. J. Whitley, of the Toronto Christian Book Centre, made these observations:]

Unknown to most North American, European and Australasian citizens is the fact that the worldwide environmental movement has been deliberately launched or co-opted by the elite, through foundational or multinational corporate financing and "semi-official" NGO standing at UN and other international political conferences, as a near-perfect instrument of social control.

Restrictions, taxes and laws which people would never accept and would vehemently protest otherwise are meekly, even enthusiastically, received if they are presented under the pretense of "environmental improvement," helping "endangered species" or "saving the earth."

This is not to say that there are not species that are endangered, or environmental concerns that need to be addressed, or that the earth should be not held in stewardship; it is to say that this otherwise laudable concern has been seized upon and harnessed by the elite to further and ensure success for their plans to:

1. Keep abundant, and sometimes inexpensively-extractable, resources out of the marketplace, thus helping to keep existing prices and profits high.

2. Ensure, through heavy "environmental impact" costs and protracted production delays, combined with extremely expensive environmental processing regulations, that new potential competitors are "taxed" out of the market almost before they can become established by crippling regulatory and other "environmental" costs of doing business — which existing elite-owned multinationals can easily meet by simply passing the costs back to us in an artificially-maintained monopolistic, or quasi-monopolistic situation.

3. Reduce the population, nation by nation as well as globally.

4. Attain their ultimate goal of de-industrialization as well as reduced world-wide living standards [except, of course, for the closeted and well-guarded elite themselves].

5. Eliminate human occupancy and activity in vast "reserves," which will be maintained as future repositories of wealth or resources for the elite and the

global corporations which they control, or as hunting or game reserves for their recreational pleasure.

6. Concentrate ownership of the most fertile or resource-rich tracts of the earth's surface in their own hands, via global environmental taxes, policies or regulations and instruments like the UN Biosphere program, the North American "Wildlands Project" [the plan to return 50% of the land area of North America to wilderness within a few decades, necessitating massive human population displacement and relocation, an estimated two-thirds reduction in the population level, and a return to virtually-medieval living standards], and financial instruments like the little-known but immensely powerful privately-owned World Conservation Bank.

7. Progressively reduce, then utterly eliminate, private automobile ownership and severely restrict individual freedom of movement.

8. Introduce and rapidly extend and increase a global taxation system based, in large part, initially on individual use of any part of "the global commons" [this taxation system can be examined in the United Nations document; *Our Global Neighbourhood*: The Report of the Commission on Global Governance.

As radical as Mr. Whitley's views may seem, there is substantial evidence to support them; and this is the point at which the eco-movement takes on global proportions.

The Millennium Summit was adjourned in New York on September 6, 2000. Its purpose, to "sign, ratify or accede" to the multilateral conventions which were earlier issued to the Secretary General of the United Nations.

Most of the 514 multilateral treaties involved had already been ratified by the U.N. General Assembly. The 25 treaties that comprise the core ideology of these pacts call for the creation of a global council that would effectively end the sovereignty and self-government of all nations on earth where environmental concerns are at stake, and there are very few national issues that are not tied to the recovery and use of natural resources. Were the United States to agree to the intent of the Millennium Summit, our rights as American citizens under the Constitution of The United States would cease to exist.

Co-Chairmen Ingvar Carlsson and Shridath Ramphal of the Commission On Global Governance (CGG) wrote in 1992:

We are not proposing movement toward a world government [but] this is not to say that the goal should be a world without systems or rules.

By 1995, the CGG had amended its official policy:

It is our firm conclusion that the United Nations must continue to play a central role in global governance.

In just a short three years, they went from "not proposing movement toward a world government," to hawking global government. One can only guess where they stand today, eight years later.

The CGG has invented the "global civil society," which, it explains, "is best expressed in the global non-governmental movement." In other words, powerful organizations in the private sector that espouse United Nations drivel. To augment this brainchild the presiding President of Earth Summit 5 selected a number of representatives from the NGOs (Non-Governmental Organizations) and the private sector for the exclusive privilege of speaking in the plenary sessions.

Among the selectees were Thilo Bode, executive director of Greenpeace, to represent the scientific and technological community; Yolanda Kakabadse, the President of the International Union for the Conservation of Nature; and Denise O'Brien, a member of Via Campesina, known for her expertise in organic farming.

These candidates are, according to the CGG, representatives vested with the responsibility of defining international policy in matters of proposed global environmental law. Where were the leaders in the business sector and institutions that monitor social needs and demographics? Where were the luminaries in our scientific communities, the legal experts and human rights specialists? Is an organic farmer, an activist in environmental agronomy, more suited to such a high profile status than, say, the head of The American Society of Agronomy or the American Horticulture Society? Who would accept a person with such credentials as a credible spokesman for American agriculture?

In any case, international meddling in United States policies of any sort seems undesirable. There shouldn't be a global police force for any purpose. But the selections made by the CGG clearly demonstrate their intent: to use the environment as the Trojan horse which provides access to all governmental bodies and subordinates them to U.N. fiat.

The U.N. deck is stacked against the United States, in the sense that the interests of the U.S. are fundamentally, and perhaps of necessity, in conflict with the interests of other nations. By the same token, one can only wonder what is signaled by the presence of Mikhail Gorbachev at the Rio de Janeiro Earth

Summit. An ex-chief of state, ex-chief of the KGB, sees the world through the lens of economics, power, and competing for strategic advantage at the highest levels; not whales and wild flowers.

You don't have to be Henry Kissinger to sense that there is more to this than meets the eye.

Expanding this same theme is an excellent article by Kim Weissman, "Global Totalitarians," which appeared April 28, 2002 on the website www.congressaction.info :

> Anyone who thought that the collapse of the Soviet Union meant an end to totalitarian efforts to dominate the world is sadly mistaken.
>
> The haters of individual liberty and freedom of choice continue unabated in their efforts to overthrow representative government and to impose their tyrannical ideology on everyone else, and in the worst traditions of despots throughout history, to destroy anyone who gets in their way. They demand total obedience to their world-view and tolerate no deviation, threatening destruction for anyone who dares disagree with them.
>
> Their ultimate objective is control not only of society as a whole and all of its institutions, but of the very minds and thoughts of everyone else, who they see as nothing more than vassals to command and control.
>
> The globalist busy-bodies claiming the most authority to impose their vision on the world operate at the United Nations. Since its creation, the U.N. has spawned a host of agencies concerned with everything from population control to gun control, environmental protection (the U.N.'s Intergovernmental Panel on Climate Change led to the Kyoto Treaty) to the International Criminal Court (ICC).
>
> The U.N. was formed to preserve "fundamental human rights," such as those protected by our Bill of Rights; many of which rights are, ironically, ignored by the ICC. Having been ratified by the requisite 60 nations (note that's a minority, constituting less than one-third of the 189 U.N. member nations, imposing this legal system on the world by fiat), the ICC officially goes into effect on July 1.
>
> The ICC is an attempt by unaccountable global bureaucrats to override national sovereignty, national laws and constitutions, and representative government. The putative purpose of the ICC is to prosecute war crimes and crimes of aggression.
>
> There is no oversight of any kind and the ICC is answerable only to itself, it claims universal jurisdiction over the majority of the world's nations that have not agreed to it and over citizens who have no input into the judges that it seats. It is not limited by any country's laws or constitutions, it has already forced some ratifying nations to alter their own laws and constitutions, and the only avenue of appeal is to its own internal Appeals Chamber.

Even then, appeals over "the fair and expeditious conduct of the proceedings" — for example, the ICC denies any right of the accused to confront witnesses against them — can only be appealed with permission of the ICC's Pre-Trial Chamber.

Congressman Ron Paul introduced H.R. 4169, the American Service member and Citizen Protection Act of 2002, and addressed U.N. claims that the ICC is authorized by General Assembly legislation. He said that the U.N. has no such legislative authority, and that the countries creating the U.N. were assured "that the body would never be able to pass laws".

But totalitarians never let small details such as legitimacy and the limits of their own constituting authority stand in their way — whether those limits are contained in our own U.S. Constitution or in the United Nations Charter itself.

In practice, the ICC will only provide a forum for the very people it is nominally intended to prosecute, from which they can launch political attacks and gain the imprimatur of respectability for their own conduct by diverting the world's attention.

The U.N. maintains sanctions against Iraq because Saddam Hussein kicked out weapons inspectors, but so-called human rights groups — the groups that never seem to notice human rights abuses by the likes of Syria, Iran, or Cuba, but never fail to find abuses by Israel and the United States — claim that the sanctions are starving children, for which they blame the U.S. Ignoring the possibility that starvation might be caused by Saddam spending his oil revenue billions on weapons of mass destruction and ornate palaces instead of food, they can simply charge the U.S. with "war crimes" by starving children, and the world will ignore Saddam's conduct, including his payments to terrorist families.

U.N. intermeddling is bad enough, but the most pervasive threat to freedom comes from radical environmentalists. Their determination to impose their ideology on the world is the most dangerous, since they cloak themselves in the guise of saviors and pursue their goals with the religious zeal of true fanatics.

The U.S. rejection of the Kyoto Treaty has caused other nations to reconsider their own support for Kyoto, fearing that if they adopt what the U.S. rejected, their industries would be at a competitive disadvantage with U.S. industry.

The anger of enviros at the U.S. rejection of Kyoto is not so much motivated by fear of a (non-existent) environmental catastrophe, but by their arrogant disbelief that when they thought they had convinced the world to jump off an economic cliff, America had the temerity not to follow. The reconsideration of Kyoto by other nations has command-and-control greens outraged, because they see a golden opportunity to drive the entire capitalist world into economic chaos slipping out of their grasp.

Climate change represents merely one avenue of the attack against civil society and capitalism being pursued by environmental extremists. Lies and fear mongering over miniscule amounts of relatively harmless chemicals and substances drive major corporations into bankruptcy.

New technologies with the potential of conquering disease and ending starvation, such as biotechnology, are mischaracterized and attacked by cynics exploiting the natural fear of the unknown.

The use of natural resources is restricted based on fantasies of non-existent dangers. Suspicion and fear dominate the public's reaction to anything new, anything that ordinary people cannot understand, and with the increasing complexity of science and the rampant spread of public ignorance, this encompasses a larger field of human endeavor every day.

But the loss of economically and socially beneficial products, the loss of jobs, even the unnecessary loss of human lives, are only part of the devastation this anti-progress mind-set wreaks. More insidious is the dampening effect on scientific innovation and risk-taking, and the stifling of objective scientific inquiry itself.

Anyone pursuing scientific innovation has to cope with the certain knowledge that opportunistic lawyers, proficient at manipulating a dysfunctional legal system and ignorant juries, are waiting to pounce and bring ruin on the innovator.

So thoroughly have environmental Luddites infected our institutions of education, politics, law, and the media, that the very concept of scientific progress is viewed with suspicion. Grade-schools are flooded with unending environmentalist propaganda, and feelings and beliefs have become preferred substitutes for critical thinking.

So conditioned by the environmentalist dogma has the general population become that anyone who dares to contradict the ideological straightjacket of anti-human, anti-development environmentalism is immediately lashed with severe public opprobrium. Even the scientific community itself has become so suborned by government grant money, tailored to the pursuit of politically and ideologically correct research, that a gaggle of government-paid scientists can always be counted on to instantly appear to condemn any hint of scientific doctrinal divergence among any of their colleagues who dare try to present their heretical ideas outside of isolated scientific journals — no matter how much factual data supports those divergent ideas.

And when those heresies are presented in a political or public forum, the proponents are portrayed either as simply ignorant, or in the pay of some insidious force bent on the destruction of the planet. The ignorance that burned witches in the 16th and 17th centuries was no worse than that which confronts scientific apostasy today.

The face of radical environmentalism also shows itself in opposition to global trade. In the guise of environmental protection and prevention of unfair trade practices, protesters seek to stop global trade and undermine free markets. If they succeed, Third World nations will be frozen into eternal poverty, with continuing human misery and further degradation to the very environment the know-nothings claim to want to protect.

Studies have shown that increased global trade raises the living standards of everyone involved, and with increased wealth comes increased concern about the environment, and the financial resources to clean it up.

When people are worried about where their next meal is coming from, about rampant disease and starvation of their children, they have little time or inclination to worry about the quality of their environment. And even if they do, they have insufficient resources to do anything about it.

An observation of conditions around the world shows that the wealthiest nations are most concerned with, and spend the most, protecting the environment, and also accomplish the most environmental remediation.

The poorest societies are the ones that suffer the worst environmental quality and the poorest sanitary conditions. If the know-nothings really cared about improving poor societies, elevating everyone's living standards, and preserving the environment, they would demand more global trade, not less. But poverty is a fertile breeding ground for socialism, and it is the spread of socialism and the destruction of capitalism that stand as the true ultimate objectives of the free trade opponents.

The United Nations is working for one global ruling body on a broad front. The environment is but one of the salient issues that they have employed to bring this to pass. There is already an International Criminal Court (ICC) with the power to prosecute "criminals" that are citizens of sovereign nations in an international venue, not the courts of their own country.

President George W. Bush has adamantly rejected the initiatives of the U.N. that would subject American citizens to the powers of the ICC, as one of the mandates of the court is to prosecute any soldier, or military unit, which engages in hostilities that are not sanctioned by U.N. resolution. Literally every American serviceman who has fought in a war, or police action, after the inception of the ICC is guilty of "war crimes," according to the court.

Let's face it, fellow Americans, most of the world is anti-American, if not openly, then behind closed doors. Our great wealth and military might are the only factors that hold the wolves at bay, and we cannot permit any issue to cross the line of American sovereignty. The European Union has installed its own Congress and they have already drafted a trade pact that replaces many American imports with inter-European products. In several of their landmark findings they have come down firmly opposed to our nation, including the impending war with Iraq.

Our rival superpowers, China and Russia, have enthusiastically thrown their support behind the international movement to create an environmental tribunal. Let's not delude ourselves... this is a strategy which will blow a gaping hole in the formidable ramparts of American sovereignty, a compromise that will signal the crumbling of our resolve. Ironically, neither of them was designated a wealthy nation in the Kyoto Protocol, that is, a nation that would be forced to bear the financial burden of that treaty, sacrifice millions of jobs, cut back on "dirty industry," regulate automobile use and fossil fuel consumption.

The rationale is logical and effective. If they can't defeat us on the economic front, nor trump the threat of a nuclear counter-strike, then let the Jolly Green Giant cripple our economy, render us dependent on foreign oil and minerals, divide our people on passionate ideological issues and compromise the source of our strength — the guiding principles of our Constitution.

The battle lines are drawn, and there is far more at stake than some obscure collection of endangered creatures. The alarmist propaganda which has stirred up this international hornet's nest has been proven a bogus issue, but it has managed to create a suitable diversion, to give our enemies the perfect excuse to incite the world's sentiment against us, an achievement that required little in way of encouragement. Americans need to stand united, and overcome the ploys that are devised to disorient and distract us; then we will remain strong.

See Appendix I — "One World Agenda," for additional documentation.

CHAPTER 14.
ECO-TERRORISM IN AMERICA

Fanaticism always resorts to violence sooner or later, and the environmental movement has its very own terrorist cells. They are clever enough to stay out of the news, for the most part; it wasn't until I began researching for this book that I became aware of the atrocities committed by these bandit gangs.

The Off-Road.com website cites an incredible piece of terrorist literature as an example of just how far radical Eco-Terrorist organizations are willing to go to stop "off-roaders" from using our public lands. The booklet, "How to Fight Motorcycles," gives instructions for fabricating and installing booby-traps along routes used by off-road vehicles — traps that would decapitate or otherwise kill or injure riders. This pamphlet is in circulation among members of "Earth First," the EDF, and others. How can any group, regardless of how strongly they differ with their fellow human beings, actually produce such a manual inciting the maiming or killing of off-road sports enthusiasts? Although it is cloaked with a "disclaimer" suggesting it's all a game about "enemy motorcyclists invading America" and how to stop "the Enemy Soldier," that sham does not fool its intended readers. Indeed, Off-Road says that people have been seriously hurt by tricks and traps like those described in the instructions. These traps are just as dangerous for children riding bicycles as they are for dirt bikers, a fact which apparently does not discourage the readers.

I could find no evidence that other environmental groups engage in this kind of violence; however, David Foreman, founder of Earth First, has been a guest speaker at environmental symposiums sponsored by many of the largest eco-groups. I could find no statement on any website that condemned these criminal acts.

David Foreman has suggested other tactics to defend the environment. The following are excerpts from the book *Eco Defense* (*Eco Defense*, 1985 — Dave Foreman. A New Ludd Book, Earth First! Books, Tucson Arizona 1985).

Cited under "Fair use":

> In some cases burning a target is the most effective way of decommissioning it.
>
> Suppose your neighborhood is infested with off-road vehicle scum or you chance upon an unattended muscle wagon where it shouldn't be. A quick slash job is in order.
>
> Powerlines are highly vulnerable to monkey-wrenching from individuals or small groups. The best techniques are 1) removing bolts from steel towers, 2) cutting steel towers with hacksaws, torches. . . . (See cutting torch article).
>
> Wooden bridges are vulnerable and are a major effort and expense to replace. They can be burned, but it takes more than a can of kerosene and a match. A huge pile of dry wood must be heaped up under the load-carrying timbers of the bridge. . .

He goes on:

> ECODEFENSE is an ongoing project. We hope to publish an updated edition every twelve to 18 months....Even communication through ECODEFENSE could be dangerous, though. In writing to us, do not use your real name or put a return address on your missive. We do not need to know who you are.
>
> After taking the information from your letter, we will burn both the letter and the envelope. Similarly, no record will be kept of orders for copies of ECODEFENSE in case a group of "plumbers" decides to take a midnight stroll through our filing cabinet. By the way, two good friends, Mr. Smith and Mr. Wesson are our security agents.

One particularly alarming aspect of Eco-terrorism is the allure it holds for bright young people, kids who have been brainwashed from infancy on the evils of capitalism and human interest which conflicts with the natural order.

America's Terrorists
by Robert Trancinski [published on Media Link – Ayn Rand Institute, 2001]
© 2001 Creator's Syndicate, Inc.

Over the past few months, several newly built Long Island homes have been burned to the ground, with graffiti left at the scene threatening future destruction. It has been a small-scale "eco-terrorism" campaign directed against the alleged evil of suburban real-estate development.

The culprits in a few of these attacks, it turns out, were four teen-age kids: Matthew Rammelkamp, 16; Jared MacIntyre and George Mashkow, both 17; and Connor Cash, 19. They are very young, relatively bright, and most of them are good students. Judging from press reports, they are not the kind of kids who normally get into trouble. Yet the three younger boys recently admitted setting fire to unoccupied homes in a campaign against "urban sprawl."

When idealistic children become terrorists, we are in big trouble. We are facing America's first real, home-grown terrorist movement.

The name of this terror network is ELF, the Earth Liberation Front. Their goal is to "defend what's sacred" — the untouched earth, in their view — against the intrusive presence of human beings.

So far, the ELF hasn't actually killed any humans, though it is only a matter of time. They have started by targeting human property, including McDonald's restaurants, test plots for genetically engineered foods, electrical transmission lines, and newly constructed homes. No, they don't want to kill people; they just want to make sure that we don't own anything, don't eat anything, don't use any power, and have no place to live.

The three Long Island arsonists admit to being "members" of ELF. But membership is self-designated in this anarchistic terror network; members receive ELF guidelines and advice over the Internet but claim to have no central leadership.

And that's what is so ominous. With no organization and no large-scale recruitment, many young idealists have signed up to commit serious crimes for the sake of their cause. The roots of terrorism have been planted much deeper in our culture than most of us suspected.

In an article written in the early 1980s, St. John's University Professor and Ayn Rand Institute writer M. Northrup Buechner asked what would be necessary for an active terrorist movement to take hold in America.

First, he wrote, the terrorists must have an ideology that demands the sacrifice of the individual to some alleged "greater good." That is the only way they can justify their destruction of property and lives and their reliance on fear as a weapon.

The environmental movement provides such an ideology in spades. ELF's mission is to defend the "sacred" earth against humans; thus, the group seeks "to speed up the collapse of industry, to scare (read: "terrorize") the rich, and to

137

undermine the foundations of the state." It is all part of the philosophy of "deep ecology."

The other requirement, Professor Buechner wrote, is that this ideology must be so thoroughly saturated in the culture that it attracts thousands willing to cooperate in terrorist crimes — and millions who are unwilling to condemn them. The terrorist ideology, he writes, "cannot be only 'in the air'; it must be in the ground."

Or it must be in the schools. Today's students are bombarded with environmentalist propaganda. They are taught that humans are a blight on the earth — that our technology and economic development lead to nothing but pollution, global warming, and the destruction of endangered species.

It is no surprise that Rammelkamp, the 16-year-old eco-terrorist, is described by press reports as a "first-rate student" who "takes advanced placement biology," or that 17-year-old MacIntyre was a bright student working on a research project on "global warming" at Brookhaven National Laboratory. These students learned their lessons well.

And what about the adults who are called upon to evaluate ELF's violent acts? A *Chicago Tribune* editorial is typical. Stopping "the spread of new construction" is "not an unworthy goal," it declares, "but eco-terrorists like those at ELF are running a serious risk at a sensitive time" because "environmentalists can't afford to lose any momentum . . . in Washington." In this view, eco-terrorism isn't evil; it's just a tactical mistake at this time.

When terrorism provokes this reaction from a culture's leaders, it is "in the ground." ELF's public mouthpiece, Craig Rosebraugh, understands this when he boasts that ELF "operates under an ideology, not a physical membership," so "it is really impossible to dissolve that ideology." An ideology cannot be dissolved — but it can be exposed. This incident is a warning that we must understand and oppose the environmentalists' anti-human philosophy — before ELF's attacks escalate.

See Appendix J — "Eco-Terrorism," for additional documentation.

CHAPTER 15.
SOLUTIONS

This book documents the conflict between environmentalist fanatics and the interests of Americans who live on the land and depend on it for their livelihood, the conflict between a stagnant federal policy and all Americans who cherish our wilderness; both those who need the wealth of nature to survive and prosper, and those who delight in the wonders of nature for recreation; skiers, snow-mobilers, fishermen, bikers, hunters, campers, adventurers, hikers, climbers, bird watchers, or just sightseers.

Over the past thirty years the U.S. government has gradually replaced the concept of "public lands" by "federal lands," a distortion which smacks of feudal tyranny, like the "King's forests" of Britain that reserved all wilderness and wildlife for the exclusive pleasure and benefit of the elite and well-fed few.

We are at a turning point in our history. We have an opportunity to distill wisdom from past mistakes and combine what we have learned with new technologies to implement a management policy that protects our wildlands without sacrificing our liberties. This is a goal that is not only possible but assured, if we work together to achieve solutions that work. This can become a reality if we remove the corrupting influence that intentionally foments animosity between those who need the environment to survive, and those who are committed to protecting it.

Solutions will demand some measure of compromise on both sides, but inflexibility will only perpetuate a counter-productive atmosphere. The environmental policies that the government enforces by the threat of punishment have proven to be destructive to the environment, and at an astronomical cost. But far worse, they have resulted in the flagrant abuse of our freedoms.

Solutions to these issues are, in some cases, simple. They involve returning to past management policies that were effective, with some changes that incorporate technology and improved methods. In other cases the solutions will only be achieved by a combined effort which brings together those who live on the land and those with a purely aesthetic and moral commitment to the natural world. Both parties share a love for the environment, and that common motive is the basis for a spirit of cooperation that will bring positive results, not bickering and hatred.

The first step, as I see it, is the need for those who have supported the environmental movement in the past to discard the illusion that ranchers and farmers, miners and oil producers, fishermen and loggers, are all greedy destroyers of nature. If this misconception were true, there wouldn't be much left to protect! The myth that eco-intensive industries have no concerns about the environment ignores the fact that they have every motive to protect it. If anything, industry is even more resolved to solve environmental issues than their antagonists are.

The second step is a sweeping change in environmental laws. We have allowed an insensitive bureaucracy to become the feudal lord of our public lands. Policy making and enforcement should be vested in local authorities. County and community leaders know the conditions in their vicinity. They are accessible to all concerned parties. Local citizens with an interest in environmental issues can participate in shaping policies. This is the process that a free people have the right to expect.

Public lands should be managed by state officials. Decentralizing the control of our lands will give all parties a voice in the decision-making process. There would be a need for a Congress of State Governors to convene and agree on a uniform body of laws, but the final decision concerning lands within state borders should remain in the hands of the state, and therefore, in the hands of the people of each state.

National Parks which span two or more states should be managed by a federal agency, but even that entity should be comprised of elected members of each state's legislature, or delegates elected by the people of a state, not appointed bureaucrats who are unaccountable to the citizenry.

The third step: the power structure in the environmental sector must be neutralized. The deep ecologists that exercise total control of non-profit organizations and federal agencies at the present time have demonstrated their fanatic disregard for both the environment and the American people. The state governments should ensure that their environmental policies are shaped by citizens of their states, and not outsiders whom have no vested interest.

Environmental cases should be confined to the state courts, and lawsuits or injunctions thrown out unless they are pursued by state citizens.

The solutions to all of our problems will only be achieved by harnessing the energy and ingenuity of every concerned citizen, whether rancher, naturalist, sportsman, birdwatcher, climber, farmer, or hunter. . . management of the land and wilderness must address the interests of all Americans, not just a fanatic fringe.

The fourth step: the massive federal agencies that currently wield so much power must be scaled down and reined in. There are still issues that require federal attention, such as remediation of toxic sites, but the charter of these agencies should be adjusted to keep them focused there, not on the regulation of environmental policy and prosecution of citizens on the basis of an arbitrary body of law. Their budgets can be distributed to state and local authorities where they will be spent for sound measures to monitor and protect the environment, and at half the cost.

The fifth step: The public should have access to our public lands, safe roads into remote areas and well-constructed bridges. Snowmobilers and dirt bikers should be free to roam wherever they like except when the fire index is high. Ranchers should be allotted much more grazing land rather than be forced to overgraze their small leases. Mining and oil companies should answer to local authorities who appreciate the infusion of revenue from their operations and, at the same time, are uniquely qualified to determine what is harmful and what is not to their indigenous environment.

The sixth step: We need to open up our vast oil reserves to exploration and drilling, and discontinue importing foreign oil. We can reduce the price of gas at the pump, create hundreds of thousands of new jobs and spark a welcome boost to our economy. Our abundant mineral deposits should also be opened to mining operations. . . More jobs means more prosperity, less dependence on foreigners, lower prices, and most important of all, unfettered freedom.

The seventh step: We must amend the curriculum in our schools to reflect these changes. Children should be learning reasonable conservation methods, not hardball politics. They should be taught that cooperation and empathy for their fellow human beings is the only acceptable means of dealing with environmental issues. The ascendancy of freedom with responsibility should be emphasized, and an appreciation for the complexities of economic reality. Free enterprise is the source of American wealth, and kids can be taught to respect that while pondering the moral responsibilities of businesses, not to simply hate all commercial interests.

Certainly, this is a broad outline that needs refinement and responsible action to implement new policies, but the central theme of these measures is sound and necessary. If we continue to travel the road we are currently on, there will be greater divisions among our citizenry, more wasted billions, more destruction to our environment, more damage to our economy, more lost jobs, and greater dangers to our national sovereignty.

Unless we change the status quo, at some point in time a violent uprising of dispossessed citizens seems inevitable. We are already seeing these passions simmering below the surface. Who can say what form this rebellion will take? It may be confined to pockets of resistance, or sweep across all of rural America.

If that sounds like a stretch, consider that we have already fought two wars over the same principle: the rights of a free people to exercise their liberties apart from governmental tyranny. Our Revolution was not just about over-taxation. The straw that broke the camel's back was the arrogant usurpation of privacy and property that the British imposed on the colonists when they quartered their troops in private homes.

Then we have the Civil War. The vast majority of confederates were not fighting to prevent the abolition of slavery. Only a tiny fraction of the Confederate Army owned slaves; that was for an elite few. They were outraged that the federal government superimposed its power over the sovereign rights of the states, and they saw that act as a great threat to their personal freedom.

Indeed, the Texas War of Independence belongs on our list. A famous flag emerged from that conflict: "Don't Tread on Me!," and perhaps the single most valiant battle in American history became the rallying cry for the people of Texas. . . ."Remember the Alamo!"

It is easy to mistake the character of the silent multitude. Millions of Americans are approaching the point where they have nothing left to lose, and they are willing to fight for these same timeless principles.

We have not known war on American soil for a hundred and fifty years, but rest assured, the usurpation of freedom will not go unchallenged if it goes too far.

If the government and the mega-rich environmental organizations continue to persecute the people of America, there will be a reckoning, and when it comes it will be too late for reasonable solutions.

DOCUMENTATION SECTION

The following appendices contain a selection of materials selected on the basis of the credibility of the sources. The individual writers have been engaged in the battle against the insidious influence of hyper-environmentalism in our society for many years; they include the top professionals in their respective fields.

LIST OF APPENDICES

APPENDIX K — Urban Sprawl
The Truth About Urban Sprawl — Samuel R. Staley

APPENDIX L — Contributor Index & Credits
A list of the contributors to this book, their credentials and affiliations.

APPENDIX M — Internet Pro-Rights Resources

APPENDIX N —Internet Addresses For Pro-Rights Organizations

APPENDIX A — THE ECONOMY

Environmentalism vs. Human Life [The following are press conference remarks by Dr. Andrew Bernstein, a senior fellow with the Ayn Rand Institute, given at the National Press Club, Washington, D.C., on Friday, April 20, 2001.]

The environmentalist movement is consistently antagonistic to the requirements of human life on earth. On issue after issue, the environmentalists hold viewpoints that oppose man's survival needs.

Man's nature requires him to continuously reshape his environment, e.g., to clear land for agricultural development, build houses and cities, engage in medical research to cure diseases, and so forth.

But the greens oppose every productive activity on which human survival depends. The leading current example of this is their crusade to block development of oil in the Arctic National Wildlife Refuge (ANWR). ANWR is an area so abundant in oil that Senator Frank Murkowski of Alaska, chairman of the Senate Committee on Energy and Natural Resources, states that it could produce oil for decades, adding as much as $325 billion to the U.S. economy and reducing imports by well over one million barrels per day.

Though geologists claim that ANWR holds over seven billion barrels, enabling it to add significantly to American energy production, its exploitation is currently blocked by environmentalist restrictions imposed for the sole purpose of protecting the wilderness, the caribou, the ice floes. Simply put, the question is, ice or oil heat — which is more important? The environmentalists are right that there is a profoundly important moral issue at stake: the requirements of man's survival vs. the value of nature as an end in itself. Because man's right to live as man is the highest value on earth it is morally imperative that the environmentalists be defeated.

Nor is the green opposition to the development of ANWR's oil the only issue on which their beliefs and actions harm human life.

Environmentalist restrictions are largely responsible for California's current energy crisis. Environmentalist groups in the state have attacked every form of energy production. Every attempt to build nuclear power plants has come under years of prohibitively expensive litigation.

The use of coal is attacked because it is too "dirty," hydroelectric power is criticized because dam construction threatens the existence of some obscure species, even the biomass industry, which employs timber chips and forest leftovers as fuel to produce electricity, has come under litigation.

The Honey Lake biomass plant was shut down last year because a lawsuit against the U.S. Forest Service originated by the San Francisco-based Earth Island Institute caused the suspension of the logging operations that provided the company its fuel source.

Prior to the shutdown, the 20 biomass companies in California could collectively have generated 600 megawatts of electricity per year. The reason environmentalists seek to deprive Californians of power? To protect the late succession/old-growth forests that are home to the California spotted owl and the Pacific fisher. Because of birds, human homes, work places and hospitals are deprived of power and exposed to all the attendant dangers.

"Green activists have worked for decades to stop the construction of major power plants in California — and have succeeded. As a result, California generates less power per resident than any other state, and "imports" about one-quarter of the energy it consumes. Since 1985 only minor power plants have been built in California, adding only 6,000 megawatts to the state's supply — hardly enough to meet an increased demand for 10,000 megawatts. If plants generating an additional 4,000 megawatts had been built in the last decade, there would be no energy crisis today. By preventing entrepreneurs from building power plants, environmentalists choked the supply of power and set the stage for crises like the current one."[1]

Further, environmentalists today continue their decades- long assault on the automobile.

Yesterday, Earth Day Network coordinated an "Earth Car-Free Day" in countries around the world, an event whose goal was to keep people from using their cars and seek alternative means of transportation.

"Across the world, people will be staying out of cars, riding bicycles, walking or participating in open-air festivals on streets blocked from cars as part of this event," said Eric Britton, head of The Commons, one of the green groups organizing the protest. Part of the purpose, say the leaders, is to protest against air pollution and global warming.

For decades, environmentalists have argued that the car pollutes the air and causes the depletion of the earth's resources. Today they add the claim that its widespread use leads to global warming.

As far back as 1970, in an essay entitled, "Warning: The Automobile Is Dangerous to Earth, Air, Fire, Water, Mind and Body," environmentalist

Kenneth Cantor claimed that "the automobile and the American public are locked in a life and death struggle." He stated that "sixty percent of all pollutants added to the air in the United States come from the internal combustion engine. In 1967, 87.4 percent of the 14,000 tons per day added to the air above Los Angeles came from gasoline-powered motor vehicles."

Cantor concluded that "the atmosphere around us has truly become a garbage dump." He went on to make similar claims regarding the relationship between automobile use and an alleged reckless depletion of the earth's non-renewable resources.[2]

Among other proposals, Cantor recommended that people use bicycles instead of cars, hitchhike and pick up hitchhikers, support programs aimed at reducing automobile use to one-tenth of then-current levels, take political action to defeat such "public abominations" as new freeways and highway bridges, eliminate the federal highway program and replace it with increased public transportation, and tax the sale of all new automobiles to fund the recycling of all old car hulks after the usable parts had been removed.[3]

These sentiments are echoed wholeheartedly by the environmentalist movement today. The so-called Earth Liberation Front recently declared war on the SUV, setting fire to a car dealership in Eugene, Oregon. "We can no longer allow the rich to parade around in their armored existence, leaving a wasteland behind in their tracks," they said. "SUVs destroy the earth."

It is clear that the development of ANWR's oil, the widespread use of the automobile and the construction of California power plants are in the best interest of human beings.

ANWR will supply the United States with a vast new source of oil; additional power plants in California will provide electricity for millions of human beings currently suffering from shortages and rolling brownouts; and hundreds of millions of people around the world will continue to get to work, play or family gatherings most conveniently by means of their cars.

Why do the greens oppose these human advances? Why do they combat similar innovations that improve man's life? Why, for example, were they against use of the Pacific yew tree, even though its bark is a source of taxol, which was considered an outstanding new drug in man's war against cancer?

Why did the EPA ban DDT, even though its own hearings established that the pesticide is harmless to man and animals, but deadly to malaria-carrying mosquitoes? Why do they oppose medical testing on laboratory mice, even though such methods were instrumental in winning the battles against polio and diabetes, and are similarly necessary for research seeking cures for heart disease, AIDS and other diseases fatal to man?

The answer is that they are not lovers of man. They value every other life form on earth as being above him, no matter if insignificant or even lethal.

David Graeber, a biologist with the National Parks Service, made clear in a Los Angeles Times Book Review essay both his contempt for man and his reverence for the natural environment as an end in itself.

He states that he and his colleagues in the green movement "value wilderness for its own sake, not for what value it confers upon mankind. . . . We are not interested in the utility of a particular species, or free-flowing river, or eco system to mankind. They have intrinsic value, more value — to me — than another human body, or a billion of them. Human happiness, and certainly human fecundity, are not as important as a wild and healthy planet. . . . It is cosmically unlikely that the developed world will choose to end its orgy of fossil-energy consumption, and the Third World its suicidal consumption of landscape. Until such time as homo sapiens should decide to rejoin nature, some of us can only hope for the right virus to come along."[4]

And speaking of viruses, it seems that they have rights, too. According to Rutgers ecologist, David Ehrenfeld the world's remaining supply of the smallpox virus should not be exterminated, since it preys only on human beings.[5]

Graeber's claim that nature has "intrinsic value," that it is worthy of our esteem, even veneration, quite apart from any utilitarian purpose it might satisfy for us, is the key to understanding the environmentalist movement.

Man, in this view, is an intruder, an eco-nuisance who inflicts harm on the sacred natural environment he inhabits. Observe the many attempts to turn environmentalism into a quasi-religion. Former New Left leader Tom Hayden taught a course at Santa Monica College entitled "Environment and Spirituality," in which he stressed that "we need to see nature as having a sacred quality, so that we revere it and are in awe of it." The Ecoforestry Institute, in a full-page ad opposing the logging of trees, claimed that trees have intrinsic value and argued that the protection of forests "is more than an economic or ecological issue. It is a spiritual one as well." Paul Ehrlich, notorious for his ceaselessly erroneous predictions of catastrophic death tolls from massive worldwide famines, predictably bases his claims in faith rather than science and reason. "It is probably in vain that so many look to science and technology to solve our present ecological crisis," he states. "Much more basic changes are needed, perhaps of the type exemplified by the . . . hippie movement — a movement that adopts most of its religious ideas from the non-Christian East. It is a movement wrapped up in Zen Buddhism, physical love and a disdain for material wealth." Carl Sagan issued a call for a religious crusade on behalf of environmentalist values. "We are close to committing — many would say we are already committing — what in religious language is sometimes called Crimes against Creation," he said. Environmentalism "must be recognized as having a religious as well as a scientific dimension."[6]

The future of human civilization depends on understanding that the environmentalists are wrong — that they are mistaken systematically, on every point and issue.

They are wrong scientifically, they are wrong logically and, above all, they are wrong morally.

Take the scientific point first. Just as they were dead wrong regarding the alleged danger of DDT, they are similarly mistaken about both hazards they attribute to the automobile — the dual claims of increased air pollution and the waste of non-renewable resources. At the time that the Clean Air Act was passed in 1970, our air was becoming progressively cleaner, not dirtier, and had been doing so for a long time precisely because of industrial progress.

According to Professor Matthew Crenson of Johns Hopkins University, sulfur dioxide pollution had been declining for decades. In 1971 he wrote, "In some cities the sulfur dioxide content of the air today is only one-third or one-fourth of what it was before World War Two."

Measurements in 14 U.S. cities in 1931-32 showed an average particulate concentration of 510 micrograms per cubic meter. By 1957 it was down to 120 micrograms per cubic meter, and in 1969 the measurement stood at 92 micrograms per cubic meter. The major reason for this positive trend was the conversion to cleaner burning fuels, such as oil and gas, from coal or wood. Improvements in technology on a free market caused this trend, not environmentalist propaganda or governmental legislation.[7]

In keeping with this pre-environmentalist trend, auto emissions had also become cleaner. The auto industry had been working on the problem for years, and by 1968 cars with significantly improved emission characteristics were already being produced, and newer anti-pollution equipment was being tested.

"By 1970, when the Clean Air Act was passed, auto emissions had already been reduced 70 to 80 percent from the level of two decades earlier."

Indeed, *environmentalist legislation worsened air quality in this country*. It introduced the catalytic converter, which produces sulfuric acid. An EPA report in 1977 presented the results of a two-year study: a 25 percent drop in carbon monoxide emissions due to catalytic converters was accompanied by an increase of 50 percent in emissions of the oxides of nitrogen.

A similar environmentalist travesty played out in the 1990s when the Clean Air Act of 1990 required many Americans to use gasoline oxygenated with MBTE and ethanol. MBTE produced so many complaints of headache and nausea from users that the governor of Alaska banned it after four weeks of use. The other additive, ethanol, produces ozone, which at low levels is a pollutant. "Even the EPA admits that ethanol produces more nitrogen oxides and hydrocarbons than regular gas."[8]

The environmentalist attack on the automobile has centered on carbon monoxide emissions. The myth they have created and spread is that the air was significantly purer before there were any automobiles or factories. This is false.

An important point is that 90 percent of the world's automobiles are in the northern hemisphere, but there is no hemispheric difference in carbon monoxide levels. Nor are carbon monoxide levels increasing on a worldwide basis. In 1978 the EPA suppressed a scientific study showing that up to 80 percent of air pollution was caused by natural, not man-made phenomena.

It took a lawsuit filed under the Freedom of Information Act to pry the report out of them.

One of the leading sources of air pollution widely ignored by the greens is volcanoes. According to Dr. William Pecora, former director of the United States Geological Survey, just three volcanic eruptions in the last 120 years (Krakatoa, Indonesia, 1883; Katmai, Alaska, 1912; and Hekla, Iceland, 1947) produced more particulate and gaseous pollution of the atmosphere than the combined activities of all the men who ever lived.

There are many such examples. Swamps are by far the greatest source of methane pollution, and *Public Works*, the official publication of Oregon's Environmental Protection Agency, states that burping cows rank as the number one source of air pollution in America, disgorging 50 million tons of hydrocarbons into the atmosphere each year. It must be made clear that Mother Nature, not man's automobiles or factories, is by far the greatest source of air pollution.[9]

The scientific facts regarding the alleged depletion of "non-renewable" resources also contradicts the environmentalists' accusations.

Starting in the 1970s and continuing today, environmentalist doomsayers have advocated a "limits to growth" doctrine which claimed that the world supply of such resources as aluminum, iron, petroleum and others would be exhausted in a matter of decades.

A brief study of the facts resoundingly refutes such nonsense. First, a minor point: the amounts of most of these natural resources existing in the earth's crust, as estimated by the United States Geological Survey, are sufficient to last for thousands of years, even at increased rates of consumption. But the most important point is that by far the greatest natural resource is man's reasoning mind that enables him to identify the properties and potential functions of raw materials.

In medieval Europe, for example, charcoal from wood was the main source of energy. When wood began to grow scarce and consequently more expensive, people sought other means of fuel. They eventually found it in chunks of black rock previously thought useless — coal.

Centuries later, in the mid-1800s, some people feared that man was running out of coal. When the price rose, innovators were encouraged to seek other energy sources. For years, farmers in western Pennsylvania had been troubled by the presence of a viscous black liquid that damaged their crops and pastures. Nobody saw any uses for it, but finally some entrepreneurs saw possibilities in it and, in 1859, formed the Pennsylvania Rock Oil Company of Titusville, Pennsylvania. Shortly thereafter, the firm was successful in digging for oil.

Today we use fiber optic cables instead of copper wire for phone lines. Such glass fibers are derived from ordinary sand. Further, we know of the enormous resources contained in sea water, and of additional supplies buried beneath the ocean floor. We know of the huge supplies of fuel available from shale and tar sands Ocean thermal power, geo-thermal energy and bio conversion — methods of generating power from the sun-warmed surface waters of the ocean, from the enormous heat contained within the earth, and by converting organic materials, especially wastes — are all feasible and represent the virtually unlimited power sources of the future.[10]

Environmentalists scoff that such claims are mere science fiction. These are the same mentalities who, centuries ago, could conceive of no possible uses for either coal or oil; who snickered at the thought that man might fly; who couldn't dream of space travel or nuclear power plants; and who would have regarded the idea that everyday sand could be employed to make fiber optic cables as the sheerest lunacy. The rational mind is man's greatest resource. When it has the freedom to innovate, it finds productive uses for every substance on earth, including waste by-products. Automobiles currently require gasoline, it is true, just as sailing ships required wood and canvas, and horses required hay and oats.

What will be the transportation vehicles of the future — and what energy source will power them? Today, nobody could predict it, just as in 1700 nobody could predict automobiles, jet travel, nuclear-powered ships or manned missions to the moon. One prediction, however, is a certainty: if men possess the political/economic freedom provided by capitalism, then the innovations of the future will dwarf such recent advances as electrical power, television, rocketry and computer technology.

The environmentalists are mistaken logically, as well as scientifically. Their use of the term "environment" involves a deadly equivocation, an unwarranted switch in the term's meaning.

"Logically, there can be no concept of an 'environment' that is not the environment *of* someone (or something). . . 'Environment' is a relational concept. It properly refers to the surroundings *of* some entity as they relate *to* that entity."

But the theory of intrinsic value holds that the environment is to be valued, even worshiped, independent of its worth to man, indeed in contradiction to his interest. The environmentalist takes in the unwary with fallacious logic. "He initially counts on its correct meaning, so that people accept a need to care about the fate of the 'environment' — which they assume in some way is *their* environment and is linked to *their* fate. This is why the movement's focus is pointedly on the 'environment,' rather than on the non- relational concept 'nature.' But once a confused public has been taken in, environmentalists re-package 'environment' to denote something upheld as existing separately from human beings."[11]

Rationally, the environment is man's surroundings or milieu, to be used in accordance with his best interests.

This leads to the moral error in environmentalism's argument, by far the most important issue of all. The intrinsic theory of nature's value holds that the environment is an end in itself, and that man's needs are to be sacrificed to it. So swamps, jungles, yew trees, spotted owls, snail darters, laboratory mice, chinook salmon, mosquitoes, even viruses are sacred, not to be disturbed; but human dams, houses, power plants are not to be built, and man's health and life expectancy are not to be protected.

Environmentalism is the most virulent form of the self- sacrifice ethics ever spawned. Communists and Nazis claim that an individual must sacrifice himself to the people or the race, but at least they argue that it is other human beings who are to benefit from an individual's self- immolation. But the environmentalists argue that *human life as such* must be sacrificed to the interest of the non-human — to the bugs, dirt and bacteria.

To fight the insanities of environmentalism it is necessary to recognize and uphold the right of an individual human being to his own life. Human life is the only moral absolute on earth. Anything else acquires worth only insofar as it benefits man.

Trees are a value only because they provide man with shade, timber, fruit, beautiful vistas, and so on.

Clean air is a value only because it promotes human health and longevity.

Automobiles are a value because they greatly increase the personal range and comfort of a man's transportation.

The extraction of oil from ANWR and the development of other natural resources are a value because they provide the raw materials with which to create modern industrial civilization.

Science, technology and industry are valuable for one reason: they greatly raise man's standard of living and increase his life expectancy. The moral principle is that man's life is the yardstick by reference to which the worth of any object, person or event is judged.

By this standard, the value of science, technology and industry is enormous and indisputable. Developments in agricultural science and the creation of modern farming equipment has led to an abundance of food in the Western world and to the Green Revolution, which produced more rice and grain in many Asian countries.

There has never been a famine in the history of the United States. When was the last time a famine occurred in any industrialized nation? Even raising such a question causes historians to scratch their heads, trying to remember. Yet a brief study of history reveals that famine was and remains a widespread occurrence in the non-industrialized countries.

The great 20th century historian, Fernand Braudel, writes that France is believed to have suffered 10 general famines during the 10th century, 26 in the 11th, 2 in the 12th, 4 in the 14th, 7 in the 15th, 13 in the 16th, 11 in the 17th and 16 in the 18th.

"Dearth and penury were continual. . . Famine recurred so insistently for centuries that it became incorporated into man's biological regime and built into his daily life."

It was not wiped out in Western Europe until the close of the 18th century, i.e., during the period of the Industrial Revolution. In the non-industrialized nations of the Third World today the same heartbreaking conditions exist. According to various charitable organizations for children, though it takes but 72 cents a day to provide a child with adequate nutrition and medical care, 30,000 children die daily from malnutrition and preventable diseases related to it.[12]

Similarly, advances in medicine have steadily raised the human life expectancy. A female child born in the United States today has a life expectancy approaching 80 years; and a male child's is mid-to-high seventies. The human life expectancy in the industrialized nations is rising, the exact opposite of what would occur if any of the environmentalist scare stories regarding the harmful effects of industrialization were true. The life expectancy is significantly lower in the countries that are not industrialized.

Further, the inventions and innovations made possible only by technological progress have vastly enriched the men of the entire Western world. The electric light, the telephone, the automobile, the airplane, the radio, television, refrigerator, air conditioner, personal computer and Internet are merely some of the advances that have made us wealthy. The anti-technology, anti-industry nature of the environmentalist movement is what marks it as a phenomenon virulently anti-human life.

Since the good is that which benefits human life, the converse also holds true: whatever harms or destroys human life is evil.

On this score, environmentalism is the most destructive doctrine ever devised. When put into actual practice, it causes harm, even death, to incalculable numbers of human beings.

By conservative estimate, the ban on DDT and other pesticides has caused the death by malaria of tens of millions of human beings. The greens' war against taxol retards man's struggle to triumph over cancer, causing untold human deaths. The same will be true if they succeed in banning medical testing on laboratory rats and mice.

Their restrictions on building power plants in California resulted in diminished electricity for hospitals, police stations, firehouses and other emergency facilities, threatening human life.

Their fight against oil development in ANWR will result in diminished heating fuel, gasoline and other petroleum products upon which modern industrialized civilization and our living standard depends. As the most anti-human theory in history, environmentalism is necessarily the most inhumane. Its virulently anti-man essence leaves us with a stark choice: human life or environmentalism. There is no middle ground.

References

1. David Holcberg, "Why Greens Are to Blame for Blackouts," www.aynrand.org.

2. *The Environmental Handbook*, ed. by Garrett De Bell (New York: Ballantine Books, 1970), pp. 197-207.

3. *Ibid.*, pp. 210-12.

4. David Graeber, "Mother Nature as a Hothouse Flower," *Los Angeles Times Book Review*, Oct. 22, 1989, pp. 1, 9.

5. Peter Schwartz, "The Philosophy of Privation," in Ayn Rand, *Return of the Primitive* (New York: Penguin, 1998), p. 221.

6. *Ibid.*, pp. 230-31.

7. Edmund Contoski, *Makers and Takers* (Minneapolis: American Liberty Publishers, 1997), pp. 193-94.

8. *Ibid.*, pp. 195-97.

9. *Ibid.*, pp. 201-04.

10. Michael Sanera and Jane Shaw, *Facts, Not Fear* (Washington, D.C.: Regnery Publishing, 1996), pp. 76-7, 79-81; Julian Simon, *The Ultimate Resource* (Princeton, New Jersey: Princeton University Press, 1981), p. 93; Herman Kahn, et. al., *The Next 200 Years* (New York: William Morrow and Co., 1976), pp. 68-76, 103-05.

11. *Return of the Primitive, op. cit.*, p. 228.

12. Fernand Braudel, *Capitalism and Material Life, 1400-1800* (New York: Harper & Row, 1967), pp. 38-40; literature from Childreach, www.childreach.org.

APPENDIX B — REGULATORY ABUSE

Property Rights, Regulatory Takings, And Environment Protection [by Jonathan H. Adler, (c) 2001, Competitive Enterprise Institute. All rights reserved.]

Executive Summary

Under current environmental laws individual Americans have been prevented from building homes, plowing fields, filling ditches, felling trees, clearing brush, and repairing fences, all on private land. Many believe that such regulations infringe upon private property rights and violate the Fifth Amendment to the U.S. Constitution's admonition "... nor shall private property be taken for public use without just compensation."

When the federal government condemns a piece of private land to create a publicly-desired resource, such as a military base, road, or wildlife preserve, it pays the land's owner for the value of the property. However when the government regulates the use of the same private land to achieve the same purpose, it rarely pays a dime. In t his manner, private land is taken for public use — through a "regulatory taking" — without just compensation.

Federal environmental laws are not the sole source of so- called regulatory takings by the federal government. However they are the most prominent. For two decades, federal land- use control has been the dominant means of achieving many environmental objectives. Two federal laws, in particular, have been the focus of the debate over compensation for regulatory takings: the Endangered Species Act (ESA) and Section 404 of the Clean Water Act (CWA), the source of regulations limiting the development of wetlands.

Private property should be viewed as the cornerstone of environmental protection. Whether the owner is seeking a profit on the property or not, self-interest still provides a powerful incentive to preserve, if not enhance, the value of the resource.

Property rights are important for both economic and environmental reasons, and must be protected from both government regulation and private malfeasance. Compensating landowners when they are deprived of the reasonable use of their land will not produce environmental catastrophe. Far from it. In many cases it will eliminate the negative environmental incentives created by the heavy hand of existing government regulations. Properly understood, property rights do not undermine sound environmental conservation, they lie at its foundation.

Businessman Fined $20 Million After Employee Spills Barrel of Oil [From *The Green Gestapo*, by Jarret Wollstein, International Society for Individual Liberty; July, 1996]

In San Rafael, California, an employee of a construction company owned by businessman Fred Grange accidentally spilled a single barrel of oil on a vacant lot. As required by law, Mr. Grange reported the spill to the EPA and local environmental agencies.

Over a dozen government agencies — including the EPA, California Highway Patrol, and local police — conducted investigations. Grange admitted he got very angry when literally hundreds of government investigators swooped down upon him. So, according to Grange, the Green Gestapo decided to make an example out of him. Fines totaling over $20 million were imposed on his business, forcing it to close.

The Kellenberger Legacy To Ohio [© Julie Kay Smithson, Founder – Property Rights Research.org, December 10, 2000]

"I've never wanted to live anywhere else. As far as can be seen from my home, the view is pleasing to the eye and a balm to the spirit. This is my home, and my family has cherished and been the best of stewards to our land."

Looking out from the front porch of Tom and Nancy Kellenberger's home, it is clear why he feels such kinship and pride in his farm. An hour south of Columbus, the Kellenberger Farm lies just southeast of Chillicothe. One of its neighbors is the Hopewell Mound Group, one of several ancient Indian earthworks found in Ohio. The view is unfettered by development, the wildlife coexists well with the human residents, and the earth has been coaxed to share her bounty.

Corn stubble exudes its own beauty, and provides nourishment and shelter for songbirds, waterfowl, and other avian residents and visitors; and a smorgasbord for the whitetail deer. Level to slightly rolling, the foothills of the Appalachians as a backdrop, it's easy to see why the Kellenbergers chose this place to sink their roots. Four generations deep, the attachment for the farm is much more than material or monetary.

The responsibility felt for the flora and fauna is not that of a mercenary, to merely deplete the resources and move on. Rather, the Kellenbergers have fought, and are fighting, to keep this place pristine for succeeding generations of Kellenbergers. The human influence on this land has been an enhancement and not a detriment, as the fine soil attests, and the mature trees that line the fields testify.

The National Park Service and the Archaeological Conservancy are united with multiple partners to separate Tom and his family from sixty-four acres of his 352-acre corn and soybean farm, including both his home and his parents home. There has never been a study done on the 64 acres to prove the existence of an earthworks, and no evidence can be found of such. Certainly, there are the occasional broken pieces of stone and flint, which exist in numerous other riverside locations in the Midwest.

It should be noted that while preserving the culture of Native Americans is admirable and necessary, it has already been done in many places in Ohio, and the need to take prime production agricultural land for another place with no ingress by the public, is questionable.

The Kellenbergers have been used by both groups, who made false statements stating that the Kellenbergers were going to donate the land in question, untruths that led to the sale of neighboring land. Over the course of nine years, Tom and Nancy have sought legal assistance, and the intervention of local groups. Nothing seems to have deterred the NPS and the Archaeological Conservancy from their chosen course, to disenfranchise the Kellenbergers from an integral part of their home and farm. The 64 acres is not only "loss of (farm) income, but also the loss of TWO family homes and the loss of a part of our lives," as Tom puts it so well.

The essence of this issue is not the preserving for research of this land, but the removal of private property rights by a federal agency and its cohorts. The current administration has, in the past eight years, locked up and removed from public use, more land than in all other administrations, put together. This is not land that a family can visit and hike, bird watch, horseback ride, or camp on. This is not land that can keep our country free from dependence on foreign oil supplies and imported products, not any more.

Our own government has stolen our country's heritage, and is doing everything possible in these last days, to make her subservient to a foreign power, the United Nations. This juggernaut of the taking of privately-owned land, the USE of privately-owned land, and the public's ability to use public lands and waters, is WRONG. The Kellenbergers stand as one Ohio example of what is happening in virtually every state in America: the siege of the American citizen, the removal of the middleclass and the backward journey into feudalism that our country was founded to thwart!

By telling their story, and many others like it, the author hopes to light a fire of curiosity and public outrage that bridges the gap between, ". . . as long as it's not in MY backyard. . . " and ". . . it's all around me, and I'd better wake up and get involved!" To expect "someone else" to attend the meetings and write the letters to the editor and make the phone calls and keep tabs on the elected officials, is to know what it's like to have it done "someone else's way." If freedom is vital for one's happiness, then one must be willing to stand up for it! The issue is no longer "if" but "when."

New York Couple Threatened With Jail Over Leaky Septic Tank
[2000 National Directory of Environmental and Regulatory Victims edited by John Carlisle, Director of the Environmental Policy Task Force of The National Center (c) 2000 by The National Center for Public Policy Research
[From *Liberty Matters*]

On January 7, 1997, Kent and Glenda Duell of Minerva, New York were sentenced to six-month jail terms and ordered to pay $340,000 in fines for "intending to pollute" a stream after their septic tank leaked. The Duells were owners of a six-unit apartment house which they rented to low-income families.

Over a period of nine years, the Duells performed repair work at least 30 times to fix leaks in the septic tank system, a system that had been designed and approved by the Department of Housing and Urban Development.

On one occasion, Kent Duell personally installed a new septic tank. Nevertheless, the couple was hauled into court on two occasions over charges of willful pollution. In both cases, the Duells were acquitted after it was determined that there was no negligence on their part, given they had even sought the assistance of the local environmental agencies in addressing any pollution problems.

However in 1996, at the request of the New York State Department of Environmental Conservation, the county District Attorney (DA) brought yet more charges against the couple. He charged the Duells with 164 counts of polluting or intending to pollute a stream abutting their property. The DA alleged that raw sewage from the septic tank had frequently been discharged on purpose into the stream.

In blatant disregard of the Duells' right to due process, their attorney, Ben Conlon, was not allowed to see the official list of charges so he could prepare a defense. Conlon was also not allowed the right of discovery to examine the evidence against his clients.

During the trial, neither the judge nor the prosecutor could determine what laws the Duells had broken. Nevertheless, a jury issued its verdicts and the couple was sentenced to six-month jail terms. During the sentencing, a tearful Glenda Duell requested that she serve her jail term first so her husband could keep his job and health insurance for another six months. The Duells have two young children.

An appellate court granted the Duells a stay pending their appeal. To pay the legal bills, the Duells sold their apartment complex and have had to sell their house to cover the $100,000 bail.

Elderly Couple Bankrupted By City Zoning Laws [2000 National Directory of Environmental and Regulatory Victims edited by John Carlisle, Director of the Environmental Policy Task Force of The National Center [(c) 2000 by The National Center for Public Policy Research]

In 1985, Harold and Iris Stone decided to sell the auto repair business they had operated in Lynn, Massachusetts for 40 years. They intended to use the money earned from the sale of the property to pay off their mortgage and enjoy retirement.

However, city regulators have made this seemingly simple plan a 13-year-long nightmare that has yet to end for the couple. Lynn officials wanted to turn the area into a development for condominiums. That was all well and good except they coerced the Stones into selling to a favored developer for $400,000, which was well below the property's actual value of $725,000.

Lynn city planners were so determined to pressure the Stones into an unfavorable sale that they resorted to using what the local press called "an illegal zoning ordinance" to scare off potential buyers who offered a higher price. The Stones used all of the $400,000 to pay off their mortgage and business accounts. The developer was supposed to pay the Stones an additional $325,000, but went bankrupt soon after the purchase — leaving the couple nothing for retirement.

In 1989, the Stones decided to repurchase their property. A real estate boom was in progress and they hoped to resell the land for a significant profit. They took out a $500,000 loan to buy back their property. Again, the city would not let them resell. City planner Kevin Geaney cut off water to the Stones' buildings and closed off the curb cuts to make it inaccessible.

Despite these unscrupulous tactics, a car dealer offered the Stones $920,000. This would have been enough for them to pay off the bank loan and still have plenty for a comfortable retirement. The City Council refused to permit the sale and the bank foreclosed on the property in March 1992. Although a jury awarded the Stones $720,000 for an illegal taking of their property, a state appeals court overturned the decision.

In April 1998, the couple went bankrupt and will soon lose their home of 38 years. Iris says, "We are just decent, hard-working people who wanted to enjoy our retirement."

APPENDIX C — FRAUD

Scientific "Research" Too Polluted At The Epa [Bonner R. Cohen, senior fellow, Lexington Institute (Letter to the Editor of the *Washington Times*, February 13, 1999)]

There is something inherently dishonest about researchers eagerly accepting government grants and then refusing to disclose the underlying data supporting their conclusions to the people who funded the enterprise: the American taxpayers... That dishonesty becomes institutionalized when federal agencies use the "scientific" conclusions based on the hidden data to justify new regulations.

The Environmental Protection Agency (EPA) has become particularly adept at this game. By passing out grants to a coterie of "usual suspects," who can be counted on to produce results following the EPA's preconceived regulatory agenda, the agency has found a way to circumvent standard scientific procedures and expand its writ in the process.

The seriousness of the problem was recognized by the EPA's own Science Advisory Board, which in a landmark 1992 report, "Safeguarding the Future: Credible Science, Credible Decisions," found that: "EPA should be a source of unbiased scientific information. However, EPA has not always ensured that contrasting, reputable scientific views are well-explored and well-documented from the beginning to the end of the regulatory process." Where all this can lead was underscored by a group of EPA employees who, in a letter to The Washington Times in June, alerted the public that "EPA regulations and enforcement actions based on poor science stand to harm rather than protect public health and the environment" ("Blowing the whistle on EPA's widespread abuse," June 10).

How does the EPA react to such internal criticism? Of the 13 EPA employees who signed that letter, six have been forced to leave the agency. Better to hide the data than to tolerate the truth.

Nwi Calls On Congress And The Administration To Take Action Against Scientific Fraud By Endangered Species Officials [National Wilderness Institute Press Release, December 18, 2001]

The National Wilderness Institute today called on Congress and the Bush Administration to investigate possible improper conduct by federal endangered species officials who reportedly falsified evidence in an effort to show that lynx were present in the Gifford Pinchot and Wenatchee National Forests in Washington state. The planted evidence was exposed when laboratory tests revealed that the fur samples officials claimed were found in the forest actually came from captive lynx.

When an endangered species is present, regulatory agencies have greatly expanded authority to restrict land management options, recreational and commercial activities in the area.

"The practice of planting bogus evidence shows how politicized and unscientific the application of the endangered species program can be," said Rob Gordon, Director of the National Wilderness Institute. "If these allegations are true, we need to know how many were in on it and remove them from government service. These charges may call into question the scientific integrity of the whole body of work done by those associated with the bogus evidence," said Gordon. . . .

According to NWI Director Rob Gordon, "Federal behavior in this case stands in stark contrast to the government's conduct in Washington, DC where NWI has had to go to court to try to halt the midnight dumping of tons of toxic sludge by a federal agency through a national park and onto the spawning beds of the endangered shortnose sturgeon."

Federal officials have refused to stop the discharges because trucking the sludge to a landfill could increase the cost to local water users and would increase truck traffic in an affluent and influential neighborhood. The discharges are flushed into the Potomac River from a water treatment facility run by the Army Corps of Engineers. It provides low cost water to the Capital area and is the only entity in the Chesapeake watershed that has a permit to discharge unlimited amounts of aluminum, iron and total suspended solids.

"There is a clear double standard when the government may have planted fake information it can use to shut down the economy of a rural community out west while in its own backyard it finds it too burdensome to have several trucks a day haul the sediment through an affluent neighborhood inhabited by government officials and influential Washingtonians," Gordon said.

APPENDIX D — RANCHERS & FARMERS

War On The West: A Call To Action, William Perry Pendley (Author, *It Takes A Hero: the Grassroots Battle Against Environmental Oppression*), President, Mountain States Legal Foundation

A New Message In The Environment

One of my favorite members of Congress is Congressman J.D. Hayworth of Arizona. During his first run for Congress, J.D. was presented with a t-shirt from a donor that read, "If two kids can have sex in the back seat of a car, why does the Spotted Owl need 50,000 acres?" He took the shirt with him on a trip to Washington, D.C., where he went out jogging.

While he was running down the mall, he saw President Clinton and his entourage approaching. Realizing that he was wearing the Spotted Owl shirt, he puffed out his enormous chest and turned in the President's direction as he passed. At first President Clinton began to smile, but then realizing that it was politically incorrect to do so, he turned solemn and looked the other way. J.D. rushed back to his hotel room where he wrote to the donor who sent him the shirt, "I went to Washington. I saw the President. I ran your message by him."

There is a new environmental message in this country, although it is now very clear either that President Clinton hasn't heard it, or believes that he can ignore it. Clinton's most recent actions in the West, including his invitation to a United Nation's delegation to visit Wyoming to evaluate western timber, tourism, mining and wildlife policies, and the Administration's increasing stridency on Congress' efforts to ease up on environmental overkill, demonstrate that Clinton is beholden to powerful environmental groups.

Yet the vast majority of the American people are increasingly disenchanted with and distrustful of this billion dollar a year juggernaut. It has not always been so.

A couple of years ago I was in New Hampshire to join with a grassroots group fighting the National Park Service's efforts to designate the Pemigewasset River as a "wild and scenic river."

By the way, the people of New Hampshire don't call it the Pemigewasset, they refer it to simply as "the Pemi." You know New Englanders are very economical in their use of the language. Remember, the skier Steve Koch — the first American to win an Olympic medal in the cross country event — who was from Vermont. He was asked if he had lived in New England all of his life. His response, "Not yet."

Following my remarks at the rally, a group of the grassroots leaders and I went out to dinner. During our discussion, one of the primary opponents of the Park Service's efforts turned to me and said, "Perry, you know what the problem with the Wild and Scenic Rivers Act is? It was never meant for eastern rivers. It was only meant for western rivers."

Suspicions confirmed. Isn't it amazing how a person's perspective changes when the rifle spins around and it's them looking down the barrel of the gun? Or, as Winston Churchill once remarked, "Nothing focuses a person's attention like being shot at and missed."

Well, people all over the country are being shot at today. It was one thing when the Endangered Species Act only applied to a bunch of loggers in the Pacific Northwest, when it was only used for activities on federal land in the West. That is no longer the case. When the Endangered Species Act was passed by Congress, it was talking about 100 species. Today, there are more than 900 listed, which affects every state in the country.

Perhaps the best example of the impact on private property, and the response of those affected, took place in August of 1994 in Texas, where 95% of the land is owned by private citizens. After Secretary of the Interior Babbitt designated 33 counties around Austin as critical habitat for the Golden Cheeked Warbler, more than 5,000 angry Texans gathered together on August 27, 1994, at the State Capitol to "Take Back Texas!" That rally, and the grassroots campaign that thereafter spread throughout the Lone Star State, is the reason why then Governor Ann Richards is today advertising Doritos.

What is the reason for the dramatic change in the public perception regarding environmental and property rights issues? There are three.

The Death Of Chicken Little

The first is that the American people are beginning to question the fundamental assumptions of the environmental movement. This began to happen in the winter of 1993-1994. Remember that winter. It was so cold in Washington, D.C. that the federal government had to close its offices. For several days the Republic was safe.

About that time I was on a talk show with Stan Soloman of WIBC in Indianapolis, Indiana. I told Stan that I wished I could be a fly on the wall of Vice President Gore's office to hear all the abuse he was taking from his friends over the brutal winter weather at the height of "global warming." Soloman said, "If you were a fly on the wall of Gore's office, you'd be the smartest creature in the room."

Which reminds me, Jay Leno recently compared Gore and former Vice President Dan Quayle. "If Quayle looks like a deer caught in the headlights of a car," said Leno, "then Gore looks like a deer hit by the car."

About that time, in January 1994, Time magazine ran an article about the cold weather under a picture of a nearly frozen over Niagara Falls and the headline stated, "The Ice Age Cometh?" In response to the question, "Whatever happened to global warming?" the article declared that, "[H]uman- induced warming is still largely theoretical, while ice ages are an established part of the planet's history."

People don't have to shovel too much global warming off their sidewalk before they begin to doubt the sky-is-falling radicals who demand they we all but destroy our civilization in order to "save the planet." People are beginning to realize they have been deceived, lied to, tricked. They have.

As Dr. Steven Schneider, one of Gore's advisers declares, "We scientists have to pick out scary scenarios and frighten the American people into action. Each one of us has to choose the right balance between being honest and being effective." That's the scientific method? No wonder the cataclysmic predictions of environmental extremists no longer produce a rush to judgment.

The End Of Environmental "Ectopia"

The second reason for the falling public support for environmental groups is the fact that the American people don't like the vision environmentalists have of the future.

For years folks believed that environmentalists sought a world in which, as my friend Bruce Vincent says, "Orphan rabbits would be raised by wolves in a sea of old growth forest from sea to shining sea." Sort of a like the lamb will lie down with the lion but won't be getting much sleep.

The American public's eyes were opened in the summer of 1994, when the forests of the American West began to burn. Nearly two million acres of woodlands went up in flames and 37 brave fire fighters were killed in the process, more than in decades.

The American people asked a reasonable question, "Why is the forest burning?" The response, "Because it is sick. Because the trees are diseased, dying or dead and now nature is taking its course, as it has for hundreds of years before the white man came West." Remarkably, environmental groups said the fires were a good thing, they were "nature's way," and we should let them burn. Most Americans did not think they were a good thing. Nor did the tiny communities that were threatened with fiery devastation.

The Clinton Administration's response to this issue is instructive. One high ranking official has declared that the fires that swept through the West are more natural than the homes in which Westerners live. How's that for a vision of the future.

It isn't just the vision environmentalist have for the West. Theirs is a dark vision for all Americans, in which we must be satisfied with less, in which government has more and more power, in which property rights are, as one former EPA official called it, "a quaint anachronism," and in which more and more land is off limits to people. Vice President Al Gore's views are a good example.

Recently, nationally syndicated columnist Tony Snow published a side-by-side comparison between the writings of the Unabomber and Al Gore. At the end of the column he switched two of the quotes and then asked his readers, "Could you tell?" I must admit, I couldn't. No wonder the American people are repelled by the vision environmentalists have of our future.

People are discovering that the battle is not about the quality of the human environment but about power and control. As Denis Hayes, one of the founders of Earth Day, said at a secret environmental conference, "We must change America's laws and its culture." Or as Al Gore said in his book, *Earth in the Balance*, he and other environmental extremists seek to achieve "a wrenching transformation of society."

No Longer "Feel-Good" And Free

The third reason for a national change in attitude on environmental issues is the fact that the American people now realize that environmental policy is no longer feel good and free. For years environmental policy was both feel good and free. Who could be against anything that is feel good and free, as long as it is consistent with the laws of God? Environmental policy is now neither.

Former U.S. Senator Russell Long of Louisiana, once Chairman of the Senate Finance Committee, said that tax policy was, "Don't tax me. Don't tax thee. Let's tax the fellow behind the tree." That was environmental policy. Environmental policy was free for everyone except the poor landowner who was discovered to have some endangered species upon his land, or whose property was coveted as a "wetland" or "viewshed" or "pristine habitat." Yet today, environmental policy is no longer free. It is no longer free because of the guarantee of the Fifth Amendment of the Constitution that "private property" may not be put to "public use" without "just compensation."

In 1992, the U.S. Supreme Court held that when the State of South Carolina told David Lucas that he could own and pay taxes on his beach front property, but could not build there, it had committed an unconstitutional taking for which it had to pay Mr. Lucas "just compensation."

The deciding moment in oral arguments occurred when Justice O'Connor asked the attorney for the State of South Carolina, "What is the nuisance you are trying to prevent?" (since outlawing a nuisance is not a "taking"). Said the attorney, "It is the possibility that a hurricane will come along, pick up David Lucas' house and throw it into someone else's house."

You don't get on the Supreme Court unless you are smart and quick, and Justice O'Connor is both. "Under that theory, couldn't you require all homes up and down the beach to be torn down?" she asked. At that point that the South Carolina attorney entered what we in Marine Corps aviation called the "dead man spiral."

In an interesting postscript to this important decision, South Carolina, after buying the property from David Lucas, sold it to the highest bidder for development purposes. The new attorney for South Carolina said, "It is beach front property. The highest and best use is development."

In 1994, the Supreme Court decided yet another vitally important property rights case that began in a suburb of Portland, Oregon. Florence Dolan sought to make use of her property.

The city told her she could get a permit to do so only if she gave the city all land within the 100-year flood plain and a 15-foot strip for a bike path and if she built the bike path. The Supreme Court ruled that that was a "taking," too, holding that even though the city was seeking to achieve something that it considered to be an environmental benefit, "there is no excuse for doing it any other way than the constitutional way."

These decisions mean that the cost of environmental policy will no longer be placed on the backs of property owners, but is a cost that must be borne by the American public. Environmental policy is no longer "free." The American people, during these tight budget times, will have to decide if they really want to save snails and flies or dry "wetlands" or if there might be something better to do with their money.

Environmental policy is no longer feel good, because the American people are learning that people are being hurt by so called environmental policy. At long last the media is starting to tell the rest of the story — our side of the story.

The watershed event in that regard was the 20/20 television story regarding homeowners in Winchester, California. As reported by Barbara Walters.

Walters reported on how armed Fish and Wildlife Service officials knocked on the doors of homeowners in southern California. The federal officials told the homeowners that they could not "disc" or plow around their homes because their yards were "occupied" by the Kangaroo Rat. When some people expressed fear that if they did not cut the debris around their homes their homes would burn down, the federal officials said if they did cut the debris they would go to jail.

Sure enough, the fires came and the homeowners who had obeyed the law lost their homes, while those who violated the law saved their homes. Concluded Barbara Walters, "Maybe this well intentioned Act has gone too far." Added Hugh Downs, her co-anchor, "Yes, Barbara; maybe next time it will be your home."

Bruce Vincent, Libby, Montana, logger, said about the 20/20 program, "We effectively torch 80,000 homes in the Pacific Northwest over the Northern Spotted Owl, and no one blinks an eye. But let 80 homes burn down in Southern California and the law has gone too far."

In my book, It Takes A Hero: the Grassroots Battle Against Environmental Oppression, I tell the stories of 57 people from 32 states and the District of Columbia who have gone from being innocent bystanders, to victims, to heroic activists because they have learned that environmental policy gone wild isn't just bad for people, it is bad for the environment.

My favorite reaction to It Takes A Hero was that of a highly educated neighbor who belongs to several environmental organizations. Said she, "I didn't think I would like it, but I did. When I see what environmental policy is doing to people, even though I have always considered myself an environmentalist, I have to say, I'm not one of them."

Today, all across America, as more and more people discover what environmental extremist policies are doing to real people, people just like us, they are saying, "I'm not one of them."

At the Forefront of the Environmental Battle

Mountain States Legal Foundation, which I am proud to represent today, does only one thing: it represents those who cannot afford to represent themselves in fighting back against oppressive policy that violates Constitutional freedoms and threatens the strength and vitality of this country. Let me share with you some of the stories of the men and women we are representing.

We are representing John Shuler, of Dupuyer, Montana, sued for $4,000 for protecting his life and his property from grizzly bears. Late one September night, John Shuler heard the unmistakable sound of grizzly bears eating his sheep. He dashed from his house clad only in his shorts and socks, but he remembered his gun.

Seeing three of them in his sheep pen, he fired into the air, and they dashed off into the night. Thinking the danger was over, he returned to his house, at which time he was confronted by the mother of all bears, or at least the mother of these three. When the bear roared up on its hind legs, John Shuler thought he would be killed. As a result, he killed the bear.

I must point out that the Fish and Wildlife Service asserted that when a grizzly bear rears upon its hind legs, it is not the sign of an imminent attack, but only what the government likes to call a scoping operation. As a result, asserts the government, that is the worst time to shoot. Moreover, when the bear comes down on all fours and charges, that, too, is a bad time to shoot since it may be a false charge.

In the administrative hearing, we claimed self defense on John Shuler's behalf. Remarkably, the judge ruled that the grizzly bear was entitled to the same legal standard as used in a criminal case. He also ruled that Mr. Shuler could not claim self defense since, by going into his own yard with a gun, he provoked the grizzly bear by entering upon, what the judge called, "the zone of imminent danger."

We are representing Dennis and Nile Gerbaz of Carbondale, Colorado. When the Roaring Fork River left its banks in the Spring of 1985, as a result of a federal water project, it flooded the land of the Brothers Gerbaz.

Their request that the federal government either take action or issue a permit to allow them to reclaim their land from the flood waters was denied. Fearing the continued loss of their land and possible jeopardy to life and after consulting with legal counsel, they restored the river to its historic channel.

As a result, they were sued by the Environmental Protection Agency which asserts essentially that their lands had become artificial wetlands that could not be dewatered without a permit. The EPA is seeking fines of nearly $200 million from the Brothers Gerbaz.

We represent a New Mexico businessman, who for years had disposed of waters produced from oil and gas operations on land he owned. He was served with a "cease and desist order" by the Environmental Protection Agency. The EPA had concluded, reversing its earlier position, that the sinkhole into which the man released the waters were "waters of the United States."

Remarkably enough, two federal courts have ruled that the man cannot challenge the EPA's finding of jurisdiction over his land without violating the cease and desist order and thereby becoming liable for $25,000 a day fines and jail time. The U.S. Court of Appeals for the Tenth Circuit held that while our public policy argument that such a policy presented a Hobson's Choice made sense, the Court did not want to undercut the enforcement authority of the EPA.

We are representing Bruce Vincent and his fellow residents of northwestern Montana and northern Idaho facing economic ruin and cataclysmic fires because of decisions of the U.S. Forest Service to cut back allowable timber harvests by 43 percent to achieve a one percent increase in grizzly bear habitat.

The irony here is that the forest is diseased, dying or dead and stands ready to burn. When the fires the locals fear come, they will destroy not just the economic underpinnings of the community, not just the forest in which they recreate, but also the habitat of the grizzly bear.

We are representing property owners in the Upper Peninsula of Michigan whose right to use the lake that abuts their property has been usurped by the U.S. Forest Service because of a nearby wilderness area. This notwithstanding, the guarantee in the Michigan Wilderness Act that "valid existing rights" will be protected, the Forest Service took the remarkable position that "valid existing rights" do not include our clients' water rights.

We are representing an owner of timberland in Texas whose property was destroyed by the failure of the U.S. Forest Service to prevent the Southern Pine Beetle from sweeping off of a federal wilderness onto private property. Government lawyers took the position that because the Wilderness Act of 1964 was passed after the statute that permits citizens to sue federal officials for negligent action, the Wilderness Act repealed the earlier provision.

In Idaho, we are representing a rancher who had one of his newborn calves killed and half eaten by a wolf imported from Canada by Secretary Babbitt. The rancher had a local veterinarian and a federal official examine the calf's remains. They both concluded that the calf had been born alive, had nursed, that its lungs were fully inflated and its hooves were hardened and covered with debris. Remarkably enough, the U.S. Fish and Wildlife Service asserts that the calf was born dead which is the only reason the wolf ate it. We have filed a "takings" action against the federal government.

We are representing the Wyoming Sheriffs Association in a challenge to the Brady Act. Our lawsuit is not about the right to own and bear arms as contained in the Second Amendment, but about whether Congress can commandeer local sheriffs and assign them duties and responsibilities. This is a key test of the issue of federalism as contained in the U.S. Constitution.

There are more, of course, but these examples are enough to reveal the breadth and importance of the cases Mountain States Legal Foundation has undertaken in defense of property rights and the guarantees of the Constitution. There is one final example, an example that illustrates that when environmental extremists assert that they are not against everything, but only the "bad" things, they are not being forthright.

On the Big Island of Hawaii, local residents faced with rolling blackouts that yielded personal and business hardship and economic uncertainty, sought to develop geothermal power. They did not want to depend on oil from Indonesia or coal from Australia, but wanted to develop local geothermal energy, a clean, efficient, home-grown resource that would yield jobs, taxes and revenues. Remarkably enough, environmentalists who have assured us that they favor such alternative forms of energy sued to stop the project claiming that if geothermal power were developed it would anger the fire goddess Pele.

A Look To The Future

Much has changed recently regarding environmental issues and property rights. However, much remains to be done. The Clinton Administration is still in charge, and Babbitt is pressing forward aggressively with regulations. Just as important, Janet Reno's Justice Department has advised environmental groups that it welcomes citizen lawsuits and is seeking to quietly and quickly settle those lawsuits to the detriment of those who use federal lands for such uses as timber harvesting.

More recently, President Clinton himself has demonstrated that he has decided to cast his lot with environmental groups. The President's recent actions in the West — his efforts to stop a mine in Montana and his officials' decision to bring in United Nations officials to determine our future — reveal that Clinton believes the one constituent group he must please and appease is the nation's environmental groups.

While Congress has changed, it has its plate full and will not be able to turn to such matters as the Endangered Species Act and wetlands policy and property rights for some time.

The one hope is in the area of appropriations. Unless and until federal bureaucrats are denied the funds to make their mischief, we will continue to suffer under unreasonable and excessive regulations. Meanwhile, there are still Senators and Members of Congress who are very favorably inclined to the environmental agenda, including many who are now in positions of responsibility. A good example is U.S. Senator Chafee of Rhode Island, now chairman of the Environment and Public Works Committee. He likes the ESA perhaps because Rhode Island is too small to have endangered species habitat.

At the Supreme Court, while the Court's decision in Lopez v. United States breathes new life into a once moribund Tenth Amendment, the Court's decision in Sweet Home Chapter of Communities for a Great Oregon, et al. v. Babbitt, et al., that the Endangered Species Act applies to the two-thirds of the country that is privately owned is devastating.

Finally, we have yet to convince many of our friends. P.J. O'Rourke, the very humorous, conservative, free market writer (he is the one who said at the height of the health care debate, "If you think health care is expensive now, wait until it's free," has a book out called All the Trouble in the World. In that book he skewers environmentalists and debunks all of their crazy ideas. He calls Al Gore, "a totalitarian twinkie with the intellectual ability of a King Charles Spaniel," for example.

Yet in his discussion of the West, he sounds like a radical environmentalist, saying we've destroyed western forests and grazing lands. If this is the view of someone we might regard as our friend, we have our work cut out for us and we do! Let me close by suggesting things we can do.

What You Can Do — A Lot

First, we must save the children from the nonsense they are learning in schools about environmental issues. We must get into the schools. We can still save the children because, unlike radical environmentalists, children are optimistic about the future and they believe in technology.

As to the future, that great environmental thinker, Ted Danson, says we only have ten years left to save the planet. Kids don't buy into such sky is falling nonsense. Although Al Gore says of technology, "we are not that clever, we never have been" (speak for yourself Mr. Vice President), children love technology. If you don't believe me, ask yourself why your VCR flashes "12:00?" The answer, the kid hasn't been through to fix it.

Second, we must spread the word within our community of the contribution our activities make to the community, economically and socially. Unfortunately, too many people don't really understand what makes their community run.

In the Pacific Northwest, when timber families pay their bills, they include slips of paper which read, "This bill paid with timber dollars." Two years ago, 48 percent of Oregonians believed that no jobs should be lost to the Northern Spotted Owl. That number is now 64 percent, a change attributable almost solely to grassroots, people-to-people contact beginning with that slip of paper.

Third, we who are employers must ensure that our employees are part of the solution, not part of the problem. Are our employees informed on the issues critical to the survival of our company or industry? They should be the best advocates in the community for you. At the very least, our employees must be made aware of the cost of environmental regulations and must know that jobs are at stake.

Fourth, we must talk with the media. We must write letters to the editor, meet with editorial boards, complain to reporters and their editors about unfair, slanted, biased or inaccurate reporting. We must get on radio and television talk shows and we must find new media opportunities to get our message out and across to the American people. If we don't, who will?

Fifth, as one of the heroes in It Takes A Hero, Bruce Vincent says, "The world is run by those who show up." We must show up! We must be there at public meetings. We must ensure that our voices are heard and our views recognized. All of us must work together, must join with one another to combat the mighty forces arrayed against us.

Such efforts have already been effective. The property rights movement, for example, helped to change the face of the U.S. Congress during the 1994 congressional elections. This is another example. Earlier this year, I had the honor and privilege of arguing a case before the U.S. Supreme Court, a case we won! During oral arguments, I took a question from Justice Breyer, the newest member of the Court.

As he was speaking, I couldn't help but think that there but for the grace of God sat Bruce Babbitt. President Clinton had decided to nominate Babbitt to the Court, but when the news leaked out all hell broke loose and the nomination was doomed. The reason was that the grassroots movement had, in the words of the highly regarded environmental writer Alston Chase, turned Babbitt into a "gargoyle."

Sixth, we must help our friends. All of us must ensure that the organizations and associations which are working to preserve economic and personal liberty are able to continue — organizations such as the one meeting here tonight. One way you could help Mountain States Legal Foundation is to purchase for only $25 a copy of my new book, War on the West: Government Tyranny on America's Great Frontier.

Never Give Up — Never Give In

Last summer we honored the fiftieth anniversary of the end of World War II — what we all know as Victory in Japan Day. Remembering that time, I could not help but reflect on the great speeches of Winston Churchill who, in some of the darkest days in history, spoke courageously and inspirationally of what the free world needed to do.

My favorite speech of his was the one he gave at his boyhood school of Harrow when he returned, in October 1941, to address the young boys who sat in the seats he once occupied. After a full afternoon of speeches, he stepped to the microphone, looked out over the young audience and said, "Never give in. Never, never, never, never, never. In things, great or small, large or petty, never give in except to conviction, honor and good sense."

Ladies and gentlemen, never give in, never give up. God bless you and good luck.

Farmers Fight 50,000 Acre Federal Land Grab [Matthew Mittan, *The Asheville Tribune, November 7, 1998]* 12 Year Old Testifies Before Senate; Tries To Save Her Family's Home.

The United States Fish and Wildlife Service has announced it's desire to create a fifty-three thousand acre wildlife refuge, much to the chagrin of local residents. Federal officials have targeted, for their refuge, some of the best farmland in the United States, land that has been farmed by some of the same families for two hundred years.

Residents opposed to the federal land designation say that the proposed refuge would dispossess hundreds of families and transform a productive agricultural economy into a non-productive service economy.

The people of Madison and Union counties in Ohio are overwhelmingly opposed to the proposal. But that has not slowed the federal agencies from pursuing the land.

Due to that fact, two local grassroots groups, Stewards of the Darby (SOD) and Citizens Against Refuge Proposal (CARP) are at the forefront of the land rights battle. Through these groups, local residents drafted a Declaration entitled "Our Land Is Our Responsibility" which reads in part, "We, the residents of the area publicized as the "Darby Prairie National Wildlife Refuge Study Area" want our voices heard! We, who live and work in this farming community, believe the impact to area businesses would jeopardize their very existence. The Madison County Auditor's Office projects the affected region generates $300 per acre, which turns over 6-7 times (in buying power) before leaving the community. This translates into a potential deficit of $90 million dollars to our area businesses.

"[Additionally,] United States Representative Ralph S. Regula asserts: 'It is simply irresponsible to take on new land responsibilities, and give grants to cities, States and private institutions, when we cannot afford to adequately take care of our primary federal responsibilities — the public lands.'

"The State Forest Department manages and protects 7.1 million acres of forest land in Ohio, for the benefit of all Ohio citizens. One hundred eighty one thousand acres of State-owned forest land are available for multiple benefits, including wildlife, recreation, timber products, and soil and water protection. In addition, there are 72 State Parks in Ohio where the public can interact with nature at its leisure.

With this great abundance of parks and wildlife areas, all supported by our tax dollars, is there really a need for more public land?

"Actual area land auctions show that a 500-acre farm is worth $1.5 million. To this initial cost, add a reasonably priced home at a cost of $85,000, and minimal equipment at approximately $641,000, and the combined start-up cost totals $2.226 MILLION. After committing to an investment of such magnitude, why would our astute, agriculturally-and family-minded farmers want to sell?

"In the case of the proposed Darby Prairie National Wildlife Refuge, most of the 53,692 acres is land that has been acquired by our farmers over many generations. This "ownership endurance" enables us to continue our conservation accredited farming skills, thus growing with our investments.

At an average of 4.5 persons per home, this equates to the possible residential displacement of over 7,500 people from the Study Area alone, with a loss of approximately 4,000 taxpayers to the community. We have a proven track record of providing Americans with a diversity of products in the global marketplace, with a combination of wheat, corn, and soybeans; there would be a loss of over 3 million bushels of grain from the Study Area!

"With well over 50,000 acres lost to food production, how many non-farmers would be willing to relinquish their combined homes and yards to replace the fertile soil that presently feeds so many, that would be permanently lost by the introduction of a National Wildlife Refuge? At some point, we will no longer have the abundance of high-quality, reasonably priced food that we now take for granted at our supermarkets.

"The growing of food to nourish our citizens is certainly as much a consideration as re-establishing a tall grass prairie. Eating is not going to go out of style, and we are not willingly going to yield our bountiful land to either developers or federal Agencies who say they are 'protecting us' from development.

"Those of us who have been entrusted with the privilege of caring for the land, know well the proper care and nurturing required to maintain, protect and preserve our farmlands, and sustain a well-established wildlife habitat through conservation management. With an eye to the future, and the experience of almost two hundred years, we know that Our Land Is Our Responsibility!"

In response to the public outcry, two bills have been introduced in the Ohio Legislature, HCR 44 (Rep. Jim Buchy) and SCR 28 (Sen. Merle Grace Kearns). Both bills seek to block the federal effort. "We are trying to send a message to the federal government that we do not want this in our state," said Julie Smithson, a career truck driver who has been closely involved with the debate.

Advocates for the protection of private property in Ohio hope that their struggle for the control of their land is not lost on the ears of citizens in other areas across the nation. "We hope that other States can take up the issue and join the bandwagon."

This fight has involved more than just the adults in the area. Sheena Pennell, a 12-year-old student, recently won an international essay contest, sponsored by Walt Disney and McDonalds, for her writings on the Darby Refuge controversy. Sheena believes that the local residents are doing just fine taking care of the land and that the Fish and Wildlife Department doesn't need to be telling farmers how best to manage their properties.

Sheena's mother Marlyne spoke to the Tribune while Sheena was at school Tuesday. She stated that Sheena has always been an independent thinker and that her daughter became very interested in the Darby dispute, researching numerous documents and asking to attend several local town hall type meetings. "She's been a 4-H'er since she was 5 years old; you learn to respect the land."

During the course of her inquiries, Sheena learned of numerous facts that caused her skepticism of the FWA initiative. "Several farmers in the area have received awards from the Fish and Wildlife Service for outstanding environmental standards, " Mrs. Pennell stated. That didn't seem to gel with the position that the FWA was coming in to "protect the land," Pennell asserted.

The Pennell family home is located on five acres that they have owned for nearly a decade. They say they chose the area to raise their family because of its small town, friendly appeal. They enjoy the traditional farming community life. However, that could soon change due to the fact that their land is within the proposed Wildlife Refuge area.

That situation, and young Sheena's essay, landed the family a seat in front of a Senate Committee looking into the Darby conflict last week. "She was a little nervous at first, but I think she feels like she's helping to make a difference," her mother told the Tribune. "She got to see [Senators] hearing her opinions."

A second round of State Senate hearings has been scheduled for mid-March.

On the federal level, written testimony was presented to the U.S. House Resources Committee recently. The testimony read as follows: "Our area is under threat of being declared a National Wildlife Refuge by the actions of corrupt officials of the U.S. Fish & Wildlife Service, acting in collusion with The Nature Conservancy, which is attempting to impose one of its restrictive 'Bioreserve' projects on our farming community.

"The Columbus Foundation and Affiliated Organizations, a consortium of urban foundations unconcerned about rural economies and the property rights of farmers, gave The Nature Conservancy a grant of $25,000 in 1996 'For Darby Bioreserve Project, including hiring RiverKeeper to promote citizen-based protection of Big and Little Darby Creeks.'

"Despite massive opposition to the Project by our local citizens, the USFWS continues to act under the influence of The Nature Conservancy and their funders, the Columbus Foundation consortium, to cripple our farm community.

"We request that Congress fully investigate this foundation- funded attempt to destroy the economy of our local farm community."

The House Resources Committee is chaired by Rep. Don Young (R, Alaska). No action had been taken on the Darby Wildlife Refuge designation as of press time.

APPENDIX E — GLOBAL WARMING

Petition Project On Global Warming

Letter from Frederick Seitz Past President, National Academy of Sciences, U.S.A. President Emeritus, Rockefeller University Oregon Institute of Science and Medicine:

Research Review Of Global Warming Evidence

Below is an eight page review of information on the subject of "global warming," and a petition in the form of a reply card. Please consider these materials carefully. The United States is very close to adopting an international agreement that would ration the use of energy and of technologies that depend upon coal, oil, and natural gas and some other organic compounds.

This treaty is, in our opinion, based upon flawed ideas. Research data on climate change do not show that human use of hydrocarbons is harmful. To the contrary, there is good evidence that increased atmospheric carbon dioxide is environmentally helpful.

The proposed agreement would have very negative effects upon the technology of nations throughout the world, especially those that are currently attempting to lift from poverty and provide opportunities to the over 4 billion people in technologically underdeveloped countries.

It is especially important for America to hear from its citizens who have the training necessary to evaluate the relevant data and offer sound advice.

We urge you to sign and return the petition card. If you would like more cards for use by your colleagues, these will be sent.

Frederick Seitz

Text Of The Global Warming Petition

We urge the United States government to reject the global warming agreement that was written in Kyoto, Japan in December, 1997, and any other similar proposals. The proposed limits on greenhouse gases would harm the environment, hinder the advance of science and technology, and damage the health and welfare of mankind.

There is no convincing scientific evidence that human release of carbon dioxide, methane, or other greenhouse gasses is causing or will, in the foreseeable future, cause catastrophic heating of the Earth's atmosphere and disruption of the Earth's climate. Moreover, there is substantial scientific evidence that increases in atmospheric carbon dioxide produce many beneficial effects upon the natural plant and animal environments of the Earth.

During the past 2 years, more than 17,100 basic and applied American scientists, two-thirds with advanced degrees, have signed the Global Warming Petition. Signers of this petition so far include 2,660 physicists, geophysicists, climatologists, meteorologists, oceanographers, and environmental scientists who are especially well qualified to evaluate the effects of carbon dioxide on the Earth's atmosphere and climate.

Signers of this petition also include 5,017 scientists whose fields of specialization in chemistry, biochemistry, biology, and other life sciences (select this link for a listing of these individuals) make them especially well qualified to evaluate the effects of carbon dioxide upon the Earth's plant and animal life.

Nearly all of the initial 17,100 scientist signers have technical training suitable for the evaluation of the relevant research data, and many are trained in related fields. In addition to these 17,100, approximately 2,400 individuals have signed the petition who are trained in fields other than science or whose field of specialization was not specified on their returned petition.

Of the 19,700 signatures that the project has received in total so far, 17,800 have been independently verified and the other 1,900 have not yet been independently verified. Of those signers holding the degree of PhD, 95% have now been independently verified. One name that was sent in by enviro pranksters, Geri Halliwell, PhD, has been eliminated. Several names, such as Perry Mason and Robert Byrd are still on the list even though enviro press reports have ridiculed their identity with the names of famous personalities. They are actual signers. Perry Mason, for example, is a PhD Chemist.

The costs of this petition project have been paid entirely by private donations. No industrial funding or money from sources within the coal, oil, natural gas or related industries has been utilized. The petition's organizers, who include some faculty members and staff of the Oregon Institute of Science and Medicine, do not otherwise receive funds from such sources. The Institute itself has no such funding. Also, no funds of tax-exempt organizations have been used for this project.

The signatures and the text of the petition stand alone and speak for themselves. These scientists have signed this specific document. They are not associated with any particular organization. Their signatures represent a strong statement about this important issue by many of the best scientific minds in the United States.

This project is titled "Petition Project" and uses a mailing address of its own because the organizers desired an independent, individual opinion from each scientist based on the scientific issues involved — without any implied endorsements of individuals, groups, or institutions.

(List of signatories of petition, alpahbetically, at http://www.oism.org/pproject/s33p333.htm)

Bush Administration New U.S. Climate Policy
(15 FEB 2002)

President George W. Bush has made an irrevocable decision to discard the Kyoto Protocol as far as US participation is concerned by announcing a separate policy on climate. He has set two priorities for the US — to clean the air, and to address the issue of global climate change in the context of scientific uncertainties.

He has flagged new 'Clean Skies' laws designed to dramatically reduce the three most significant forms of pollution from power plants, namely sulphur dioxide, nitrogen oxides and mercury. According to Bush, "We will cut sulfur dioxide emissions by 73 percent from current levels. We will cut nitrogen oxide emissions by 67 percent. And, for the first time ever, we will cap emissions of mercury, cutting them by 69 percent. These cuts will be completed over two measured phases, with one set of emission limits for 2010 and for the other for 2018."

His approach aims to 'protect the environment', 'prolong the lives of thousands of Americans with asthma and other respiratory illnesses, as well as with those with heart disease', and to 'reduce the risk to children exposed to mercury during a mother's pregnancy'. The new laws will operate via a market-based cap-and-trade system for which he expects to have broad support in Congress.

But on climate, he was more circumspect — "Now, global climate change presents a different set of challenges and requires a different strategy. The science is more complex, the answers are less certain, and the technology is less developed. So we need a flexible approach that can adjust to new information and new technology."

His stated goal is to reduce America's greenhouse gas emissions "relative to the size of the US economy," by cutting greenhouse gas intensity (or how much is emitted per unit of economic activity) by 18 percent over the next 10 years.

This latter approach is somewhat vague in comparison with his Clean Skies proposal. But then Bush states his bottom line. "Our nation must have economic growth — growth to create opportunity; growth to create a higher quality of life for our citizens.

Growth is also what pays for investments in clean technologies, increased conservation, and energy efficiency." This is in direct contrast to the Kyoto approach which was manifestly anti-growth. "We will promote renewable energy production and clean coal technology, as well as nuclear power, which produces no greenhouse gas emissions. And we will work to safely improve fuel economy for our cars and our trucks."

In effect, he is demanding that any climate policy must work within normal economic activity, not cripple it as the Europeans would do with the Kyoto Protocol. Looking to the future, he added — "If, however, by 2012, our progress is not sufficient and sound science justifies further action, the United States will respond with additional measures that may include broad-based market programs as well as additional incentives and voluntary measures designed to accelerate technology development and deployment." Note his caution about 'sound science', implying that a lot of the 'science' around today is anything but sound, a caution this website fully endorses.

As for the Kyoto Protocol, Bush was scathing and uncompromising — "My approach recognizes that economic growth is the solution, not the problem. Because a nation that grows its economy is a nation that can afford investments and new technologies. The approach taken under the Kyoto Protocol would have required the United States to make deep and immediate cuts in our economy to meet an arbitrary target. It would have cost our economy up to $400 billion and we would have lost 4.9 million jobs. As President of the United States, charged with safeguarding the welfare of the American people and American workers, I will not commit our nation to an unsound international treaty that will throw millions of our citizens out of work."

However, Bush also promised that the United States would "not interfere with the plans of any nation that chooses to ratify the Kyoto protocol," a clear reference to the European Union which will now have to fund, on their own, all the grandiose wealth transfers and economic growth cuts which the Protocol envisioned.

Summarising what could become the 'Bush Doctrine' on climate, he said — "To clean the air, and to address climate change, we need to recognize that economic growth and environmental protection go hand in hand. Affluent societies are the ones that demand, and can therefore afford, the most environmental protection. Prosperity is what allows us to commit more and more resources to environmental protection. And in the coming decades, the world needs to develop and deploy billions of dollars of technologies that generate energy in cleaner ways. And we need strong economic growth to make that possible."

Soon after Bush's speech, Australia's Prime Minister, John Howard, made a public statement that Australia would not ratify the Kyoto Protocol without US and developing country's participation. Since President Bush has read the final funeral oration on the protocol as far as the US is concerned, it is now a dead letter here in Australia too.

The Heidelberg Appeal

Background — The Heidelberg Appeal was publicly released at the 1992 Earth Summit in Rio de Janeiro. By the end of the 1992 summit, 425 scientists and other intellectual leaders had signed the appeal. Since then, word of mouth has prompted hundreds more scientists to lend their support. Today, more than 4,000 signatories, including 72 Nobel Prize winners, from 106 countries have signed it. In spite of this spontaneous and growing support from the world's scientific community, the Heidelberg Appeal has received little media attention.

Neither a statement of corporate interests nor a denial of environmental problems, the Heidelberg Appeal is a quiet call for reason and a recognition of scientific progress as the solution to, not the cause of, the health and environmental problems that we face. The Appeal expresses a conviction that modern society is the best equipped in human history to solve the world's ills, provided that they do not sacrifice science, intellectual honesty, and common sense to political opportunism and irrational fears.

The Heidelberg Appeal Text

We want to make our full contribution to the preservation of our common heritage, the Earth.

We are, however, worried at the dawn of the twenty-first century, at the emergence of an irrational ideology which is opposed to scientific and industrial progress and impedes economic and social development.

We contend that a Natural State, sometimes idealized by movements with a tendency to look toward the past, does not exist and has probably never existed since man's first appearance in the biosphere, insofar as humanity has always progressed by increasingly harnessing Nature to its needs and not the reverse. We full subscribe to the objectives of a scientific ecology for a universe whose resources must be taken stock of, monitored and preserved.

But we herewith demand that this stock-taking, monitoring and preservation be founded on scientific criteria and not on irrational preconceptions.

We stress that many essential human activities are carried out either by manipulating hazardous substances or in their proximity, and that progress and development have always involved increasing control over hostile forces, to the benefit of mankind.

We therefore consider that scientific ecology is no more than extension of this continual progress toward the improved life of future generations.

We intend to assert science's responsibility and duties toward society as a whole.

We do, however, forewarn the authorities in charge of our planet's destiny against decisions which are supported by pseudoscientific arguments or false and nonrelevant data.

We draw everybody's attention to the absolute necessity of helping poor countries attain a level of sustainable development which matches that of the rest of the planet, protecting them from troubles and dangers stemming from developed nations, and avoiding their entanglement in a web of unrealistic obligations which would compromise both their independence and their dignity.

The greatest evils which stalk our Earth are ignorance and oppression, and not Science, Technology, and Industry, whose instruments, when adequately managed, are indispensable tools of a future shaped by Humanity, by itself and for itself, overcoming major problems like overpopulation, starvation and worldwide diseases.

SIGNATORIES of the Heidelberg Appeal (* Denotes Nobel Prize Winner)

Here are some of the more than 4000 signers:

*Bruce N. Ames, Director, National Institute of Environmental Health Sciences Center, Berkeley-Biochemistry-U.S.A. * Phillip W. Anderson, Nobel Prize (Physics), Princeton University- Physics-U.S.A. * Christian B. Anfinsen, Nobel Prize (Chemistry), John Hopkins University-Baltimore-Biology-U.S.A. Henri Atlan, Professor, Head of Nuclear Medicine Department, Hotel Dieu, Paris-Nuclear Medicine-France * Julius Axelrod, Nobel Prize (Medicine), Lab. Of Cell Biology Nat. Institute of Mental Health-Cell Biology-U.S.A. Aden Bauleiu-Inserm, Ac. of Sciences, France, National Institute of Sciences, U.S.A. Lasker Prize- Endocrinology-France * Baruj Benacerraf, Nobel Prize (Medicine), National Medal of Science, President, Dana-Farber, Inc.-Cancerology-U.S.A. * Hans Albrecht Bethe, Nobel Prize (Physics), Emeritus Professor, Cornell University-Ithaca-NY-Nuclear Physics-U.S.A. *Sir James W. Black, Nobel Prize (Medicine), Professor Of Analytical Pharmacology King's College, London- Pharmacology- Grande-Bretagne * Nicholas Bloembergen, Nobel Prize (Physics), Harvard University- Physics-U.S.A. Sir Hermann Bondi, Emeritus Professor Of Mathematics King's College University Master of Churchill College Cambridge- Mathematics-Grande-Bretagne * Norman E, Borlaug, Nobel Prize (Peace), Sc. Consult CAMWOOD, Mexico Pdt. Sasakawa African Assoc.-Agriculture-U.S.A. Pierre Bourdieu, College de France-Sociology-France * Adolph Butenandt, Nobel Prize (Chemistry), Hon. Pres. Max-Planck Institute-Chemistry-Allemagne * Thomas R. Cech, Nobel Prize (Chemistry), University of Colorado- Chemistry-U.S.A. Carlos Chagas, Academia Pontificia, WIS- Medicine-Bresil * Owen Chamberlain, Professor, Nobel Prize (Physics), Emeritus Professor, University Of California-Berkeley-U.S.A. * Stanley Cohen, Nobel Prize (Medicine), Distinguished Professor, Department of Biochem., Vanderbilt University- Biochemistry- U.S.A. *Sir John Warcup Cornforth, Nobel Prize (Chemistry), School of Chemistry and Molecular Sciences, Brighton- Chemistry-Grande-Bretagne * Jean Dausset, Nobel Prize (Medicine), Ac. of Sciences, France, Pres. U.M.S.E., W.I.S., Paris-Immunology-France * Gerald Debreu, Nobel Prize (Economy), Emeritus Professor of Economics and Mathematics, University Of California-Economy-U.S.A. * Johan Deisenhofer, Nobel Prize (Chemistry), University of Texas, Southwestern Medical Center, Dallas-Biochemistry-U.S.A. Sir Richard Doll, Emeritus Professor Of Medicine, Radcliffe Infirmary, Oxford-Epidemiology-Grande- Bretagne * Christian de Duve, Nobel Prize (Medicine), Biology-Belgique * Manfred Eigen, Nobel Prize (Chemistry), President of Max Plank Institute, Gottingen-Chemistry-Allemagne * Richard R. Ernst, Nobel Prize (Chemistry), Swiss Federal Institute of Technology, Zurich- Chemistry-Suisse * Pierre-Gilles de Gennes, Nobel Prize (Physics), Ac. of Sciences, Professor,*

College de France, Paris-Physics-France * *Ivar Giaever, Nobel Prize (Physics), Institute Professor, R.P.I.-Physics-U.S.A.* * *Donald A. Glaser, Nobel Prize (Physics), Professor of Physics, University of California-Physics-U.S.A. Francois Gros, Professor, College de France, Ac of Sciences, France, Vice President of WIS, Paris — Biology of development-France* * *Roger Guillemin, Nobel Prize (Medicine), Whittier Institute, La Jolla-Medicine-U.S.A.* * *Herbert A. Hauptman, Nobel Prize (Chemistry), Pres. Med. Found. of Buffalo, Professor of Biophysics Sc-Biophysics-U.S.A. Harald zur Hausen, Professor, Dr., Director of German Cancer Research Center, Heidelberg-Cancerology-Allemagne Mrs. Francoise Heritier-Auge, Professor, College de France, Pres Cons Nat. Sida Dir, Ehess-Anthropology-France* * *Dudley R. Herschbach, Nobel Prize (Chemistry), Baird Professor Of Science, Harvard University, Cambridge-Chemistry-U.S.A.* * *Gerhard Herzberg, Nobel Prize (Chemistry), National Research Council of Canada, Chemistry — Canada Benno Hess, Professor, Doctor, Honorary Senator and Former Vice President, Max-Planck Society, WIS — Biophysics-Allemagne* * *Anthony Jewish, Nobel Prize (Physics), Professor, Cavendish Laboratory, Cambridge University Physics — Grande-Bretagne* * *Roald Hoffman, Nobel Prize (Chemistry), Professor Of Chemistry, Cornell University-Chemistry-U.S.A.* * *Robert Huber, Nobel Prize (Chemistry), Max-Planck Institute for Biochemie, Biochemistry-Allemagne* *Sir Andrew Fielding Huxley, Nobel Prize (Medicine), Formerly President of London, Medicine-Grande-Bretagne Serguei Petrovich Kapitza, Professor of Sciences, Institute for Physical Problems, WIS-Physics, electrodynamics-Russie* * *Jerome Karle, Nobel Prize (Chemistry), Chief Scientist, Lab for Structure of Matter, Chemistry-U.S.A.* *Sir John Kendrew, Nobel Prize (Chemistry), Professor, The Old Guildhall, Cambridge, Molecular Biology-Grande-Bretagne* * *Klaus Von Klitzing, Nobel Prize (Physics), Professor, Max-Planck Inst. Solid State Research, Stuttgart-Physics-Allemagne* * *Aaron Klug, Nobel Prize (Chemistry), M.R.C. Lab. of Molecular Biology, Cambridge-Chemistry-Grande-Bretagne* * *Edwin G. Krebs, Nobel Prize (Medicine), Professor Emeritus, Department of Pharm & Biochem, University of Washington-Biochemistry-U.S.A.* * *Leon Lederman, Nobel Prize (Physics), Director Emeritus, Fermi Nat'l Accelerator Laboratory, Nuclear Physics-U.S.A.* * *Yuan T. Lee, Nobel Prize (Chemistry), Professor of Chemistry, University of California-Berkeley-U.S.A.* *Jean-Marie Lehn, Nobel Prize (Chemistry), Professor, College de France, W.I.S. Chemistry-France Pierre Lelong, Professor, Ac of Sciences, W.I.S.-Mathematics-France* * *Wassily Leontief, Nobel Prize (Economy), Professor, New York University-Economy-U.S.A.* * *Rita Levi-Montalcini, Nobel Prize (Medicine), Ac Lincei, Ac Pontificia, W.I.S.-Neurosciences-Italie Andr Linchnerowicz, Professor, Ac of Sciences France, Ac Lincei, Ac Pontificia, President of W.I.S., Mathematical Physics-France Richard S. Lindzen, Professor, US National Academy of Sciences, M.I.T., W.I.S.-Meteorology-U.S.A.* * *William N. Lipscomb, Nobel Prize Winner (Chemistry), Professor Emeritus, Harvard University, Cambridge-Chemistry-U.S.A.* * *Harry M. Markowitz, Nobel Prize (Economics), Speizer Professor of*

*Finance, Baruch College-U.S.A. * Simon van der Meer, Nobel Prize (Physics), Geneva-Nuclear Physics-Suisse * Cesar Milstein, Nobel Prize (Physiology), Dr Cambridge-Physiology-Grande-Bretagne *Sir. Nevil F. Mott, Nobel Prize Winner (Physics), Emeritus Professor, Cambridge University, Physics-Grande-Bretagne * Joseph Murray, Nobel Prize (Medicine), Professor, Dr Surgery, Harvard Med School-Cell Biology-U.S.A. * Daniel Nathans, Nobel Prize (Medicine), Professor, John Hopkins Un, School of Medicine, Baltimore-Molecular Genetics-U.S.A. Daniel W. Nebert, Professor, Director, Center for Environmental Genetics, University of Cincinnati, Genetics-U.S.A. * Louis Neel, Nobel Prize (Physics), Physics-France * Erwin Neher, Nobel Prize (Medicine), Doctor, Director, Max-Planck Institute, Biophysics, Goettingen-Biophysics-Allemagne * Marshall W. Nirenberg, Nobel Prize (Medicine), National Institutes of Health, Bethesda-Medicine-U.S.A. * George E. Palade, Nobel Prize (Medicine), Professor, Division of Cellular & Molecular Med, Cell Medicine-U.S.A. * Linus Pauling, Nobel Prize (Chemistry, Peace), Professor, Linus Pauling Institute Sc and Med, Chemistry-U.S.A. Jean-Claude Pecker, Professor Hon, College de France, Ac of Sciences, Royal Ac of Belgium, W.I.S.-Astrophysics-France * Amo A. Penzias, Nobel Prize (Physics), Professor, Bell Labortories, Murray Hill-Physics-U.S.A. * Max Ferdinand Perutz, Nobel Prize (Chemistry), MRC Laboratory of Molecular Biology, Cambridge-Biochemistry- Grande-Bretagne Julian Peto, Professor, Head , Section of Epidemiology, Institute of Cancer Research, London-Epidemiology-Grande-Bretagne Richard Peto, Professor of Medical Statistics & Epidemiology, University of Oxford-Epidemiology-Grande-Bretagne * John Charles Polanyi, Nobel Prize (Chemistry), Professor Of Chemistry, University of Toronto-Chemistry-Canada *Lord George Porter, Nobel Prize (Chemistry), Professor, Chairman, Photomolec, Sc Imperial College, London-Chemistry- Grande-Bretagne * I. Prigogine, Nobel Prize (Chemistry), Professor, Director, Institute Intern. de Phys. et de Chim, Bruxelles-Chemistry-Belgique A. Prochiantz, Pr, Director of Research CNRS, Ecole Normale Suprieure, Paris, W.I.S.-Pharmacology-France Ichtiaque Rasool, Jet Propulsion Laboratory, Pasadena-Physics-France * Tadeus Reichstein, Nobel Prize (Medicine), Professor Emeritus, Org Chemistry, University of Basel-Organic Chemistry-Suisse * Heinrich Rohrer, Nobel Prize (Physics), IBM Research Laboratory, Physics-Suisse * Bert Sakmann, Nobel Prize (Medicine), Professor, Max-Planck Inst for Med. Forschung, Heidelberg-Cell Biology-Allemange * Abdus Salam, Nobel Prize (Physics), International Centre for Theoretical Physics, Italie Jonas Salk, Distinguished Pr., Dr., International Health Sciences-Biology-USA Evry Schatzman, Professor, Ac of Sciences-France-Astrophysics-France * Arthur L. Schawlow, Nobel Prize (Physics), Stanford University-Physics-U.S.A. G. Schettler, Professor, Director, Former President, Academy of Sciences, Heidelberg-Cardiology-Allemagne Elie A. Shneour, Professor, Director, Biosystems Research Institute, San Diego, California-U.S.A. * Kai Siegbahn, Nobel Prize (Physics), Physics-Suede S. Fred Singer, Professor of Environmental Sciences, University* *of Virginia, Director of the Washington S.E.P.P., EnvironmentalSciences-U.S.A. * Richard Laurence Millington Synge, Nobel Prize (Chemistry), Biochemistry- Grande-Bretagne GP Talwar, Professor Emeritus, Nat Inst of Immunology, Ac of Sciences, India, W.I.S.- Immunology-Inde * Jan Tinbergen, Nobel Prize (Economy), Economy-Pays-Bas *Lord Alexander Todd, Nobel Prize (Chemistry), Chemistry-Grande-Bretagne Alvin Toffler, Author-Futurist-Futurology-U.S.A. * Charles H. Townes, Nobel Prize (Physics), W.I.S. Professor Emeritus, Physics, University of California, Berkeley-Physics-U.S.A. Ren Truhaut, Professor, Pharmacology Facult des Sciences, Pharmaceutiques, Paris-Toxicology-France *Sir John R. Vane , Nobel Prize (Medicine), Professor, Chairman of William Harvey Research Institute, London-Endocrinology-Grande-Bretagne * Harold E. Varmus, Nobel Prize (Medicine), Professor of Microbiology, University of California, San Francisco-Microbiology-U.S.A. * Thomas Huckle Weller, Nobel Prize (Medicine), Professor Emeritus, Harvard-Medicine-U.S.A. * Elie Wiesel, Nobel Prize (Peace), University of Boston Literature-U.S.A. * Torsten N. Wiesel, Nobel Prize (Medicine), Professor, Lab of Neurobiology, Rockefeller University of New York, Neurobiology-U.S.A. * Robert W. Wilson, Nobel Prize (Physics), Head, Radio Physics Res Department, AT&T Bell Laboratories-Physics-U.S.A.*

KEY ISSUES IN THE GLOBAL WARMING DEBATE

Computer models forecast rapidly rising global temperatures, but data from weather satellites and balloon instruments show no warming whatsoever. Nevertheless, these same unreliable computer models underpin the Global Climate Treaty, negotiated at the 1992 Rio de Janeiro "Earth Summit," and are the driving force behind United Nations efforts to force restrictions on the use of oil, gas, and coal.

The Third Conference of Parties (COP-3) to the Framework Convention on Climate Change (FCCC) (a.k.a. Global Climate Treaty), meeting in Kyoto, Japan, in December 1997 agreed to set mandatory limits and timetables. Politicians were told that the science is "settled" and "compelling," when in reality, scientific experts still strongly disagree on the evidence.

Considering the economic damage from energy rationing and taxation, the plans are drawing strong negatives in the U.S. Congress. Without firm evidence that an appreciable warming will occur as a result of human activities, or that its consequences would be harmful, there can be no justification for bureaucratic remedies or any action beyond a "no-regrets" policy of energy efficiency and market-based conservation. For additional commentary, see articles on Global

Warming and the Btu Tax. See also Hot Talk, Cold Science: Global Warming's Unfinished Debate and the convenient 12 point summary of Global Warming: Unfinished Business. We also refer you to the Scientific Case against the Climate treaty in English and in German.

The IPCC Controversy: In May 1996, unannounced and possibly unauthorized changes to the latest United Nations report on climate change touched off a firestorm of controversy within the scientific community.

The Intergovernmental Panel on Climate Change (IPCC), the science group that advises the United Nations on the global warming issue, presented the draft of its most recent report in December 1995, and it was approved by the delegations. When the printed report appeared in May 1996, however, it was discovered that substantial changes and deletions had been made to the body of the report to make it "conform to the Policymakers Summary." The clandestine changes put a spin on the report's conclusions that "the balance of evidence suggests a discernible human influence on global climate."

Lead authors of the crucial — and doctored — Chapter 8, dealing with the detection and attribution of climate change, have since backed off from this conclusion and now admit that it may take 10 years or more before any human influence on climate can be detected.

Regulatory Excess

In response to a lawsuit filed by the American Lung Association, an EPA-funded lobbying group, the U.S. Environmental Protection Agency has imposed ever more stringent standards on ground-level ozone and particulates.

These standards are based on inadequate science and wildly unrealistic cost/benefit figures, yet EPA Administrator Carol Browner ignored comments put forth during the formal review process and zealously moved ahead. This puts the Clinton Administration in a bind.

Opposition is building among labor unions and industries, city mayors and members of Congress. In part, the fear is that Browner's extreme measures will stall current efforts to deal with urban air pollution by forcing revision of existing plans. But more important, if costly federal regulation forces industry to flee the inner cities, the loss of jobs and the effect that will have on the municipal tax base could exacerbate poverty and destroy efforts to revitalize urban neighborhoods.

Ozone Depletion

Although environmental pressure groups have made exaggerated claims that the stratospheric ozone layer is being eaten away by chlorofluorocarbons (most notably Freon) wafting into space, scientists have yet to see any increase of solar ultraviolet radiation at the Earth's surface.

Actually, even the worst-case scenario (the one that spawned all those bogus stories about blind sheep, blind rabbits, blind trout, plankton death, dead plants, autoimmune disorders, and melanoma epidemics), would have resulted in only a minor increase in UV — one you could experience by driving just 60 miles closer to the equator, say from Washington, D.C. to Richmond, Virginia.

Nevertheless, the Bush Administration hastily imposed a ban on CFC production, costing U.S. consumers up to $100 billion. And to make that sound like a good deal, the EPA is claiming a preposterous health benefit of $32 trillion. Meanwhile, a hugely profitable black market has been created because of the high cost of CFC substitutes and retrofitting air conditioning systems.

Indeed, news reports say the border traffic in "hot" Freon is running a close second to cocaine. Worse, Third World countries, exempt from the ban, are still using CFCs and building factories to produce more. Combine the two and it's unlikely that the ban has produced any benefit to stratospheric ozone.

Now that all the handwringing has led to an international protocol, however, the issue is no longer in the public eye. As in the case of acid rain, another minor problem "fixed" by an expensive non-solution, hype has triumphed over substance.

APPENDIX G — WETLANDS

Protecting Wetlands, Destroying Freedom, Joseph L. Bast, President, The Heartland Institute (*The Heartland Institute Environment & Climate News*, May 2002)

Anti-business groups, smart-growth advocates, anti-market environ-mentalists, and NIMBY (not in my backyard) activists are organizing around the country to back state legislation to "protect wetlands" in the wake of a U.S. Supreme Court ruling that limits the federal government's authority over wetlands.

In Illinois, for example, the Openlands Project is asking its supporters to lobby for the Wetlands Protection Act, a bill pending in the Illinois House. The legislation is necessary, the action alerts says, because "many of [Illinois'] remaining wetlands are now vulnerable after a United States Supreme Court decision eliminated federal protection over them."

Oh, really?

The court decision at issue, SWANCC v. U.S. Army Corps of Engineers, handed down on January 9, 2001, found the Corps had over-reached its statutory authority to regulate "navigable waters" by attempting to stop development of land adjacent to wetlands and seasonal ponds that were plainly not navigable. Federal authority to protect wetlands on federal land and adjacent to rivers and lakes remains intact.

The court's decision did not leave wetlands in Illinois or other states unprotected. Land use historically has been regulated by private property rights, markets, tort law (laws concerning trespass and nuisance), and local governments. These four institutions contain all the rules and incentives necessary to protect the environment and ensure that one person's use of his land does not interfere with his neighbor's same right.

Anyone who owns a home or commercial property manages that property with an eye toward its resale value. We personally suffer a financial loss, either at the time of sale or when we attempt to tap the value of the property as collateral for a loan or line of credit, if we fail to properly maintain it.

The same is true with recreational, scenic, or ecological value to others. Hundreds of millions of acres of forests and wetlands in the U.S. are protected by private property owners so they can be enjoyed by current and future generations.

If our land use activities interfere with the right of our neighbors to enjoy their property, we can be sued and forced to change our conduct, pay for the damage we've caused, or both. In cases where development of wetlands might cause flooding or other problems for nearby properties, recourse can be had through local planning authorities as well as the courts.

Private ownership of property also ensures that valuable wetlands and other natural sites are preserved voluntarily, by those who value them, rather than via the roulette wheel of politics.

Private ownership works because it ensures that the costs and benefits of development are borne or enjoyed by those responsible for making the decisions. If the authority of government is needed at all, it is best exercised locally, by elected officials who are more accountable to voters and more likely to have knowledge of local facts and opportunities than state legislatures or federal bureaucracies.

The Wetlands Protection Act is a radical departure from this liberty-based system of private ownership and local governance. It would authorize the state to impose a fee of $1,000 per acre being developed, require buffers of at least 50 feet between development and a wetland, and demand at least 1.5 acres of wetlands be created or restored for every one acre developed.

These rules assume that someone other than the individual land owner actually "owns" the property, and therefore has the right to decide how to use it. There is a name for this doctrine of "social" property rights: feudalism.

It prevailed in Europe for many centuries, discouraging trade and commerce and elevating privilege over individual freedom. It was finally overthrown in the 17th century by the doctrine of natural rights, which held that private property is so important to individual liberty that it must remain outside the control of the state. The doctrine of natural rights is enshrined in the Declaration of Independence.

The folks who are backing these Wetlands Protection Acts may enjoy dreaming that the environment can be protected by taking rights away from private property owners and giving them to the state.

But the history of feudalism and more recently the former Soviet Union demonstrate that "social" property does not work. People do not invest in maintaining property they do not own, and people who do not bear the consequences of errors do not make decisions wisely. Violating private property rights disrupts the incentives and undermines the basic freedoms that made us a prosperous country.

A year ago, the U.S. Supreme Court struck a blow for property rights. State governments should not be allowed to undo this small victory.

The following cases of environmentalist abuses of individual property rights should sound a warning to every American. If these intrusions into our personal liberties are allowed to continue, then no American, anywhere, will be safe from the tyranny of an environmental policy which ignores our fundamental rights.

The following stories are excerpted from The National Center for Public Policy Research's 2000 National Directory of Environmental and Regulatory Victims, edited by John Carlisle. The entire directory is available at http://www.nationalcenter.org/VictimDirectory00.html."

WETLANDS RULING COSTS LANDOWNER USE OF 80% OF HIS PROPERTY

2000 National Directory of Environmental and Regulatory Victims edited by John Carlisle, Director of the Environmental Policy Task Force of The National Center (c) 2000 by The National Center for Public Policy Research [from *Defenders of Property Rights*]

Howard Dean owns 4.8 acres of commercially-zoned property in New Baltimore, Michigan. In 1988, Dean sought permission from the Michigan Department of Natural Resources (DNR) to fill a portion of the property in order to build a medical office. His a application was denied because part of the property contained a wetland, a ruling which was later upheld on administrative appeal.

Michigan's wetland statute ostensibly exempts wetlands smaller than five acres. However, the DNR found that, although Dean's property is smaller than the minimum size, the wetland was part of a larger wetland "system" and thus required special protection.

That ruling, however, is blatantly arbitrary. Dean's property is the last undeveloped commercial property in the area and none of the other nearby owners were prevented from developing their tracts. The state still allowed these owners the full use of their land despite the fact that the DNR found that their properties also contained wetlands that should have been part of the same wetland "system."

As for Dean, he can only build on the upland portion of his property, which consists of two isolated hills totaling less than 20% of his property.

ELDERLY WOMAN PREVENTED FROM BUILDING HOME

2000 National Directory of Environmental and Regulatory Victims edited by John Carlisle, Director of the Environmental Policy Task Force of The National Center (c) 2000 by The National Center for Public Policy Research [from *Defenders of Property Rights*]

Peggy Heinz gets emotional when she talks about her ordeal in building her retirement home. That's because her neighbors have been using environmental regulations to stop construction.

Heinz's land is located in one of the driest regions of Washington State. The lot itself is typically dry. But it has been designated a wetland because the high clay content of the soil makes drainage slower than usual.

Heinz, who lives on a fixed income of $1,000 a month, has already spent thousands of dollars to secure permits for her home, including one year's income on septic permits and a month's wages on fill issues. But she still can't build.

Neighbors who live in houses on similar land have testified against Heinz before the county's Shoreline and Sensitive Areas Committee. They apparently fear that the construction would obstruct their view of the ocean. One even told her, "I don't have to buy your land; I can just see to it that you never use it."

NEW YORK FARMER SEES PROPERTY RIGHTS PUT OUT TO PASTURE

2000 National Directory of Environmental and Regulatory Victims edited by John Carlisle, Director of the Environmental Policy Task Force of The National Center (c) 2000 by The National Center for Public Policy Research from *Defenders of Property Rights*]

Thomas Cogger owns an 11-acre farm in the town of New Castle, New York. He has farmed this land since 1976. But Cogger has been forced to wage a major legal fight against local ordinances that deny him the full use of his property. One of these ordinances prohibits property owners from allowing their animals to graze within 250 feet of the lot line of their property. Another prevents owners from allowing animals, other than livestock, from grazing on land judged by the town to be a wetland.

Cogger was convicted in September 1996 of violating both of these ordinances. His "criminal" conduct consisted of allowing two sheep and a goat to graze within 250 feet of the lot line, and allowing two horses (not considered "livestock" by the court) to graze in a brook deemed by the town to be a "wetland." The trial court disregarded evidence presented by Cogger that the effect of these ordinances is to restrict the allowable area for grazing to a mere 19,000 square feet — not enough to support even one animal.

Cogger is currently appealing his conviction to the Supreme Court of New York on the ground that these ordinances are illegal because they take property for public use without providing just compensation.

Designation Of Property As Salt Marsh Costs Florida Woman $60,000 [Source: Sean Paige, "Almost Paradise," *Insight*, April 6-13, 1998, p. 10]

Nine years ago, Regina Gonzales, a sales engineer from Coral Springs, Florida, paid $60,000 for two lots in the Florida Keys. She intended to build a house for herself and another for her parents.

However, her lots have since been declared a "salt marsh" even though the parcels are completely landlocked and seemingly dry. Furthermore, says Gonzales, her plots are directly across the street "from a $500,000 home with a tennis court and swimming pool." Although she is prohibited from building, Gonzales still has to make $688 monthly mortgage payments for the useless property.

Baptist Preacher Faces Jail Term For Filling In A Horse Pasture [Jeremy Pearce, in "Land Owner's Conviction Puts Focus on State's Fight to Preserve Wetlands," *The Detroit News*, February 5, 1998]

James Headd, a retired Baptist preacher, faces up to one year in jail after being convicted for filling in a horse pasture on his property that the state claimed was a protected wetland.

Headd says that when he purchased the 4.6 acre plot for $4,200 from the state Department of Natural Resources (DNR) in 1987, the DNR never said anything about a wetland. Furthermore, he said, it had already been used as a farm.

Headd then built a three-bedroom house, dog kennels and a barn. The tiny plot in contention is an area where he cut down trees behind the house to make a pasture for his horses. Eventually, he noticed water started collecting in the pasture.

He started dumping rubble at the edge of the collecting water but never filled it. "That's when my troubles began," says Headd. The Michigan Department of Environmental Quality charged Headd with purposely destroying a wetland. As far as Reverend Headd is concerned, "The state has perpetrated fraud against me and my family.

We have not been prosecuted — we've been persecuted." In February 1998, Headd was found to be criminally guilty of filling in a wetland. He could get a year in jail, be ordered to pay thousands of dollars in fines and be forced to pay for restoring the wetland.

Legal experts were surprised by the criminal sanction. Says David Favre, an environmental law instructor at Michigan State University, "Penalties like this aren't common. Filling wetlands isn't like drunk driving." Headd plans to hire a lawyer to appeal the conviction. He represented himself originally because he never thought he would lose. "You can't go to jail for a wetland that was never there."

Wetlands Designation Costs Construction Worker $38,000
2000 National Directory of Environmental and Regulatory Victims edited by John Carlisle, Director of the Environmental Policy Task Force of The National Center [(c) 2000 by The National Center for Public Policy Research]

In 1994, Nick Chiusolo of Park Ridge, Illinois decided he wanted to sell a plot of property he owned in the community. His most recent tax assessments showed the property was worth $40,000.

However, the Lake County Assessor told Chiusolo that the Army Corps of Engineers claimed the lot was a wetland. As a result, the property was worth no more than $2,000. Chiusolo was astounded. When he bought the parcel in the mid-1970s, nobody told him it was a wetland.

Furthermore, he couldn't understand how the property, which measured 100 feet long and 275 feet deep, could possibly be a wetland. Surrounded by homes on virtually identical land, Chiusolo's property simply had a few trees and grass, nothing that could distinguish it as a wetland.

Chiusolo contacted the local authorities to get help. Chiusolo says he never got a straight answer from anyone as to why his property was deemed a wetland. Officials claimed at one point that he knew it was a wetland when he bought the property. Chiusolo says this is untrue. He is currently talking to his state and federal representatives in an effort to get the ruling reversed.

Veteran Finds Himself Fighting Domestic Threat To Freedom On His Own Property

2000 National Directory of Environmental and Regulatory Victims edited by John Carlisle, Director of the Environmental Policy Task Force of The National Center (c) 2000 by The National Center for Public Policy Research [from *Defenders of Property Rights*]

In 1980, James Fritch purchased approximately 50 acres of lake property in Michigan. Shortly thereafter, Fritch contacted the Michigan Department of Natural Resources (DNR) to determine whether he should build a bridge or a culvert to access the property.

The agency did not respond. Fritch decided to build a bridge rather than filling up a portion of the river for a culvert. His rationale was that the bridge would disturb less land than a culvert.

Unfortunately, the bridge was not built to DNR standards, so Fritch was taken to court. He was fined. After putting a road on the property to reach the lake front, Fritch settled in and lived undisturbed on the land for about five years. About this time, he began to sell off parcels of the land, all with the appropriate permits.

A short time later, an employee from the DNR visited Fritch and explained to him that until he removed the driveway that he had built from the road to his home, he would not be given any more permits to sell parcels. The official said the area could be considered a wetland. In addition to having to spend thousands of dollars to get rid of his road, he lost the use of nearly all of his property.

"Being an ex-serviceman from the Korean War, I couldn't believe this. I went to service to save some other country from having their land confiscated only to come home and find my own government taking my land," said Fritch. To make matters worse, because Fritch relied on this property to fund his retirement, he has virtually no means of generating income.

Mud Puddle On Man's Property Earns Wetland Designation and Slashes Value

2000 National Directory of Environmental and Regulatory Victims edited by John Carlisle, Director of the Environmental Policy Task Force of The National Center (c) 2000 by The National Center for Public Policy Research [from *Oregonians in Action*]

Bill Roberts owns a four-acre property in Happy Valley, Oregon just outside of Portland. In 1997, city officials hired a wetlands expert to drive around town examining mud puddles to determine which ones could be officially designated as wetlands.

Unknown to Roberts, the expert found a promising mud puddle on his property and summoned additional experts to take samples of dirt for analysis. They determined that Roberts's mud puddle was indeed a wetland and informed Happy Valley City Hall.

Roberts had no idea what was going on until he decided to sell the property when his health prevented him from maintaining the land. A potential buyer told him he would offer far less than the market price because the property was a wetland.

Roberts is angry at the city because someone not only trespassed on his property but never bothered to inform him of the status of his land. What he finds most galling, however, is that the so-called wetland was actually the city's fault.

The mud puddle, it seems, is formed during the rainy season because a culvert next to a nearby public road gets filled with garbage and the city fails to clean it up. Roberts contacted one of the experts who examined the puddle and asked him to come back for a second opinion. The expert replied that he wasn't in fact sure if it was a wetland but if Roberts would pay him $2,500 he would do another study.

APPENDIX H — ENDANGERED SPECIES

Nationwide Assaults On Property And Human Life [Jarret Wolstein, "The Green Gestapo" (excerpt), International Society for Individual Liberty; July, 1996]

In Colton, California, a fly brought economic development to a screeching halt. This town of 45,000 slipped into economic depression when a local military base closed. Unfortunately for its human residents, Colton is also home to the Delhi Sand fly, which is listed as endangered. To protect the fly, state authorities have blocked construction of a new hospital and industrial park that would have brought over $171 million in new capital and thousands of jobs. Any major development in Colton is now impossible because of the fly. [Source: Contra Costa Times, 6/16/97, pp. A-10.]

According to the Mountain States Legal Foundation, over 1,300 species — including a number of flies and rats — are now listed as "endangered" and hence protected. Kill one, and you risk a $300,000 fine and two years in prison.

Salmon Protection Sacrifices $30 Million In Agricultural Productivity

2000 National Directory of Environmental and Regulatory Victims edited by John Carlisle, Director of the Environmental Policy Task Force of The National Center [(c) 2000 by The National Center for Public Policy Research]

Citing the need to protect salmon, the National Marine Fisheries Service (NMFS) denied an application for irrigation water withdrawals from the Columbia River system by the Inland Land Company (ILC).

ILC had proposed irrigating 20,000 acres which would produce $30 million worth of crops each year. The state approved the eastern Oregon irrigation application, but NMFS said the company could not put new irrigation intake pipes into the Columbia River unless it found ways to replace the water during the dry years.

Environmentalists are suing in state court to block the project. Columbia River Association executive director Bruce Lovelin says the denial of irrigation rights completely fails to take into account the economic needs of the region's businessmen and farmers.

Federal Efforts To Protect Grizzly Bear Ruin Economy of Montana Community

2000 National Directory of Environmental and Regulatory Victims edited by John Carlisle, Director of the Environmental Policy Task Force of The National Center (c) 2000 by The National Center for Public Policy Research [from *Bruce Vincent*]

Ten years ago, the United States Fish and Wildlife Service (USFWS) proposed a plan to increase the Grizzly Bear population in the area around Libby, Montana. Concerned citizens immediately organized themselves into a coalition and demanded the government's assurance that the increased bear population would pose no threat to people or hurt the economy.

In 1990, the USFWS and the United States Forest Service (USFS) officially stated that increasing the Grizzly Bear population from about four to 90 bears would not negatively affect the economy of Libby. Libby took the government at its word. But just one month later the USFWS changed its position, stating that human activity would infringe on the projected Grizzly Bear population.

As a result, the USFWS closed 56% of the county roads and severely restricted the logging and mining activity on which the local economy depended.

One of the first victims was the saw mill in Libby. It was forced to close, throwing 600-700 people out of work. Since Lincoln County, where Libby is located, has only 15,000 people, the closure of the saw mill alone severely affected the local economy. That was just the beginning, however.

Bruce Vincent, a Libby resident, says the USFWS has cost the county more than 1,800 jobs. Double-digit unemployment is the norm and the Food Bank ran out of food, unable to meet the demand. Incredibly, the USFWS refused to admit that its efforts to augment the Grizzly Bear had affected Libby's economy — although the USFS did admit as much. It wasn't until March 1998 that the USFWS belatedly admitted that its policies probably had a negative impact on the economy.

Placing Animals Above People: The "Buffalo Commons"

2000 National Directory of Environmental and Regulatory Victims edited by John Carlisle, Director of the Environmental Policy Task Force of The National Center [(c) 2000 by The National Center for Public Policy Research]

Mention the names Frank and Deborah Popper in almost any rural Great Plains or Western community and you are likely to freeze from the icy glare. In the Dakotas, Wyoming and New Mexico, Colorado and Montana, thousands of rural Westerners have heard quite enough, thank you very much, of the Professors Popper and their very serious proposal for the "Buffalo Commons."

The professors have concluded, from their vantage point in one of the most congested areas in the world — Frank teaches at Rutgers in New Brunswick, New Jersey, Deborah at New York University in New York City — that mankind was never meant to live upon the Great Plains. The Poppers believe that sooner or later most of the folks living on the Great Plains will be gone.

The Poppers don't want to wait that long. To hasten the process, they advocate a massive government program to "deprivatize" 110 counties in nine states in which 400,000 people live so that the buffalo may return to roam freely across a vast area of once private land.

The audacity of the Poppers' proposal stems not only from the effrontery with which it is offered — that is, without regard to the people who populate the region — but also from the Popper's conclusion that "the Great Plains' experience has implications for much of the rest of the Western and rural United States."

Notwithstanding their repeated conclusion — that the exodus from the region is already occurring — the facts do not bear them out. The Center for the New West, for example, has concluded that just the reverse is true — although the Professors Popper have given up on the Great Plains, others have not.

How do the Poppers propose to "reinvent" the Great Plains? They have an assortment of weapons in their arsenal: designating vast areas for single use; purchases by the federal government's land agent, the Nature Conservancy; outright purchases by the government; regulating cattle and sheep off federal lands; and using the Endangered Species Act to lock up land.

Despite their assertion that the free market is helping to achieve Buffalo Commons, the Poppers admit that of the "potential building blocks for the Buffalo Commons, most of them [are] federal."

The weapon of choice, of course, is the Endangered Species Act (ESA), or as it is called by environmental extremists, "the pitbull of environmental laws."

The False Hope of Tourism

While environmental groups and federal officials use such laws as the Endangered Species Act to stop economic activity and to limit and constrain the use of private property in the West, they hold out tourism as the answer — the brass ring for which small resource producing communities should reach. One such community is Libby, Montana.

Libby, a tiny logging town surrounded by other tiny logging towns and by a once abundant and thriving forest, is scrambling. The surrounding forests have been virtually shut down to logging and an attempt by a major mining company to develop a world-class deposit are being stymied by environmental extremists as well as the U.S. Fish and Wildlife Service.

Libby would like to develop a ski hill for alpine and cross-country skiing, but fears what the Fish and Wildlife Service would demand as "mitigation" for disturbing grizzly bear habitat.

Other development is also on hold due to the demand of the Environmental Protection Agency that Libby improve its air quality. Libby's air quality suffers from its inversion layer and the burning of wood for heat, the only fuel many Libby residents can afford. Libby is in a "Catch 22" situation. They cannot afford cleaner burning fuel without better jobs; they cannot have better jobs without cleaner air.

Moreover, the recreational pursuits of the people of Libby are being limited because the national forests that surround them are restricted by the same approach to grizzly bear management that is taking away their jobs. The U.S. government asserts that grizzly bear habitat can only have .75 miles of road for every square mile of forest land, so U.S. Forest Service roads are being gated and closed.

As if that weren't enough, the largest nearby body of water, Lake Koocanusca 90-mile-long reservoir that has been a magnet for fishermen and campers — is now being used to provide water to "save" the salmon downstream. The 300-yard barrier of knee-deep mud surrounding the falling lake has caused the locals to refer to their lake as "Whocanuseit."

Today, Libby residents are searching desperately for new jobs so that the men and women who love the isolation of their remote and beautiful community can continue to live there. One solution, they are told by the environmental groups and their allies from academe who are responsible for closing the forest to logging, is tourism.

It is an answer Westerners repeatedly hear when they ask how they are to survive once their industries are destroyed. It is a lie.

A recent study conducted in connection with the University of Montana School of Economic Research, however, reveals that, in order to replace the timber jobs already lost, 675,000 visitors to Libby would have to spend more than $100 each on their way through town. Which has led one resident to jest, "We're planning to set up roadblocks to make sure we get that amount from everybody passing through."

Tourism is an important part of the economy of the West. But it is not now and will never be the complete answer.

For one thing, many Westerners like what they do for a living and have no desire to change. Thus when environmental activists like Oregon's Andy Kerr come into ranching towns like Lakeview, Oregon, and say that "more espresso [will be] sold than barbed wire [in the future in Lakeview]," it sounds more like a taunt than sound advice.

For another, portions of every Western state will never be year-round, or temporary, tourist attractions, even if they wanted to be. The Denver Post reported that for every Aspen, Vail, or Telluride, there is a Lake City which, while conducting a reasonably good tourist business in the summer, all but rolls up its sidewalks during the winter.

Ironically, some of the environmentalists who agitate for a "New West" totally dependent upon tourism will often turn around and condemn some of the results. In a New York Times commentary, Hollywood's vocal environmentalist Robert Redford attacked "mining, logging, grazing and the newest shovel on the block, real estate development."

Nonetheless, environmental extremists and their allies in Congress and in the various federal agencies continue to claim that, as Bruce Vincent of Libby says with bitter irony, "tourism is our future."

However, there is a great difference between what those inside the Washington, D.C., beltway promise and what they deliver. Perhaps the best example is the promises made to the people of northern California about the creation and expansion of the Redwood National Park astride Highway 101 north of Arcata, California.

Environmental groups asserted that federal acquisition of 30,000 acres necessary for the creation of the park would not result in job loss, claiming that increases in tourism and higher allowable timber harvest levels on the Six Rivers National Forest would make up for any park-related unemployment.

The environmental groups that advocated the acquisition of private land for the park were bullish on tourism, as was the National Park Service: "After establishment of such a park, assuming adequate development, total attendance is estimated at 1.2 million visitor days by the fifth year of operation, and 2.5 million by the fifteenth year. . . ."

Every prediction was false.

To begin with, the total cost to the taxpayers of the 1968 taking was over $306 million — two-and-a-half to three-and-a-half times greater than the U.S. government estimated and six to ten times greater than the various estimates of the Sierra Club.

Actual job losses due to a decline in timber industry employment were 718 local and 2,039 regional jobs. Between 1980 and 1986, jobs with the National Park Service fell, from a high of a hundred full-time and 232 part-time, to 73 full-time and 139 part-time jobs.

The greatest difference between the abstract and the actual was what happened regarding tourism. Ten years after the park was created, visitor days reached slightly more than 39,000 — less than 4 percent of what the National Park Service had predicted.

More telling, the National Park Service numbers revealed that the vast majority of those counted as visitors to the Redwood National Park came to visit areas that were attractions before the park was formed.

One reason the park has so few visitors is that, contrary to their public pronouncements regarding tourism, environmental groups and the government moved to limit and discourage use of the park.

Superintendent Robert Barbee, for instance, apparently believing that two thousand annual visitors to the Tall Tree grove area of the park were "too many," curtailed access to the area to a day's hike along a foot path. (When the area was private property, people could drive right up to the Tall Tree Grove.)

There are other ways to prevent people from using parks. The U.S. Fish and Wildlife Service has placed the wolf in Yellowstone National Park. Over the opposition of thousands of rural Westerners, Secretary of the Interior Bruce Babbitt is taking steps to ensure that eventually one hundred wolves will roam throughout Yellowstone, with two hundred more in both Idaho and Montana.

Perhaps realizing that most Americans are not in touch with the thrill of returning the "wild" to Yellowstone, the federal government is now asserting that introducing the wolf will increase tourism. Oh? The wolf is known to be a reclusive, nomadic creature of the night. How can such a creature be seen by tourists in a 2.2 million-acre national park, only a small portion of which is accessible by roads? It can't.

This assertion, like the promised jobs in the Redwood National Park area, is the bait before the switch. The switch in this case will be to close portions of the park to protect the wolf's habitat from being disturbed by humans.

To put it bluntly, environmental extremists don't want tourists to see the wolf. At least one of them has even admitted that part of the reason for placing the wolf in Yellowstone is to frighten away tourists.

Mark Obmascik, environmental columnist for The Denver Post, wrote: [T]he plan also will bring back another ingredient that has been vanishing from the western back country. The ingredient is fear. Wolves are killers. They run in packs and rip the guts out of their live prey.

They don't think fawns are cute and cuddly; wolves look at Bambi and see fresh meat. Sometimes wolves look at humans the same way. Although wolves usually try to avoid people, they have been known to order up an occasional course of homo sapiens, especially foolish specimens of the species. . . . [This] could serve as a rude awakening for hordes of recent western visitors who now view the back country as an adventure theme park. . . . People will think twice before traipsing into the back country.

Recent studies have indicated that the time of the long, two week, drive-across- the-country-and-see-the-sights vacation may be a thing of the past, becoming more and more rare. The more likely vacation is the long weekend holiday at a nearby spot. Lately, for many Westerners, tourists have been their neighbors.

All this makes the definition Dave Rovig of Billings, Montana, gives for "tourist" highly relevant: "someone with a job." No matter how attractive we may make our Western towns to visiting tourists, no matter how willing federal officials are to cooperate in providing the types and kinds of facilities that will attract tourists, we who live here and are the most likely visitors won't be making the trip, unless we too have jobs. As the old saying goes, "We can't all be pressing each others' pants."

Conclusion

Those outside the West should be concerned about the war on the West because it puts constitutional freedoms at risk and because it is being waged by an increasingly tyrannical government that abuses federal laws. We should be concerned because the war on the West will hurt the economy of the entire nation, decrease the quality of the human environment, and obliterate recreational resources. Most of all, we should all be concerned because the war on the West is being waged not just against fellow Americans but against fellow human beings.

APPENDIX F — TERRORISM

American Eco-Terrorism: Another Threat? Or Is It A Promise?
By Tim W. Rhodes, M.Sc., EMT-P, Chairman, Ada County Terrorism Taskforce-Boise, Idaho

"On behalf of the lynx, five buildings and four ski lifts at Vail were reduced to ashes on the night of Sunday, October 18th. Vail, Inc. is already the largest ski operation in North America and now wants to expand even further. The 12 miles of roads and 885 acres of clearcuts will ruin the last, best lynx habitat in the state. Putting profits ahead of Colorado's wildlife will not be tolerated.

This action is just a warning. We will be back if this greedy corporation continues to trespass into wild and unroaded areas. For your safety and convenience, we strongly advise skiers to choose other destinations until Vail cancels its inexcusable plans for expansion."

You might think these words are from a radical terrorist group such as the IRA or the Islamic Jihad. In a certain sense, you might be right. They are the words of a domestic terrorist organization, the ELF (Earth Liberation Front), after they took responsibility for the October 18th arson of the Vail ski resort.

What began as an environmentalist originated legal battle to prevent expansion at the Vail Colorado ski resort, ended in $12 million of damage due to an "environmentalist" perpetrated act. The ELF destroyed five buildings and four chair lifts when a court decision allowed the Colorado Company, Vail Associates, to expand the world famous resort.

The ELF's message makes it very clear why they oppose the Vail ski resort expansion. At the center of the dispute is the North American Lynx, which is considered threatened by the U.S. Fish and Wildlife Service.

The lynx is expected to be reintroduced into the Vail area. According to many environmentalists, the ski resort expansion, which includes clearcutting and road expansion, may endanger that reintroduction by limiting the lynx's habitat and survival rate.

According to analysts at North American Research based in California, the ELF is a splinter group of Earth First!, a radical environmental activist movement who participants endorse "front-line, direct action to get results."

Like many domestic militia and anti-government groups, the ELF is an underground organization whose members adhere to the "leaderless resistance" principle made famous by Louis Beam and other right-wing paramilitary

215

activists. According to Katie Fedor, a spokeswoman for the Animal Liberation Front (ALF), the ELF works in "small groups of closely connected colleagues that they trust, literally, with their freedom."

Fedor reports that the Animal Liberation Front and the ELF have worked together in past, citing examples of arson of a U.S. Department of Agriculture building in Washington and the release of 300 mink from a private biomedical research company.

The ELF and ALF designate the week before Halloween "the seven nights of Earth night." The groups threaten to step up eco-sabotage for those seven nights. According to one Internet site that supports the eco- terrorism, the ELF also promotes April 1st-7th as "April Fools Day Bash".

The "fools" are those who desire action against "Earth's abusers" and advocate revenge on those who "are destroying the Earth and its inhabitants." The author of the Internet message cites the "abusers" such as McDonalds, highway departments, anti-environmentalists, elected officials, medical researchers, and habitat destructors as targets for retaliation during the seven nights

Eco-terrorists, such as the ELF, have exchanged their empiric action of civil disobedience, sit-ins and chaining themselves to trees to being prepared to use violence and massive destruction to convey their beliefs and principles.

What explains this change in behavior and adherence to this new belief structure? At root, it's a not-so- new notion that pristine nature possesses "intrinsic value." As David Graber (a biologist with the U.S. National Park Service) stated it: "We are not interested in the utility of a particular species, or free-flowing river, or ecosystem to mankind. They have intrinsic value . . . "

This "intrinsic value" morality means that pristine nature should be preserved "for its own sake," regardless of any value or dis-value to humans. Cutting down trees or filling in a mosquito-infested swamp to erect houses and hospitals, or mining ore to build machines and medical instruments, or constructing dams to generate electricity, or drilling sour gas wells to fuel cars and heat homes-all industrial activities and those who propose it — are immoral because they harm the "intrinsic value" of the non- human environment.

According to one ELF member in Idaho, "If pristine nature possesses "intrinsic value," then human values are inconsequential. Since man survives by conquering nature, man is an intrinsic dis-value-an inherently evil creature that warrants hatred."

This belief that many environment extremists share forms the basis of a nature-worshiping, man-hating doctrine. According to David Graber, "I know scientists who remind me that people are part of nature, but it isn't true.

Somewhere along the line . . . we quit the contract and became a cancer. We have become a plague upon ourselves and upon the Earth . . . Until such time as Homo sapiens should decide to rejoin nature, some of us can only hope for the right virus to come along."

These "extremists" are consistent practitioners of the "intrinsic value" philosophy underlying environmentalism. While it may be true that the bombers/arsonists are extremists seeking a moral justification for their nihilistic hatred, the fact is that the perpetrators believe that environmentalism offers them that moral justification.

The Vail ski resort is not the first incident of its kind. The following list of incidents that the ELF and ALF have taken credit for, which by no means is exhaustive, shows the trend for violence and motivation for destruction that eco terrorists are increasingly adhering:

July 3, 1998 — 310 Animals were released from a research center in Washington June 21, 1998. Two U.S. Department of Natural Resources facilities in Washington state were bombed causing $1.9 million in damage.

July 31, 1994 — Near Olympia, Washington. Log skidder, two fire trucks and a bulldozer were torched about 2:45 p.m. Damage, over $80,000. On August 9, the Washington Contract Loggers Association's answering machine tape held a message spoken by a computer-generated robotic voice: "The recent destruction of logging equipment was retaliation by the Earth Firsters to protect the planet earth from logging."

March 1994 — Two fires; Olympia, Washington. Allan Wirkkala Logging Company, $8,000 damage. ELF claims responsibility.

March 1994 — Quinault, Washington. Tobin Logging, $10,000 damage. ELF claims responsibility.

April 1994 — Snoqualmie Pass, Washington. Bill Burgess Logging, arson fire, $50,000 loss. ELF claims responsibility.

April 2, 1993 — Near Flagstaff, AZ. Dump truck belonging to High Desert Investment Company of Flagstaff destroyed. Letter left behind said, "This letter is to inform you that your 1977 dump truck was not destroyed by young vandals, it was monkey-wrenched." It was signed, "Coconino Clyde and his merry band of eco-warriors."

September 8, 2001 AZ: ALF claimed an estimated half million in damage at a McDonald's arson in Tucson. "ALF," "ELF," obscenities and swastikas were spray-painted on the buildings in the attack.

August 29, 2001 New Zealand: The 34th International Congress of Physiological Sciences in Christchurch, attended by over 3,000 scientists, received a death threat aimed at California Michael Stryker, a sleep deprivation research scientist. Animal rights protesters amassed to protest the conference and police responded with sufficient force to keep a lid on violence throughout the conference. An anonymous letter received by government officials and the press stated that a "good California doctor" was targeted and that before leaving New Zealand, ". . . he may be dead."

August 21, 2001 Norway: An ALF press release claimed credit for releasing about 1,200 mink from a farm in Telemarken, Norway, southeast of Oslo. Almost all of the animals were recovered.

August 21, NY: ELF claimed credit for damage in a misguided attempt to vandalize a site they believed to be carrying on genetic research. The Cold Spring Harbor Laboratory, involved in cancer research, sustained an estimated $15,000 in destruction.

August 16, 2001 UK: One of the three men who assaulted Brian Cass, managing director of Huntingdon Life Sciences, at his home, received a sentence of three years in jail for his part in the attack. David Blenkinsop and two others donned ski masks and ambushed Cass as he arrived home, bludgeoning him with wooden staves and pickaxe handles. DNA on the handles and Blenkinsop's clothing helped convict him of the offense. Police are still searching for the other two attackers.

July 28, 2001 UK: Glynn Harding, a 26-year-old schizophrenic, admitted three charges of causing bodily injury by explosives and 12 counts of sending an explosive with intent. He also admitted to possessing bomb making materials. His participation in a highly publicized letter bomb campaign last winter and this spring blinded one woman in one eye and left a six-year- old girl scarred.

July 4, 2001 MI: An ELF act of arson gutted a Weyerhaeuser office in protest over support for the genetic engineering work on poplar and cottonwood trees conducted by Oregon State University and the University of Washington. An communiqué claimed credit for the attack, along with responsibility for the destruction of eight Ford Expeditions by arson at Roy O'Brien Ford in June, and the destruction of two plate glass windows and a drive-through at a newly-built McDonald's, also in June.

June 14, 2001 AZ: Mark Warren Sands was arrested and indicted on 22 counts for setting fires to eight homes in Phoenix and Scottsdale between April 9, 2000 and January 18, 2001. Some of the luxury homes, under construction when torched, were valued at over a $million each. Sands claimed at his initial hearing hat "God's work has to be done."

June 12, 2001 AZ: Four luxury homes burned overnight in a construction project inside an upscale gated community. Authorities are looking for ties to previous arson fires of luxury homes by eco-terrorists. The initials CSP, standing for "Coalition to Save the Preserves," were sprayed on at least one home. Two of the homes had been sold and two were still on the market. None were occupied yet, and damage was estimated at $2 million. The four homes in total were valued at $5 million.

June 12, 2001 OR: Jeffrey Michael Luers, age 22, was sentenced to 22 years, 8 months in prison for his part in arson attacks in Eugene last year. Another activist apprehended in the same arson, Craig Marshall, entered into a plea bargain agreement last November and is now serving a 5-year sentence.

Luers's defense that he took pains not to injure people and was frustrated about the growing ecological destruction of the planet did not mitigate the measure 11 mandatory sentencing guidelines or otherwise soften his sentencing. The same auto dealership that Luers was convicted of torching went up in flames again on March 30, 2001, damaging 35 SUV's and producing over a $1 million in damage.

June 6, 2001 OR: Jeffrey Luers, charged and convicted of 5 counts of arson for attacks on the Joe Romania truck lot and the Tyee Oil Company last year, faces a possible sentence of 7 1/2 years in prison. The Romania lot was the target of a second arson by others still at large this past March, with damages estimated at $1 million.

June 5, WASHINGTON, DC: At a joint-university news conference MSU's director of the Agricultural Biotechnology Support Project estimated that the university would spend more than $1 million in security improvement and repairs as a result of the arson that destroyed her office in January, 2000.

APPENDIX J — ONE WORLD AGENDA

Excerpts from Our Global Neighborhood: The Report of the Commission on Global Governance (This report may be obtained from Oxford University Press. ISBN 0-19-827997-3, 410 pages.)

Next to life, liberty is what people value most. The impulse to possess turf is a powerful one for all species; yet it is one that people must overcome . . . [G]lobal rules of custom constrain the freedom of sovereign states, . . . sensitivity over the relationship between international responsibility and national sovereignty [is a] considerable obstacle to the leadership at the international level, . . . Although states are sovereign, they are not free individually to do whatever they want.

Maurice Strong, presiding Chairman of the 1992 environmental conference in Rio de Janeiro, and the Chief Aide to Secretary General Annan, wrote in an essay entitled Stockholm to Rio: A Journey Down a Generation: "It is simply not feasible for sovereignty to be exercised unilaterally by individual nation-states, however powerful. It is a principle which will yield only slowly and reluctantly to the imperatives of global environmental cooperation."

The NGO machinery of global governance is at work in America. Their activity includes agitation at the local level, lobbying at the national level, promoting the celebration of the UN's 50th anniversary, producing studies to justify global taxation, and paying for television ads that elevate the image of the UN.

The strategy to advance the global governance agenda specifically includes programs to discredit individuals and organizations that generate "internal political pressure" or "populist action" that fails to support the new global ethic.

The national media has systematically portrayed dissenting voices as right-wing-extremist, militia-supporting fanatics. Consequently, the vast majority of American citizens have no idea how far the global governance agenda has progressed.

This year, 1996, may be the last opportunity the world has to avoid, or at least to influence the shape of global governance. The United States is the only remaining power strong enough to influence the United Nations. Those voices now speaking for all Americans in the United Nations are cheering the forces that would diminish national sovereignty and render individual liberty and property rights relics of the past.

If the current voices representing the United States continue to push for global governance, the world will be committed to a course which will truly transform society more dramatically than the Bolshevik revolution transformed Russia.

The recommendations of the Commission, if implemented, will bring all the people of the world into a global neighborhood managed by a worldwide bureaucracy, under the direct authority of a minute handful of appointed individuals, and policed by thousands of individuals, paid by accredited NGOs, certified to support a belief system, which to many people — is unbelievable and unacceptable.

Report on The Kyoto Protocol — America's Participation (from www.sovereignty.net, 2002)

November 12, 1998

BUENOS AIRES — The Kyoto Protocol was officially signed today by Peter Burleigh, acting UN Ambassador. The event, widely anticipated at COP4, signaled a commitment by the United States to the conference participants, even though the White House has characterized the signing as "symbolic," with "no obligation to implement" the treaty.

Michael Cutijar, Executive Secretary of the UN Framework Convention on Climate Change, says that signing the treaty indicates that a nation "intends to become legally bound by it, and is committed not to act against the treaty's objectives before being so bound."

The U.S. press office said flatly that President Clinton "will not submit the Protocol to the Senate until there is meaningful participation by key developing countries." The term "meaningful participation" has not been defined or quantified. To date, 59 of the 171 nation Parties to the Convention have signed the Kyoto Protocol; two nations have ratified it: Fiji, and Antigua.

Confirmation of the signing came early this morning. Immediately, there was a noticeable relaxation of tension among the delegates and NGO observers. Delegates who are unfamiliar with America's Senate ratification process assume that the United States is now on board. Those who know how the U.S. government works, realize that once again, the White House has out-maneuvered the Congress.

By signing the treaty, the White House has clearly accepted "international obligations." By refusing to submit the treaty to the Senate for an up-or-down vote, the President is free to implement administratively whatever programs he wishes without fear of rejection by Congress. It is not likely a coincidence that Executive Order 13083, scheduled to take effect this month, lists "international obligations" as one of many justifications for triggering federal supremacy over state and local governments.

Signing the treaty draws a new battle line between the White House and Congress. The act is seen by many Congressmen to be a slap-in-the-face of the U.S. Senate, which, last year passed by a vote of 95 to 0, a Resolution saying it would not ratify a treaty which did not include requirements for all nations, nor one which imposed significant economic costs. The Kyoto Protocol requires nothing of 137 developing nations, while imposing substantial costs on the American economy.

Last year, after passage of the Senate resolution, the President appeared on national television and said firmly that he would not accept any treaty that did not conform to the requirements of the Senate resolution. Today, by signing the Protocol, the President did what he said he would not do.

The press announcement also said that "new findings have reinforced the strong scientific consensus that human activities are affecting the climate." The most recent statement from the scientific community says. "There is no convincing scientific evidence that human release of carbon dioxide, methane, or other greenhouse gases is causing (or will in the foreseeable future cause) catastrophic heating of the Earth's atmosphere and disruption of the Earth's climate." This statement has been signed by more than 18,000 American scientists. (See "Petition Project" on our Climate Change page.)

Americans have now become accustomed to hearing their President declare a statement to be true, on national television, and subsequently finding that it is proven to be false. Americans are familiar with the White House spin machine that launders language with a process guaranteed to distort black or white to a shade of gray that makes the White House dingy.

Author's Note: By law, non-profit organizations are not required to reveal their sources of revenue, thus accurate figures are very difficult and time consuming to compile. The following tables, which are the only records I was able to find, are offered as evidence that control of the environmental movement is vested in private foundations and corporate America, primarily. I might also note that in the 12 - 15 year period since these figures were compiled, the number of environmental organizations in America has topped an astronomical 700,000, and the revenues of the largest ones have probably tripled, or more.

Table 1: Environmental Groups' Organization Revenues (U.S. dollars, 1990, 1991)

Foundation	Revenue
African Wildlife Foundation	$ 4,676,000
American Humane Association	3,000,000
Center for Marine Conservation	3,600,000
Clean Water Action	9,000,000
Conservation International	8,288,216
The Cousteau Society	14,576,328
Defenders of Wildlife	6,454,240
Earth Island Institute	1,300,000
Environmental Defense Fund	16,900,000
Greenpeace International	100,000,000
Humane society	19,237,791
Inform	1,500,000
International Fund for Animal Welfare	4,916,491
National Arbor Day Foundation	14,700,000
National Audubon Society	37,000,000
National Parks Conservation Assoc.	8,717,104
National Wildlife Federation	77,180,104
Natural Resources Defense Council	16,926,305
Nature Conservancy	254,251,717
North Shore Animal League	26,125,383
Planned Parenthood	383,000,000
Population Crisis Committee	4,000,000
Rails-to-Trails Conservancy	1,544,293
Sierra Club	40,659,100
Sierra Club Legal Defense Fund	8,783,902
Student Conservation Association, Inc.	3,800,000
Trust for Public Land	23,516,506
Wilderness Society	17,903,091
Wildlife Conservation International	4,500,000
WWF/Conservation Foundation	60,000,000
Zero Population Growth	1,600,000
Total	$1,177,656,571

Sources: Buzzwork, September/October 1991- Chronicle of Philanthropy, March, 13, 1992

TABLE 2

224

Table 2: Who Owns The Environmental Movement? Foundation Grants To EDF And NRDC (U.S. dollars, 1988)

Foundation	EDF	NRDC
Beinecke Foundation, Inc.	850,000	
Carnegie Corporation of New York	25,000	
Clark Foundation	150,000	
Columbia Foundation	30,000	
Cox Charitable Trust	38,000	
Diamond Foundation	50,000	
Dodge Foundation, Geraldine	75,000	10,000
Educational Foundation of America	30,000	75,000
Ford Foundation	500,000	
Gerbode Foundation	50,000	40,000
Gund Foundation	85,000	40,000
Harder Foundation	200,000	
Joyce Foundation	75,000	30,000
Macarthur Foundation	600,000	
Mertz-Gilmore Foundation	75,000	80,000
Milbank Memorial Fund	50,000	
Morgan Guaranty Charitable Trust	5,000	6,000
Mott Foundation, Charles Stewart	150,000	40,000
New Hope Foundation, Inc.	45,000	
New York Community Trust	35,000	
Noble foundation, Inc.	0,000	35,000
Northwest Area foundation	100,000	
Packard Foundation	50,000	37,000
Prospect Hill Foundation	45,000	
Public Welfare Foundation	150,000	
Robert Sterling Clark Foundation	50,000	40,000
Rockefeller Brothers Fund	75,000	
San Francisco Foundation	50,000	
Scherman Foundation	40,000	50,000
Schumann foundation	50,000	
Steele-Reese Foundation	100,000	
Victoria Foundation	35,000	

Virginia Environmental Endowment	25,000	
W. Alton Jones Foundation	100,000	165,000
Wallace Genetic Foundation	80,000	65,000
William Bingham Foundation	1,000,000	150,000
Total*	2,885,000	3,236,000

*The total includes some smaller foundation grants not listed here.
Source: The Foundation Grants Index — 1989, 1990

Table 3: Top 15 Recipients In Environmental Law, Protection, And Education

Recipient Foundation	Grant in $
World Resources Institute Macarthur Foundation	15,000,000
World Resources Institute Macarthur Foundation	10,000,000
Nature Conservancy R.K. Mellon Foundation	4,050,000
Nature Conservancy Champlin Foundations	2,000,000
Oregon Coast Aquarium Fred Meyer Charitable Trust	1,500,000
International Irrigation Mgmt Inst. Ford Foundation	1,500,000
Open Space Institute R.K. Mellon Foundation	1,400,000
International Irrigation Mgmt. Inst. Rockefeller Foundation	1,200,000
Chicago Zoological society Macarthur Foundation	1,000,000
Native American Rights Foundation Ford foundation	1,000,000
Wilderness Society R.K. Mellon Foundation	800,000
World Resources Institute A.W. Mellon Foundation	800,000
University of Arkansas W.K. Kellogg Foundation	764,060
National Park Service Pillsbury Co. Foundation	750,000
National Audubon Society A.W. Mellon Foundation	750,000

SOURCE: *Environmental Grant Association Directory, 1989*

APPENDIX K — ENVIRONMENTAL POLITICS

The Political Sacrifice Zone — Bruce Babbitt

By Dave Skinner (a freelance journalist from Whitefish, Montana), The Paragon Foundation Website, 1996

"We must identify our enemies and drive them into oblivion." Given the full-page ads attacking Gale Norton, George W. Bush's nominee for Interior Secretary, it might not surprise you that the president of the League of Conservation Voters said that. But it wasn't Deb Callahan, LCV's current president who made this extremist declaration of political war. Bruce Babbitt made it in 1991 — the very man Norton has been nominated to replace.

Many Westerners hope Norton will be confirmed. After Babbitt, and a Clinton Administration bent on using rural America as a Political Sacrifice Zone, the West is in dire need of a friend.

In January of 1993, Washington Post reporter Tom Kenworthy wrote: "Babbitt's record suggests he would push the reform envelope as far as the politics permit." Turns out Kenworthy was right. Babbitt pushed as hard as he could — using the power of Interior Department agencies and laws such as the Endangered Species Act to drive as many of his enemies into oblivion as possible — without spurring Congress into action.

Ranchers were the first "enemies" Babbitt went after. Through "Rangeland Reform," Babbitt made all public lands ranchers vulnerable to having their grazing leases blocked through environmental appeals by any number of anti-grazing law firms. Miners were next on Babbitt's enemies list. When Congress would not go along with the Secretary on repealing the 1872 Mining Law Babbitt decreed it was "no longer in the public interest to wait for Congress" and "changed the rules of the game."

Both ranchers and miners are small voting blocs. Even in mining states such as Montana and Colorado, newspapers endlessly repeat the fact that "only" one percent of jobs are mining jobs (that pay twice the state median wage).

The wildlife lobby Defenders of Wildlife claims 750,000 members — while there are only 20,000 public lands ranchers. In politics, that's a no-brainer.

Babbitt came into office empowered with the Endangered Species Act, and did much to keep that power. Instead of encouraging the sort of brutish enforcement that hard-line Green activists wanted, and which would have alienated the vast, reasonable bulk of the American public, Babbitt went about negotiating Habitat Conservation Plans to lock businesses into difficult terms that they could at least survive with. He often presided over species listings as "threatened" rather than "endangered," then publicly pitched the situation as "local control" versus "top-down." What he never mentioned is that if state wildlife and environmental agencies did not do what the feds wanted, species could be upgraded to full-endangered status overnight.

It wasn't until after President Clinton's midnight proclamation of the Grand Staircase, Escalante National Monument in Utah, that Babbitt truly showed his sick genius — by adopting the Antiquities Act as his own. He began by proposing mineral moratoriums on BLM lands, and then rode into town, demanding that local Congressional delegates shape a monument proposal to his liking or he would sic the President on them.

Babbitt's abuse of the Antiquities Act was masterful, always just short of spurring a Congressional repeal, or action overturning any designations. Babbitt didn't give the environmental lobby all it wanted...but he has kept the Antiquities Act intact, retaining the Political Sacrifice Zone Monument option open for future presidents looking to score some cheap environmental votes.

Babbitt jokes about someday being able to visit the West and have people wave at him with "all five fingers." While that may seem self- deprecating, it's actually sad. During his "farewell" tour around the West last week, one event was cancelled because 300 local opponents to yet another possible monument had staked out the hamlet of Selma, Oregon — raising what reporters called "security concerns." Handfuls were allowed to travel the 45 miles to Medford for an audience, safely within Babbitt's security ring. I doubt anyone appreciated the possible ironies of a civil rights riot in another Selma, but there it is.

When the leaders are afraid to face the citizens, something is terribly wrong. When leaders view citizens as enemies to be identified and obliterated, that's criminal.

Irs Audits on SUV Owners Date: February 13, 2003

The Sierra Club on February 11, 2003 issued a press release beginning: "The Sierra Club today urged the Internal Revenue Service (IRS) to aggressively audit the returns of taxpayers who take advantage of a tax loophole subsidizing their purchases of gas-guzzling SUVs.

In a letter to the IRS, the group stressed the need for the IRS to ensure that these vehicles are in fact being used for business purposes at least 50% of the time, as the tax code requires. Already, many individuals have taken advantage of the loophole to drive off the lot with a luxury SUV, often for personal use, assured that they will be able to pass on to taxpayers up to $25,000 of the cost of the vehicle."

The release continues, in part: "A long-standing provision of the tax code lets small business owners write off a portion of certain business expenses. Vehicles weighing over 6000 pounds are eligible so that small business owners who need work trucks and delivery vans can take advantage of the provision.

But many S.U.V.s weigh over 6000 pounds, and since that loophole — which [the Sierra Club's Daniel] Becker described as 'a loophole big enough to drive a Hummer through' — came to light last year, a growing number of individuals are using it to buy S.U.V.s for what may be personal — not business — use. According to Taxpayers for Common Sense, the SUV tax loophole costs the federal government $1 billion for every 100,000 vehicles that exploit the deduction."

APPENDIX L — URBAN SPRAWL

THE TRUTH ABOUT URBAN SPRAWL

Samuel R. Staley (excerpt from: "The Sprawling of America: In Defense of the Dynamic City," Policy Study 251, Reason Public Policy Institute National Center For Policy Analysis, Monday, March 24, 1999)

Urban sprawl has sparked a national debate over land-use policy. At least 19 states have established either state growth-management laws or task forces to protect farmland and open space. Dozens of cities and counties have adopted urban growth boundaries to contain development in existing areas and prevent the spread of urbanization to outlying and rural areas. The Clinton administration has proposed to make urban sprawl a federal issue.

Although a clear definition of sprawl remains elusive, public debate over sprawl is driven primarily by general concerns that low-density residential development threatens farmland and open space, increases public service costs, encourages people and wealth to leave central cities and degrades the environment.

However, evidence suggests that suburbanization — which might be defined as urban-like development outside central urban areas — does not significantly threaten the quality of life for most people and that land development can be managed more effectively through real-estate markets than comprehensive land-use planning.

Are Open Spaces Threatened?

Historically, the most rapid rate of suburbanization occurred between 1920 and 1950. By the 1970s and 1980s, the trend was moderating, according to a study of more than 300 fast-growth rural counties. Despite widely cited reports on the pace of urban growth, urban land remains a very small part of overall land use, and urban development does not threaten the nation's food supply.

Less than 5 percent of the nation's land is developed and three-quarters of the population lives on 3.5 percent of the land. Only about one-quarter of the farmland loss since 1945 is attributable to urbanization.

Predictions of future farmland loss based on past trends are misleading because farmland loss has been moderating since the 1960s, falling from a 6.2 percent decline in farmland per decade in the 1960s to a 2.7 percent decline in the 1990s. In addition, with dramatic increases in agricultural output, American farmers are producing almost 50 percent more food than in 1970, using less land.

Rural parks and wildlife areas have increased as dramatically as urbanized land. More than three-quarters of the states have more than 90 percent of their land in rural uses, including forests, cropland, pasture, wildlife reserves and parks. Acreage in protected wildlife areas and rural parks exceeds urbanized areas by 50 percent.

Does Suburban Growth Increase Public Service Costs?

Many studies of the cost of development exaggerate the effects of suburbanization on local government costs. Most costs are recovered through on-site improvements made by developers. Local governments often do make conscious policy decisions not to recover the full costs of development, when officials and voters decide for one reason or another to subsidize development through general revenues. The evidence is mixed on infrastructure costs and whether low-density development causes them to increase.

While some infrastructure costs (street maintenance, for example) fall as density increases, as a rule increases in density are accompanied by increases in population and in the level of general spending.

Is Suburban Growth Responsible For The Decline Of Cities?

Sprawl has been blamed for the decline of big cities and older, inner-ring suburbs. But while large cities have a number of features that attract businesses and people — roads, cultural activities, diverse and sometimes inexpensive housing opportunities and easy access to mass transit — many cities suffer from poorly functioning school systems, high tax rates, anticompetitive regulations and deteriorating housing stock.

Studies show that for many families, particularly working-class families, the poor quality of central city schools is the driving factor in their moves to the suburbs. Concerns about public safety in general and crime in particular also drive many people from cities.

Does Suburban Growth Damage The Environment?

Some critics of low-density residential development maintain that it means more pollution, more congestion and fewer preserved natural resources. They believe that higher-density compact development would mitigate those impacts. However, population density does little to alleviate auto-caused smog. Metropolitan areas with the lowest population densities have the fewest air pollution problems. Furthermore, population density or compactness has little relationship to how much commuters depend on automobiles.

More than 75 percent of commuter trips are by car in every area except New York — and more than 90 percent are by car in the vast majority of areas. Studies show that the number of vehicle miles traveled actually increases with population density in the United States.

Thus a policy strategy that attempts to increase population density could lead to more traffic congestion, exacerbating air pollution levels and potentially causing more areas to fail to meet federal clean air goals.

Another important environmental objection to suburbanization, the potential loss of open space, overlooks the fact that limiting development often accelerates the loss of open space inside urban areas. To overcome the shortage of land, developers eventually do projects on odd-shaped parcels and other lands that would ordinarily have remained vacant lots and the equivalent of mini-parks. In addition, plans to increase population density may call for the destruction of most farmland inside an area selected for high-density development, reducing urban open space still further.

Can We Trust Policy Planners To See The Future?

Policy recommendations using a 20-, 30- or 50-year vision for a state or community inevitably adopt top-down planning tools and government control of land to achieve state policy goals. However, there is little evidence that governments are better suited than real estate markets and private conservation efforts to provide the kinds of homes and communities people want. Indeed, many planners have acknowledged that "bad planning" (for example, large-lot zoning) was a significant contributor to the urban sprawl they now want to eliminate. Ironically, many reformers expect state and local governments to operate differently once the "right" urban planning reforms are in place.

APPENDIX M — CONTRIBUTOR INDEX & CREDITS

Contributors:

Johnathan H. Alder (Competitive Enterprise Institute)

Howard Aubin (Author, Lecturer)

Joseph L. Bast (President, Heartland Institute)

Radley Balko (Cato Institute)

Dana Berliner (Senior Attorney - Institute for Justice)

David Brown (Reporter, Pittsburgh Tribune-Review)

Scott Bullock (Senior Attorney - Institute for Justice)

Henry N. Butler (Professor of Law and Economics, University of Kansas)

John Carlisle (ex-Director, Environmental Policy Task Force, The National Center for Public Policy Research)

Katie Cobb (Journalist)

Dr. Bonner R. Cohen (Senior Fellow, Lexington Institute)

Don Comis (Journalist)

Chad Cowan (National Center For Public Policy Research)

Bryan Denson (Reporter, The Oregonian)

Tom DeWeese (Author and President, American Policy Center)

Dan Eggen (Journalist, Washington Post)

Rob Gordon (Executive Director, National Wilderness Institute)

Joseph Farah (Editor, Whistle Blower Magazine, WoldNetDaily.com)

Honorable Helen Chenoweth-Hage (U.S. Congresswoman, retired)

William F. Jasper (Author, Columnist - The New American)

Jeff Jacoby (Reporter, Boston Globe)

William Robert Johnston (Reporter, Brownsville Herald)

Dr. Jo Kwong (Environmental Research Assitant, Atlas Economic Research Foundation of Fairfax, Va)

Henry Lamb (Executive Vice President, Environmental Conservation Organization, Columnist - NetWorldDaily.com)

William La Jeunnesse (Fox News Staff)

Yale Lewis (Journalist)

Russell Madden (Instructor in Communications, Mercy College)

Rogelio A. Maduro (Fox News Staff)

John P. McGovern (Director, National Center for Public Policy Research)

Patrick J. Michaels (Professor, Environmental Sciences, University of Virginia & Senior Fellow, Cato Institute)

Matthew Mittan (Reporter, The Asheville Tribune)

Robert H. Nelson (Professor, Univ. of Maryland)

David Neuendorf (Author)

William K. Niskanen (Chairman, Cato Institute)

Sean Paige (Insight Magazine)

William Perry Pendley (President, Mountain States Legal Foundation)

Jeremy Pierce (Reporter, Chicago Tribune)

Roger Pilon, Ph.D., J.D.(Senior Fellow and Director, Center for Constitutional Studies, Cato Institute)

Tom Randall (National Center for Public Policy Research)

Tim W. Rhodes (Chairman, Ada County Terrorism Taskforce-Boise, Idaho)

Joyce Russell (Journalist)

Rabbi Yisrael Rozen

Ralf Schauerhammer (Journalist)

Peter Schwartz (Ex-President & Senior Fellow, Ayn Rand Institute)

Ryan Sager (National Center For Public Policy Research)

Frederick Seitz (Past President, National Academy of Sciences, U.S.A. President Emeritus, Rockefeller University)

Glenn Shaw (Atmospheric Scientist & Professor, KSU)

Dave Skinner (Journalist)

Samantha Smith (Journalist)

Julie Kay Smithson (Founder, Property Rights Research)

Hans F. Stennholz (Director, Department of Economics, Grove City College)

Jim Streeter (National Wilderness Institute)

Ralph de Toledano (Columnist, Washington, D.C.)

Robert Trancinski (Journalist)

Bruce Vincent (President, Alliance for America)

Robin Wallace (Fox News Staff)

Zane Walley (Paragon Foundation)

J. Whitley (Author)

Jarret B. Wollstein (Founder, Society For Individual Liberty)

Glen Worcenshyn (Journalist)

Jack Yetiv (Journalist)

A heartfelt thanks to the following individuals and organizations for their support and encouragement on this project.

Andrea Sengstacken and the Staff of Algora Publishing, New York

Janet Tompkins, Louisiana Forestry Assn.

Mike W. Smith, Congressional seat candidate, 49th Dist., WA

George Passantino, Reason Public Policy Institute

Sue Kocsis, Chairwoman - AASPO Land Rights Committee

Tom Knapp, Director of Partner Services - Free-Market.net

Jacqui Krizo, Oregonians in Action

Bill Moshofski, President - Oregonians in Action

Steve Milloy, author & Founder of junkscience.com

Marc Moreno, Reporter, CNSNews.com

C.J.Hadley, Publisher - Range Magazine

Colorado State Shooting Assn.

David Crisp, Editor - The Billings Outpost

Morris Halliburton, President - British White Cattle

Bart Frazier, President - The Future of Freedom Foundation

Richard Ebeling, Editor - Freedom Daily Magazine

Colleen Cahill, Stewards of the Range

Michael Patty, Reviews - Blue Ribbon Magazine

Bill Pickell, President - Washington Contract Logger's Assn.

Amy Ridenour, Co-founder - Ntl. Center for Public Policy Research

Mark Da Cunha, Editor - Capitalism Magazine

Diane Bast, Co-Founder - Heartland Institute

David Neuendorf, Author

Julie K. Smithson, Founder - Property Rights Research

Angela Lyons, President - Oregon State Shooter's Assn.

Don Harkins, Editor - The Idaho Observer

Dan Frank, Editor - Gun News

Lucky Johnson, President - Inland Shrimper's Assn.

Paul J. Tetreault, Jr., Citizen Soldier

Rick Rydell, Keni-Radio, Anchorage, AK

Dave McKay, WQLK/WHON Radio, Richmond, IN

Roger Olson, KFAB Radio, Omaha, NE

Steve Jason, Citadel Broadcasting, Charleston, SC

Brett Bonner, KGMI Radio, Bellingham, WA

Chandler Van Voorhis, GreenWave Radio, Middleburg, VA

John R. Smith, The Talk Station, Morehead City, NC

**Note: *The titles following these names are the latest information available to the author at this time. I apologize for any out-of-date information or failure to acknowledge any one contributor's current status.*

APPENDIX N — INTERNET LINKS.

TO PRO-RIGHTS ARTICLES

The Clinton/Babbitt Law (BLM 3809), *signed on their last day in office, which limits the rights of individuals to access their own properties, or mining claims, if they must cross federal lands.* http://roadrunnergold.com/politic04.htm

A discussion forum *of late breaking eco-abuses from the victims themselves, friends, etc.* http://www.cfis.org/ubb/Forum6/HTML/000043.html

Stop Federal Land Grab Org. *A current listing of property rights abuses.* http://www.stopfedlandgrab.org/index.html

House Committee On Energy And Commerce Health And Environment, *Subcommittee Statement of Hon. Thomas J. Bliley, Jr. July 21, 1993. Congressional testimony on the abuses of the EPA regarding smoking, lies to the public, deception.* http://www.pipes.org/Articles/Bliley.html

The Commons: *One page of this site has an extensive essay on EPA abuses* http://lists.bcn.net/pipermail/the-commons/1999-June/000134.html

Grant's Pass Irrigation Project: *One of many projects under fire by the EPA, this page exposes property rights abuses and other regulatory overkill issues* http://home.echoweb.net/Mike/gpid_new/lb_memo7.htm

Clairmont Institute: EPA; *Definition of Tyranny* http://www.claremont.org/publications/eastman000925.cfm

Free Market Net: *Pro-freedom news and articles supporting free enterprise* http://www.free-market.net/spotlight/takings/

Fox News: *One man's 20 year battle against the EPA* http://193.78.190.200/10b/epa-no.htm

Washington Post *Ex-EPA Administrator, Carol Browner, destroys documentation and other evidence of her regime under the Clinton Administration.* http://193.78.190.200/10b/landmark.htm

Excite.com *Australia Doctors refusing smokers surgery and treatment until they quit smoking.* http://193.78.190.200/10/au.htm

Sky News *Australian smoker dies after doctors refuse him treatment* http://193.78.190.200/10/au2.htm

Junkscience.com *The account of Bill Clinton's covert actions against whistleblowers in his administration.* http://www.junkscience.com/mar99/whistle.htm

To Pro-Rights Organizations:

Cato Institute: *Federal Regulatory Abuse Property Rights Congress. Excellent resources documenting property rights abuses.* http://www.freedom.org/prc/

Cato Institute: *Distinguished professionals testifying before Congress, written articles supporting freedom issues.* http://www.cato.org/research/natur-st.html.

Interactive Citizens United: *Property rights resource center* http://home.inreach.com/rgierak/prop.htm

Land Owners of North Dakota: *Promoting property rights in ND* http://www.ndland.org/

Liberty Matters : *An array of freedom issues* http://www.libertymatters.org/

Regulatory Policy Center: *Property rights & regulation* http://www.regpolicy.com/

Stop Taking Our Property: *Indiana land owners coalition* http://members.aol.com/jwaugh7596/STOPwatch.html property

Take Back Kentucky : *Kentucky property owners coalition* http://www.takebackkentucky.org/

Treekeepers : *Stressing environment and human compatibility* http://www.treekeepers.org/

Minnesota Landowners Rights Assoc. : *Property rights focus* http://www.rrv.net/mlra/

Montana Grassroots : *Property rights in Montana* http://www.montana-grassroots.com/

Pennsylvania Landowners Assoc.: *Property rights in Pennsylvania* http://www.pa. landowners.org/

Property Rights Foundation of America: *Dedicated to property rights* http://www.prfamerica.org/

National Association of Reversionary Property Owners : *Property Rights Advocates:* http://home.earthlink.net/-dick156

Off-Road.com : *Defending recreational activities on public lands* http://www.off-road.com/

Paragon Foundation : *Speaking out on property rights* http://www.paragonpowerhouse.org

Property Rights Research : *Excellent property rights research tools and articles, email alerts* http://www.propertyrightsresearch.org/

Sawgrass Rebellion: *A coalition against the "re-wilding" of Florida.* http://www.sawgrassrebellion.org/

Marine Conservation Rights Institute: *Committed to conservation within the framework of citizen's property rights* http://www.mecri.org/

Environmental Perspectives, Inc. : *Consulting firm against one world domination and infringement of personal rights* http://www.epi.freedom.org/

Timeline to Global Governance: *Excellent source of material on global government agenda* http://www.sovereignty.net/timeline.html

American Land rights Organization : *Patriotic and pro-rights site* http://www.landrights.org/

American Policy Center: *Sources of articles on many key issues pertaining to freedom* http://www.americanpolicy.org/

The Grange Connection: *Links to many Grange organizations, promoting freedom* http://www.grange.org/

Camp America: *"Where God's Truth and Patriotism Go Hand In Hand"* http://www.campamerica.org/

Defenders of Property Rights: *Dedicated to property rights protection* http://www.defendersproprights.org/

Frontiers of Freedom : *Many sources on freedom in all categories* http://www.ff.org/

Mountain States Legal Foundation: *Acclaimed defenders of the victims of regulatory abuse* http://mountainstateslegal.com

Ayn Rand Institute: *Education & articles on free enterprise* http://www.aynrand.org

Center For Defense of Free Enterprise: *Free market, property rights and limited government* http://cdfe.org

United Property Owners: *Articles & source materials – property rights* http://unitedpropertyowners.org

Oregonians In Action: *Land use and regulatory reform* http://www.oia.org

American Land Rights Association http://www.landrights.org

National Center For Public Policy Research

Restoring America

    CLAW
    Forfeiture Endangers American Rights
    Capatalist Magazine (Marc Da Cunha)
    Property Rights Coalition
    Utah Private Property Ombudsman
    Houston Property Rights Association
    Citizens For Private Property Rights
    CEIL
    Reason Public Policy Institute
    PERC
    American Enterprise Institute
    American Association of Small Property Owners
    American Institute For Economic Research
    Atlas Economic Research Foundation
    Brainstorm Magazine
    Brookings Insitute
    Center For the New West

Citizens Against Government Waste
Citizens For a Strong Economy
Competeitive Enterprise Institute
Evergreen Magazine
Foundation For Economic Education
The Federalist Society
Free Market.com
The Future of Freedom Foundation
Great Plains Public Policy Institute
Heritage Foundation
Hoover Institution
Hudson Institute
Independent Institute
Eastern Oregon Mining Association